THE
Art OF

A CHRISTIAN COUPLE'S GUIDE TO SEXUAL INTIMACY

INTIMATE
MARRIAGE

& TIM KONZEN

DR. JENNIFER KONZEN

Published by Konzen Publishing
San Diego, CA

Cover Design by Beth Weeks
Layout Design by Dylan Wickstrom, DoubleYou Design
Layout and Publishing Support by Beth Lottig, www.elizabethlottig.com

ISBN: 978-0-692-73070-6
Printed in the United States of America

ACKNOWLEDGMENTS

We have four children. In some ways, this book feels like another birth. And so many dear people have been with us in the delivery room. We have had wonderful direction in our own sex life since our engagement and throughout our married life. Thank you to those in the early years who bared your hearts and gave us the specifics we needed: Dave and Judy Weger, Marshall and Marina Hopkins (we will see you there, Marshall), and Ralph and Angie Boaz. What a wonderfully fun foundation they all helped us set.

As we began to plan on doing this work of helping others with their marital and sexual lives, we had some amazing support. Thank you Guillermo and Terry Adame for the immeasurable ways you have literally saved our souls (with special attention to me, Tim) and believed in us through everything.

We have some incredibly supportive, lifelong friends who also gave their time to reading this book to make sure we did not mess up too much. Thank you, Ron and Linda Brumley, Paul and Kerry Schultz, and Janet Schalk. Thank you also to Robin Weidner for the wonderful direction and editing help. It was vital to us that this book would not only be helpful but would be grounded in an accurate understanding of Scripture. All of you helped us make that happen.

Our gratitude also goes to those who provided Jennifer's early training in sexual medicine—thank you, Irwin Goldstein—and vital input to the technical sexual details in this text—thank you, Debra Taylor and Rose Hartzell. We are so grateful to those who used their design and artistic skills to make this book look great. Thank you Dylan Wickstrom for the book design and Beth Weeks for the incredibly beautiful cover and design elements. And, of course, we are very grateful to our editor, Beth Lottig, for her enthusiastic support and direction.

Sex as God designed it is a beautiful thing, and for us it has resulted in four beautiful people. Our children have had to explain many times to their friends why there are all these books about sex on our shelves (and on our floor and behind that chair). So in light of all the embarrassing conversations you have had to have, we appreciate your patience with us and love you deeply beyond words. This book is dedicated to you. It is our hope and prayer that each of you will have the joy and victory in your marriages that God has generously granted us. Our prayer is this—that all of you who are reading here will ... *"Glorify the Lord with me. Let us exalt His name together."* —Psalm 34:3

CONTENTS

THE Art OF

A CHRISTIAN COUPLE'S GUIDE TO SEXUAL INTIMACY

INTIMATE
MARRIAGE

INTRODUCTION:

The Art of Intimacy

"We love each other, but it is so hard to talk about our sex life."

"We have a happy marriage, but our intimate life is a source of pain, frustration, and disappointment."

"We have had some physical challenges that have affected our sex lives, and we don't know how to overcome them or talk about them."

"There's been a lot of damage that's happened in our marriage, and we're having a really difficult time being intimate with one another, not just in our sexual relationship, but overall as well."

"Sex is going fine, but we have always wanted our intimacy to be great. We could use some help with how to get there."

Maybe you picked up this book because these words describe how you're feeling about your sex life. Or maybe you're just looking for ways to make things more fun! You may be searching for answers. Genuine intimacy in marriage is like a beautiful masterpiece. For thousands of years, it has been rendered in paintings, music, and sculpture. Like a fine artist, creating that kind of beauty in the marital relationship usually takes practice and dedication. Within these pages, you will find some direction to help you learn the art of marital intimacy.

It's been said that when sex is good, the influence sex has on how satisfied partners are in their relationship is 15–20 percent. But when sex is not going well, the influence swells to 50–70 percent.[1] This highlights the importance of dealing with the very real challenges that come up in the sexual relationship. But what is a fulfilling sexual relationship? Over the years, we have talked with many married couples in the ministries we have led about their sex lives, both about the fun and joy they are experiencing and the problems that have caused anxiety. In the midst of meeting these kinds of needs in our ministry, Jennifer became a marriage and family therapist and a sex therapist. In both of these areas, in our professional and ministry lives, we found that many couples were having challenges in their sexual relationship, but that the resources for help from a biblical view were scarce.

The good news is that God has a beautiful plan for creating and maintaining a great sexual relationship in marriage. When you look at the Scriptures, the words God uses to describe sex include passion, burning, honor, pleasing, satisfying, and intoxicating. God is very sex positive. Though many of the Bible verses on sexuality are about the many different ways people can sin sexually, for a married couple, the Bible shows us how to honor one another in the sexual relationship and how to enjoy the intoxicating pleasure of sexual intimacy. When we look deeply at the descriptions of the sensual relationship between the beloved and the lover in Song of Songs, we find a beautiful, romantic, and erotic picture of what God intends for your marriage.

Things may be going well in this part of your marriage. As a couple, you are a great intimate team. This book may help you explore new ways to deepen that intimacy. For others, you may look at the picture painted in Song of Songs and feel you are starving for that kind of intimacy—starving for someone to hear you, someone to care, someone to understand, someone to want you, someone to touch you. An incredibly common refrain we hear is "We just aren't close," "He/she doesn't really get me," "We live like roommates," and "We rarely touch." Married couples are often looking for a starting point to deepen their intimate connection, to create one they feel has never been there, or to repair one that has been severely damaged.

So together we will focus on intimacy—the kind of intimacy God intends when two of His children marry. Yes, we'll be sharing a lot about sex, but sexual intimacy truly resides within the quality of overall intimacy in marriage. But what exactly is intimacy?

How's Your IQ? Your Intimacy Quotient

God created us to be intimately connected. In Psalm 139, God expresses His intimate knowledge of us when He describes how intimately He knows us in Psalm 139, saying that He knows our thoughts, discerns when we lay down, and created our innermost parts. Through the prophet Isaiah, God calls us beloved, tells us that we are engraved on the palm of His hand, reminds us that He carries us close to His heart, and says, possessively, "You are mine!" (Isaiah 40:11, 43:1, 49:16).

God also created us to be intimately connected with others and to enjoy sexual intimacy with our spouse. The reality is that people can have sex and not feel intimate. That is not God's plan. The very words used by God in the Bible for sex connote a deep and intimate knowing of one another (for more detail, see chapter two, *So What Does the Bible Say About Marital Sex?*). For many, they need to feel intimately and emotionally connected before they can really enjoy sex. For others, having sex is the *sine qua non*, the indispensable ingredient, of marital intimacy. Having the experience of that skin-on-skin loosing of the self within the other in the midst of orgasm is what makes them feel intimately bonded with their spouse.

Matthew Kelley, in his book *The Seven Levels of Intimacy*, divides intimacy into seven levels: clichés, facts, opinions, hopes/dreams, feelings, faults/fears/failures, and needs. He mentions that most couples do not go below the first three levels. What researchers have found is that only 15 percent of married couples experience these deeper levels of intimacy in their marriage.[2] Another 25 percent experience intimacy only during times of trial, such as illness or funerals. That leaves the majority of us sharing facts and opinions with our spouse but rarely sharing our fears, hurts, hopes, mistakes, and dreams. John and Karen Louis, in their book *I Choose Us*, describe this lack of deeper intimacy as the Mutual Affection phase. They describe how couples at this point are in danger of disintegration if they do not learn to stoke the fire in their marriage. We hope to help you identify and remove obstacles so that you can put more logs on and stoke that fire. We pray you will rediscover sexual intimacy from the midst of a deeper, loving connection—the unique treasure of marriage. To do this will require examining how you are doing in your overall intimacy skills, your intimacy quotient, and then improving those skills in both your emotional connection and your sexual relationship in order to reflect on what is found in the Scriptures.

The Risks

The reality is intimacy comes with serious risks. What if you share the depths of your heart with your spouse, things you are feeling, fears you have, and dreams and hopes you cherish, and your spouse says, "Uh, OK ..." What if you expose the sexual desires and needs you have and your spouse dismisses or ignores them? Baring yourself to someone and disclosing your vulnerable parts can be scary, especially if they do not seem to understand you or appreciate your gift of openness or your expression of need. It is an honor when your partner is vulnerable and exposes their very self to you. But remember, it is dangerous for them to do so. The word *vulnerable* comes from the Latin root *vulner,* which means *wound.* When you make yourself vulnerable, you are making yourself woundable. Husbands, wives, it is vital that you hear this. When your spouse shares their hurts, dreams, fears, hopes, frustrations, and joys, they are letting you into the depths of who they are. When your spouse opens their body to you sexually, they are allowing you into an even deeper, more vulnerable part of themselves. Sex is such a risky, tender area of the marital relationship. Can you imagine a more vulnerable time, when you have exposed the most private parts of your body to someone you love? And then you're supposed to tell them what you want them to do while you are laying there so exposed? You have the power to do incredibly beautiful things in those moments or terribly destructive things. Be careful with that power and use it well.

So tread lightly and lovingly with all you learn here. Be careful that the contents of these pages are not used as any kind of weapon. Surround yourselves with help as you explore these passages; stay close to God in your time with Him, and draw near to other couples involved in your life who can help you safely navigate these waters. Take what you learn and pray about it. Meditate on God's Word and focus on the areas you see that you need to change. Pray and allow God to work in your spouse's life. When you put the exercises found in these pages into practice, remember they are but guidelines to steer the course; there is no test, and you will not be graded. You definitely won't want your spouse to feel like they are being graded either. Taking this journey will be an exploration; so be curious, be loving, and be kind.

Not My Story

The reality is, you may read the words above about the unique treasure found in marriage in the sexual relationship, and you may feel sad, discouraged, angry, or frustrated. As followers of Christ, you may have anticipated marital sexuality to bring great delight, but instead it brought disappointment and conflict. Or you may be married to someone who is not a believer. This book may be a hard read. You may have gone to multiple marriage classes or retreats and walked away feeling hopeless, trampled, and completely left out of the picture every time someone taught about the sexual relationship. You may be someone who avoids reading Song of Songs because it is just too painful; it brings up everything that is *not* in your marriage. We hear you, and our recommendation as you seek to implement *The Art of Intimate Marriage* is to read slowly and prayerfully, taking each of the parts of this book to God and asking Him to work in your marriage, in your heart, and in your spouse's heart. Like we've mentioned above, share what you are learning with those you trust and are close to and ask their help with the things you are seeing and learning. We can't urge you enough to be open, be honest, and get help with how to speak the truth in love.

What Is Contained in These Pages?

Finding sexual fulfillment starts with embracing a biblical view of sexuality and then putting what you believe into practice. This will require facing issues from your family background and how experiences with sexual violations, sexual sin, or sexual betrayals influence your sexual relationship now. In many of the chapters, you will read about real people with very real problems in their sex lives and how they have overcome those challenges. Their names and details have been changed. We have also included results from several research studies Jennifer has conducted, including the personal words of many of the participants.

However, this work will have missed its mark if we have helped you improve the physical act of sex without deepening your intimate connection. So we will lay a foundation by looking at the overall picture of intimacy in marriage, sharing ways to resolve conflict and deepen your connection in the midst of conflict, and helping you grow in touch and affection. Then we will be ready to explore sensual and sexual touch, the necessary ingredients to mutually intoxicating sexual arousal.

We also realize we've missed the mark if we don't address the distress that is caused by the very real physical and medical challenges that come up in the sexual relationship. Therefore, we will cover issues with erectile dysfunction, premature ejaculation, low sexual desire, sexual pain, difficulties with orgasm, and medical and age-related challenges with sexuality. The pinnacle of this journey will be practical and creative ways to make your sex life fun, romantic, and exciting (although by this point, we hope you will have already seen your sexual relationship become more thrilling, satisfying, and life-giving).

Will This Stuff Really Help Us?

That is such a valid question. God promises that when we change, it brings about refreshment and restoration (Psalm 23:3; Acts 3:19). It is also true that how much things improve in your marriage may depend on how much each person is willing to do what is needed to bring about change. However, another part of the challenge with change is that sometimes the things we use just aren't very effective. Most of us have given in and bought that red-light special that turned out to be useless. It is usually a good idea to know if something really works before you invest too much.

With that in mind, we wanted to share about some of what is behind the book that you are reading.

Our primary desire has been that anything we teach or write on marriage and sexuality be based on God's Word. It is God who causes growth in our lives (1 Corinthians 3:7). We have therefore included a large number of scriptures throughout the book so that you can examine them yourself. We also wanted the book to contain solid, well-founded direction and information on sex. For this, we relied on established medical, psychological, and sex therapy literature as well as on the results from Jennifer's research. In the process of her work, Jennifer has had the opportunity to conduct a few research studies. One study examined married Christian women's experiences of shame in connection to sexuality.[3] Some of the results of that study are included in the chapters of this book. Jennifer also ran a research study (a randomized controlled trial) of the sex therapy model she had developed to help Christian couples with their sexual relationships.[4] One of the goals was to see if her model of treatment helped couples improve in their overall intimacy and in their marital and sexual satisfaction. The results were substantial and showed that couples improved significantly. In the professional fields of medicine and mental health, practitioners strive to provide care that has been proven to be effective—that is evidence based. The evidence-based model of sex therapy that Jennifer developed and uses in her private practice is at the core of many of the exercises found in this book. Enjoy!

So Who Are We?

From Tim: Jennifer's got a number of impressive credentials, and this isn't just coming from a biased husband; she's amazing. She's a doctor of psychology, a licensed marriage and family therapist, a certified sex therapist, a nationally award-winning sex researcher, a certified chemical dependency counselor, an international speaker, and a professor. And, oh yeah, she also has a Bachelors of Music in Musical Theater. She always jokes that her next book is going to be entitled *Sex, Drugs, and Show Tunes*. But on top of that, or as she will tell you, more importantly, she is a disciple of Jesus, a wife (lucky me), and a mother of four children. Those are her favorite jobs.

From Jennifer: Tim has a lot of credentials as well. Not only has he been an attentive and devoted lover through the years, and I can say that because I'm his wife, but he has supported me in all the crazy adventures I've had in learning to help people. Through our years together, he's been a small group leader, a married ministry leader, a financial adviser to the ministry leadership, and a deacon. His integrity and hard work as a program manager and business owner make him a great provider. But it is his genuine love for God and his sincere determination to stay faithful to his commitment to God, to me, to his children, and to God's kingdom that I truly love, need, and admire.

Together we have enjoyed twenty-three years of marriage and parenting four great kids. Like many of you, we have struggled to keep our marriage bed pure from anger, sexual sin, unfaithfulness, selfishness, worldliness, resentment, criticalness, and pride. There have been so many who have helped us along the way. We hope we can be one of the many for you—one of the many resources you find in your life to help your marriage bring glory to God and to help your sex life be the life-giving joy that God intends it to be.

As disciples of Jesus, we have the opportunity to have a deeper understanding of God's loving heart through being deeply known and erotically bonded with our spouse. *The Art of Intimate Marriage* is designed as a road map to help you experience growth toward a more rewarding, spiritual sexual relationship. Let's get started!

1

Sexuality and Your Family of Origin

"Yeah, we had a sex talk. My dad basically said, 'So you know how it all works, right, the whole birds and the bees thing? Great.' And that was about it. Both my parents were too embarrassed to talk about sex."

"My mom would tug my brother's hands out when they were down his pants and swat his hands, and say, 'That's dirty down there.' "

"My dad told me, 'Get a good look at her mom before you get her pregnant or marry her, 'cause that's what you're gonna end up with.' "

"My mom used to say, 'Where did you get those thighs?' and continually tell me not to eat this or that or I'd get fat and men wouldn't be attracted to me."

"I could hear my parents arguing about sex. My dad would beg my mom, and my mom would just ignore him, and then he'd get angry."

"My dad had Playboy and Penthouse hidden in his closet. We went to church every week, and heard a lot about how Satan tempts us to have sex, and we need to never think about it 'til we were married. So I got this double message."

"My mom never talked about it with me. Ever. The message I got early on was that it was a taboo subject."

"I think my parents thought if they avoided the topic long enough, I'd figure it out on my own."

"My dad's only words of advice were, 'Wear a condom.'"

"When I started to develop, my dad would make comments about my breasts getting bigger. I felt really uncomfortable. He would always make sexual jokes too. My mom would just laugh him off."

"My mom used to say, 'All men are pigs.' She had a lot of boyfriends. Several of them violated me; they made comments or touched me in really awful ways."

"Most of what I learned about sex was from sitcoms. The clear message I got was that men want sex and women don't, but grudgingly give it to them to keep the relationship."

"I heard at church ... they taught at school ... my friends always said ... I once saw ...."

Do any of these words sound familiar? There are many different things that can influence how sex is going in your marriage, and there is no question that what we experience in the area of sexuality during childhood and adolescence is a big part of that influence. The simple lack of talking openly about sex while growing up can create difficulties in how someone experiences sexuality as an adult.[1] Experts in the field of sexual development have found that negative sexual events during those formative years have an effect on how an individual views sexuality as an adult.[2]

The messages at the opening of this chapter may have come from parents, from society, from peers, or from a religious upbringing. However, the reality is that most of us have gone through a number of different experiences during childhood and adolescence that gave us a skewed view of sexuality.

Researchers on the sexual self-schema, that internal map one has of oneself as a sexual person, define this self-schema as the way someone thinks about sex, how they view themselves when they have sex, and how they feel and respond to their own sexual arousal or to their spouse's arousal and desire.[3] It may also include what someone thinks when they see their own body and their own genitals or the internal dialogue someone has while having sex (sexual scripts).

Negative sexual events during development that influence the adult sexual self-schema can include a number of different experiences:[4]

- the lack of openness talking about sex
- a lack of physical, affectionate touch
- harsh or shaming responses to typical childhood exploration of the genitals (i.e., when playing doctor)
- lack of open discussion about changes during puberty or negative comments about the child's or adolescent's changing body
- rigid gender expectations ("Boys don't do that," "Girls are supposed to...")

Other negative events include:[5]

- dehumanizing or humiliating sexual experiences or violations
- witnessing adult sex (intercourse or masturbation)
- harsh attitudes about the body
- sexual abuse
- a lack of belief or support from a parent or caregiver when a child or adolescent tells about being molested

The women in Jennifer's research study[6] shared a number of experiences that created negative feelings and beliefs about sexuality:

"Nobody ever gave me the sex talk, nobody ever told me ... I just wish somebody was there to say, 'Guys want this from you, and they're gonna do this and they're gonna say that'... It would have been nice, you know."

"That's how I grew up. That sex is what you do because you're supposed to. It's not anything voluntary. You just submit to it to have kids."

"My mom said... 'You have sex with everybody that walks in this house,' and my stepmom said 'You will be pregnant by the end of summer.'"

"I remember doing it and feeling very guilty and a lot of shame, and I would come home and get on my knees and say 'God, I'm really sorry.' With my first husband, I remember us doing that a little bit in the beginning; and on our wedding night, we had sex, and I just cried and cried and cried. 'Cause I was like, how can this... I'm supposed to feel so great about it when I felt so bad about it for so long."

"Just the desire to have it [sex] to me was really sinful, really wrong."

"I think also my Mom didn't like any kind of physical affection in front of us, so it made me think it was really dirty or wrong. She didn't like my dad kissing anything, touching or anything ... her pushing him away, getting

frustrated or flustered when he tried. So I would say I kind of grew up thinking, ewww ... ewww."

"I had the abuse when I was little, and... I always had it in my mind that that was my fault because I was a flirt ... I remember even feeling then, What did I do that made him think that that was OK?"

"I think growing up, even thinking about sex was wrong ... So I couldn't ask questions."

"I grew up thinking that I wasn't supposed to have it or want it. It's all on the guy's part. They have the desire, and we're just there to fulfill that desire."

"[My mom] heard us looking at each other in the garage, looking at each other's vaginas. Obviously, she'd heard us. But she didn't say much about it. We just didn't go there. She just said, 'If you ever want to know anything about your body or about sex, you know you can always ask me.' And I remember thinking, I would love to talk about that."

"I think, had it been... not so condemned and not so ashamed, but more understood and taught, I think there wouldn't have been the shame and the guilt and the tears and the fear."

"At some point she handed me this book called You Take the High Road, but we really didn't talk about it."

"I was probably on my period for a whole year before I told her. I just kind of hid it because we didn't have that kind of open communication."

"He was kind of talking to me and kind of following me, and it started feeling a little weird; and he followed me and grabbed me and kissed me, and I like pushed him away and ran. But I would never tell [my parents] cause we didn't talk about that stuff. I was sure I had done something wrong. If he would do that, then I must have done something wrong."

"Dad had been very hands on; I mean, we played. He picked me up and threw me around. I sat on his lap. When I was younger. But as I matured, it was very much hands off. Since he didn't want to be inappropriate. I get that to some degree. I didn't have the closeness with my dad anymore. And I really thought there was something wrong with me."

"I think the lack of communication communicated very clearly it wasn't something you could bring up."

"You didn't want to look attractive to anybody. That was sinful. You could cause a brother to lust after you."

Demeaning comments, discomfort with talking about sex, guilt, shame, negative parental sexual relationships, sexual molestation—each of these things skews the development of healthy sexuality. Though the words above are from women, the reality is that many men experience significant negative sexual events as well. When men talk about their own experiences, they also share about the lack of communication about sex in their families. They talk about the shame or embarrassment they experienced with masturbation and pornography, being handed a book to read but no talking about it, and hearing their parents argue about sex. Negative comments about the body for boys usually centers around their size, their musculature or lack of muscles, and the size of their penis. Though the percentage of women who experience molestation and sexual abuse is significantly higher than for men, men also share about having other boys or older men or women violate them with demands for oral or anal sex or being forced to engage in sexual touch and sexual contact with others.

For instance, think about the development of your own sexual self-schema (or sexual self-concept). In your own upbringing, was sexuality a taboo subject in your family, or was it spoken about in ways that felt demeaning, crude, or invasive? Did you experience molestation or rape? Did you hear negative comments about your body, especially during puberty, or were negative comments made about other people's bodies? What was your family's level of comfort discussing the physical and sexual changes during puberty, if they discussed them at all? Did your family respond negatively when, as a child, you began to explore sexual sensations and feelings (i.e., genital touching of self or others)? Were there rules in your family or in the spiritual environment you were raised in that were never explained, such as whether you should dance, wear certain clothes, go on dates, listen to certain music? Were you exposed as a child or adolescent to exploitative sexuality, violating sexual comments, or pornography, etc.?

Learning where your beliefs and feelings about sexuality come from is not the fix-all for problems in your marital sexual relationship, but it can definitely shed some light on patterns and responses you may currently engage in. It can bring understanding and compassion into such a potentially explosive, sensitive area. Exploring this helps broaden the picture of what you need in order to experience sexuality as God intended.

In the midst of exploring how these negative sexual events may have influenced you, remember God's compassion toward us and our pain. Consider the compilation of scriptures below that express God's heart in regards to the broken experiences we have in our lives. These are His promises and this is how He cares. As Piper and Taylor[7] have said: "To those for whom sexual experience has resulted in unholy pain, Christ says: *I understand well your experience. I hear the cry of the needy, afflicted, and broken. Come to me. I am your refuge. I am safe. I will remake what is broken. I will give you reason to trust, and then to love. I will remake your joy*'" (Psalm 10, 147; Jeremiah 33; Amos 9).

EXERCISES

About the Exercises in This Book
Some of the exercises, as in the first one below, are for the individual to do. Most of the exercises are for the couple. It is best when both husband and wife genuinely commit to doing these exercises. Though spouses who are reluctant at first can become engaged after trying something, it may not be of benefit to your marriage to use compulsion to get your spouse to grudgingly participate.

Talk together with your spouse about reading this book at the same pace and then about how you would like to incorporate the exercises found here. For those of you who are reading this book to improve your marriage yet your spouse is not interested in reading with you, you may want to consider asking if she or he would be willing to read certain portions (i.e., chapter six, *Talking About Sex*) and discuss it together.

The first exercise includes some questions to help you explore psychosexual events during your childhood and adolescence and to examine how they may have influenced your adult view of sexuality. Before reading or answering these questions, you may need to think ahead of time of someone you can call and speak with if these questions bring up any painful or difficult memories and feelings. If you find yourself becoming emotional or having a challenging time, make sure to take a break and breathe. Then consider if you should talk to a friend or support person before you go on, or whether you need to seek some professional support.

Sexual Background Exercise 1: Questions to Ponder and Journal

1) Did you have a time with a parent or a caregiver when they openly explained about how babies were made and how sex worked (The Talk)?

2) When you were going through puberty, was there openness in your family to discuss some of the physiological changes happening to your body? Did you feel able to ask questions?

3) Was there much affection in your family (between your parents/ caregivers, toward you, among other family members)?

4) During childhood, when you began exploring sexual sensations, or touched your genitals, or explored yours or other children's bodies, did you experience any responses from your parents or caregivers that were negative or that left you feeling shame?

5) When you had sexual questions, did you have anyone you could go to and ask?

6) Did you receive any negative comments about your body (not just sexually, but overall), or did you get negative messages about your body or the body overall from any other sources?

7) Did you experience any sexually unwelcome or violating experiences (touches, comments, interactions, pornographic material, genital contact, penetration, molestation, rape)?

8) Have you experienced any sexual interactions that left you feeling shame? When you think about the words *shame* and *sex*, have you had any experiences that associate feelings of shame and embarrassment with sex?

Journal: It may be helpful to take some time to journal your answers to these questions. After answering, explore and write about how you think these experiences may have influenced the way you interact around sexuality now as an adult.

Sexual Background Exercise 2: As a Couple

With your spouse: When things in your relationship are in a good place, it might be quite beneficial to take some time away, when you can be uninterrupted, to share your answers to the questions above with each other.

Spouses: When your spouse shares their answers, experiences, and thoughts, listen and merely reflect what they share with you. This would not be the time to interpret or fix or explain your thoughts or view. Simply give your spouse a compassionate, listening ear.

This can be quite an intimacy building time together. If emotions or tears are expressed, ask your spouse if they just want you to be there and listen, if they need to be held, or if you can take their hand. Sometimes all your spouse may want is your presence without any touch.

2

So What Does the Bible Say About Marital Sex

Don't do it until you're married.
Sexual sin will send you to hell.
If your spouse wants it, you better do it.
Otherwise, they will struggle with sexual temptation.
Or they will leave you and go find it somewhere else.

That is about the sum total of what most people think the Bible says about sex. However, in His Word, God addresses sexuality in a much deeper and finer way. Some of you may be eager to learn God's perspective on sex. You may wish you knew more about what the Bible teaches about sex and God's view of sexuality. However, some of you may find the whole topic uncomfortable or embarrassing. For others, you have read books on sex and gone to numerous marriage retreats where sex was one of the topics, but talking about sex has become discouraging and something you would rather avoid. You have heard lots of lessons about how sex should be great, that everyone should be having sex often, and that you need to spice up your sex life. This can sometimes lead to hopelessness. You may have some serious areas you are working on in order to develop a mutually fulfilling sex life. We pray that these words will give you a new life-transforming view of sexuality. This may include reexamining your beliefs and coming to a new understanding of the biblical view of marital sexuality. Let's take a deeper look at the Scriptures in the Bible on sex in order to bring how you are living out your sexual relationship closer to what God intends.

Sexuality and God

One of the areas about sexuality that can be very confusing for Christians is how to fit God in the picture. For many of us, it seems that our thoughts about sexuality have little connection to our thoughts about God. Sex is over here on the far right, and God is over here on the far left, and they never interact. Even the two words, God and sex, in the same sentence seem kind of inappropriate. This is even truer for the words sex and Christ. When you think about it, really, *Jesus never even had sex*, so it seems so inappropriate or even sacrilegious to put sex and Christ in the same sentence, right? What do the two have to do with each other? Yet that is not what we find in the Bible. Jesus is to be Lord over every area of our lives, God speaks to us in every area of our lives, and that includes sexuality. We do not have to divorce ourselves from God and Jesus in the middle of sex in order to allow ourselves to experience the full, sensual enjoyment possible during sex.

We personally have hundreds of books and articles on sexuality on our bookshelves, some from a Christian perspective and some not. This is only a very small amount of the information that exists on this incredibly important area of the marital relationship. Our journey to understand this has included a continual search, both personally and professionally, for grounding in the Scriptures and for finding what really works in helping couples improve their sexual relationship. Before beginning to specialize in sexuality, Jennifer took some extensive time to look up every scripture that referenced sex and marriage. If you are a married couple, and this is an area of difficulty for you, this is our first recommendation. If you are a therapist working from a Christian perspective, or a ministry leader wanting to help married couples, and you want to grow in your competence in working with sexuality, this is our first recommendation. Ground yourself in what the Scriptures say about sex. To help you, we have included quite a few scriptures that you can compare to your view of sexuality.

There are many books out there in the Christian publishing industry that have differing perspectives and theological stances about the marital and sexual relationship. Although there is some helpful information out there, it is important to take a very critical stance when reading them. Some of those books, though the motivation of the author(s) may be to help, contain some biblical, psychological, and physiological errors. Others take stances that may be contrary to the heart of the Scriptures and the heart God has about sexuality between a husband and wife. We hope you take the same critical view of what will be shared here.

In our work with couples and in doing workshops—both professionally and in the ministry—we have found that there is usually a lot of learning and relearning that has to happen in order to grasp God's perspective on marital intimacy. Couples often have to work through false beliefs about sex and the incredible pain that often surrounds this area of an individual's and couple's life. Be a noble Berean (Acts 17:11) and look up the scriptures and spiritual principles found in this book so that you can feel confident, convinced in your own mind (Romans 14:5), of what the scriptures teach.

A Biblical View of Sexuality

> *"The language and imagery of sexuality are the most graphic and most powerful that the Bible uses to describe the relationship between God and his people—both positively (when we are faithful) and negatively (when we are not)."*
> —Piper and Taylor, *Sex and the Supremacy of Christ**

One of our favorite texts for helping people understand the biblical and spiritual view of sex is *Sex and the Supremacy of Christ* by Piper and Taylor. The authors have kindly given permission to briefly review two major points from their book here: "God has designed sexuality as a way to know Him fully," and "Knowing God guards and guides our sexuality." As you read this, watch for how God has used the language and imagery of sexuality to communicate with us and to help us know Him. Note how our knowledge of God protects and directs how we live out our sexuality.

"God Has Designed Sexuality as a Way to Know Him More Fully"

This idea is found in the first chapter of Piper and Taylor's book. Please take a moment now to read Ezekiel 16 and then Ezekiel 23. When God is speaking about the nation of Israel and their worship of other idols, He uses words and phrases such as "prostitute," "lavished your favors," "degraded your beauty," "offering your body with increasing promiscuity to anyone who passed by," "your young breasts were fondled," "genitals ... like those of donkeys," and "emission, like that of horses." Why would God use such graphic sexual language? He is describing the spiritual choices Israel has made in idol worship, and He is using sexual language to depict what they had done. Let's explore this together.

For many couples, the biggest fear they have or the greatest emotional pain they have faced is the idea or experience of their spouse being unfaithful. We have sat with couples who have expressed the devastating pain of sexual betrayal in their marriage, of finding out that their spouse has intimately touched another man or woman in a way only they should be touched. When God talks here about the incredible pain of Israel's betrayal with idols, He uses the language of sexual betrayal and adultery, and He talks about it by using the physical, sexual body—words such as breasts, genitals, and emission. Why? Because He wants us to understand the level of pain He feels when we choose to worship something other than Him, when we choose to turn our backs on Him and His love for us ("you became mine" Ezekiel 16:8). Because we understand the pain of betrayal in marriage, God uses these pictures and words to describe the pain of betrayal He feels when we commit spiritual adultery, or idolatry, against Him. God uses sexual language to communicate His heart, who He is, and how He feels, so that we can understand and come close to Him. He wants us to know Him deeply.

This is similar to how God communicates to us overall. He uses the creation to tell us who He is (Romans 1:20, Psalms 19:1-3). He shows us who He is through making us in His image (Genesis 1:27), and He ultimately wanted us to know Him so well that He incarnated Himself into the physical body of Jesus to show us His very nature, the essence of who He is (John 1:14, Isaiah 9:6, John 14:9, Colossians 1:15). God uses the physical to express the spiritual. He also uses the physical language of sexuality to tell us about Himself and to communicate to us.

Knowing God

"I know my sheep and my sheep know me, just as the Father knows me and I know the Father" (John 10:14). God knows us. Jesus knows us. Jesus knows God and God the Father knows Jesus. The word *know* here is *gnosko* in the Greek, which means firsthand knowledge through personal experience; to learn, to recognize, to perceive. *Gnosko* is the word used here to describe the depth to which God and Jesus know each other. This is an intimate understanding of the other at an indescribably deep level. What is interesting is that *gnosko* is the same word used to describe the sexual interaction between Joseph and Mary. "He (Joseph) did not know (gnosko) her (Mary) until she gave birth to a son" (Matthew 1:25; parenthetical references added). *Gnosko* not only describes how well Jesus knows us, and how well Jesus and God know each other, but the depth to which Joseph and Mary knew each other.

We see something very similar in the Hebrew language. "No longer will a man teach his neighbor... 'Know the Lord,' because they will all know me" (Jeremiah 31:34). The Hebrew word here for *know* is *yada*, meaning to know, acknowledge, and understand through all the senses. And guess what? We find it also in Genesis 4:1. "Adam knew (*yada*) his wife Eve." So in both the Greek and Hebrew, the word for *know* describing how God knows us, how we know Jesus the Shepherd, how Jesus knows God, and how God wants us to know Him is also used to describe the sexual relationship between Adam and Eve and between Joseph and Mary. In many translations the word *know* is no longer used and has been variously translated to say "lay with her," or "had relations with her." The latest translation of the NIV says, "made love to." This is not to say in any weird way that our relationship with God or the relationship between God and Jesus has a sexual expression. That is what the pagan world did with false gods through their temple worship with temple prostitutes. But this does help to convey how God understands the sexual relationship. The depth of intimate knowing between Jesus and God, the depth to which He knows us, the depth to which God wants us to know Him, is the depth of intimacy God intends for us in our marital sexual relationship—a deep emotional, spiritual, and physical intimacy. These are the words God uses to describe sex.

This puts the importance of sexuality on a whole different level. John 17:3 says, "This is eternal life, that they *know* (gnosko) you, the only true God, and Jesus Christ." The biblical definition of eternal life here is the word *know*. We will spend eternity in an intimate knowledge and understanding and closeness with God and Jesus. Wow! And we believe that God gives us a taste of that in our sexual relationship. The level of intimate knowing that we can attain when we are ecstatically, intimately, and erotically bonded with our spouse during sexual intimacy, and at orgasm, is only a taste of the depths and levels of the wonderful, intimate connection we will have with God for eternity. God uses the physical to express the spiritual so that we may *know* Him.

"Knowing God Guides and Guards our Spirituality"

Piper and Taylor do an amazing job of describing this truth in their book. The *knowing* we wrote about above is the foundation God uses to guard our sexual choices and to guide our sexual lives. When we have that deep, intimate connection with our Father, He directs us in how we should live our lives overall and in the sexual arena. When we do not retain our knowledge for God, this disorders our sexual lives. "God gave them over in the sinful desires of their hearts to sexual impurity for the degrading of their bodies with one another. They exchanged the truth of God for a lie...Since they did not think it worthwhile to retain the *knowledge* of God, He gave them over to a depraved mind, to do what ought not to be done" (Romans 1:24-25, 28; emphasis added). The word *knowledge* here has the same root, *gnosko.* When we do not retain or nurture our *gnosko*—our knowledge, our intimate knowing of God—it messes us up sexually.

So let's review. God communicates to us and teaches us who He is through the language of sexual intimacy. His goal is for us to know Him intimately but also for us to know one another intimately within marriage. That knowledge of who God is, coupled with a life-giving knowledge of each other, can then guard and guide our sexual relationships. As we progress, we will learn that the Bible includes a wealth of other clear directions on how to live out our sexuality as God intends. This includes what we might have on our sexual menu, what sensuality in marriage could look like, how to please one another and be good stewards of each other's bodies, and the kind of fire and intoxication the Scriptures say can happen in your sexual relationship.

What to Include on Your Sexual Menu: What's Allowed

As we have learned, sexuality fosters an intimate connection between the husband and wife. Most of the scriptures in the Bible about sex are about what not to do: Don't do it with a goat, and don't do it with your father's wife. In other words, the scriptures in the Bible that do address how to live out our sexuality according to God's plan are *only* about sex within the marital relationship. This is very important. Biblical sexuality is about intimate connection. It is not just about the sex act itself. The overall purpose of sexuality found in the Bible, the overarching theme of God's plan for sexuality, is to bring about and nourish the intimate connection in the marital relationship. Any choice of what to engage in sexually should therefore be guided by that overarching principle. Does what we engage in sexually draw us closer together, does it build our intimate connection?

Couples often ask us what we think God allows in the marital bed. Are there prohibitions in the Bible about what a married couple can engage in sexually? Rather than tell couples what they are allowed to do, we give them a set of scriptures to go over together and, by doing that, make a decision together about what to include in their sexual repertoire (see the exercise and the scriptures used below). The questions are often about oral sex, anal sex, using toys or vibrators, or the use of aids such as lubricants, medications such as Viagra, and testosterone. We also get asked about role playing and dressing up, mutual watching of pornography, mutual masturbation and individual masturbation, and engaging in phone/text/email sex (i.e., phone sex and sexting) with a spouse.

Because one of the common questions we get is whether an individual or couple should engage in individual masturbation, we will use that as an example of how to make choices about what to include sexually. We have gotten this question from single individuals who masturbate but say they do not fantasize during masturbation. We also get this question from married individuals who say that this is how they manage the discrepancy in sexual desire, where one spouse desires sex more than the other; they engage in masturbation rather than continually asking their spouse, who does not have the same level of interest or desire for sex. This also comes up with couples with a spouse who travels a lot or is out on deployment. These are just a few of the scenarios.

So what does the Bible say about masturbation? Absolutely nothing.

The practice of masturbation is not addressed in the Scriptures. It is from here that it is important to look at the overarching view of sexuality in the Bible. Does this practice, in whatever fashion we/I engage in it, create connection and intimacy between us as a married couple? What is the fruit of choosing to include this in our sexual repertoire? Consider a husband who has a background in masturbation and pornography, a practice that he believes God does not desire him to engage in. Let's say he begins to include individual masturbation in his sexual practices, with his wife's support, when they are not able to have sex together. However, if he is drawn back to engaging in practices he believes are wrong, such as masturbating to pornography, then including masturbation may not be a good spiritual choice for this man. The fruit of this choice may not bring benefit. At times, the use of masturbation, or allowing a spouse to masturbate, can also be a way to *avoid* genuine giving. In other words, it may come from a place of selfishness. Some say they would rather their spouse masturbate than continually ask them for sex.

A better goal may be to develop a way to include masturbation in the couple's relationship as a mutual activity while they are in the same room. In our experience, when both spouses are not included in a sexual activity, such as individual masturbation, then the **masturbation becomes a missed opportunity for connection.**

Consider this scenario for that husband who has a greater sex drive than his wife. When you, the husband, feel the desire/drive for a sexual release, instead of masturbating on your own, include your spouse. Curl up together in bed with your wife. Husband, give your wife some time, even a short time, whatever she would enjoy, of sensual touch or massage. Wife, now hold his scrotum within your hand as he brings himself to orgasm manually. Kiss him, and off you both go to sleep. Or consider this scenario: When you, the wife, desire a second or third orgasm after engaging sexually with your husband, rather than take care of it on your own because you do not want to burden your already tired spouse, have him take you in his arms as you stimulate yourself to a further, perhaps more intense orgasm. Doing this usually brings up a lot of feelings about self-stimulation in front of someone else and the guilt that can come cascading in or that can make someone uncomfortable. However, consider what it may do for your sexual relationship to give yourself and your spouse the permission to bring yourself to sexual release right before their eyes. Vulnerable? Oh yes. Bonding? You might be surprised. Bottom line? Any sexual practice, including masturbation, that does not include your spouse, or that does not promote that deep intimate connection between you, may not be reflecting God's plan for sexuality in the Bible. You may be missing out on a great opportunity to deepen God-given eroticism between you.

Remember, similar to what we mentioned above, if either of the above scenarios lead to bad fruit, consider whether you want to continue. So use the questions below, talk about them together, and explore. If you decide to try something and feel it is not prohibited by Scripture or does not go against someone's conscience, yet you find that after trying it, your connection and intimacy is not enhanced, then toss it out. If it does draw you closer together and make your sexual relationship even more enjoyable, that is wonderful indeed.

Song of Songs

As we mentioned, most of the scriptures about sex are about what NOT to do. Don't do it with your father's sister, with an animal, with someone you are not married to, or with anyone other than your husband or wife. This is all very clear from the scriptures. So, when you do have sex, what kind of direction does God give? Well, the Bible is the only world religion scriptural text that devotes an entire book to sensuality and sexuality. The Song of Songs is full of much that is helpful. We will cover some of that in different chapters, but it is important to notice here that God, even in how He handed His Word to us, prioritizes the marital sexual relationship by writing an entire book about it. We need to take note of that. Sensual touch and sensual talk is all over the Song of Songs. Both the Lover and the Beloved describe each other in sensual, poetic terms. They also use poetic language to describe the delights of the sexual relationship. Note the scriptures below:

Lover: "How beautiful you are and how pleasing, O love, with your delights! Your stature is like that of the palm, and your breasts like clusters of fruit. I said, 'I will climb the palm tree; I will take hold of its fruit.'" The Lover here speaks of climbing the palm tree (her body) to grasp the fruit (her breasts).

The Lover says: "You are a garden fountain, a well of flowing water, streaming down from Lebanon." And the Beloved responds: "Blow on my garden, that its fragrance may spread abroad. Let my lover come into his garden and taste its choice fruits." The Lover here describes the flowing streams of her garden and the Beloved calls him to blow on the garden and taste its fruit. This is considered by many to be a clear allusion to their enjoyment of the act of oral sex and the flowing waters of her lubrication and orgasm.

God has intended for us to thoroughly enjoy sexuality and the erotic sexual bond we can have with our spouse. More on Song of Songs in a later chapter.

Pleasing Your Spouse: Stewards of Each Other's Bodies

"But a married man is concerned with ... how he can please his wife ... A

married woman is concerned about ... how she can please her husband."
— *1 Corinthians 7:33-34*

*"The husband should fulfill his marital duty to his wife, and
likewise the wife to her husband ... Do not deprive each other
except by mutual consent for a time, so that you may
devote yourselves to prayer. Then come together again so that
Satan will not tempt you because of your lack of self-control."*
— *1 Corinthians 7:3, 5*

*"The wife's body does not belong to her alone but also
to her husband. In the same way, the husband's body
does not belong to him alone but also to his wife."*
— *1 Corinthians 7:4*

These scriptures in 1 Corinthians 7 have been some of the most specific, helpful, and misunderstood scriptures of the Bible on sex. So let's go over a few important points.

God wants us to live our sexual lives focused on the pleasure we can bring to our spouse. That doesn't mean you don't have likes and dislikes, preferences and turn-offs, and that you should just shut those down and only think about your spouse. In fact, it is crucial to communicate openly and honestly about what you prefer. We're going to devote quite a bit of space in these chapters to that exact issue. However, God does call us to consider one another better than ourselves and prioritize the interests of others (Philippians 2:3-4). If both the husband and wife kept that as their focus, many of the difficulties in the sexual relationship would go much more smoothly.

In a similar way in Corinthians, Paul, though he understood that a celibate life was not what many would choose, emphasized how someone could be more productive in God's work here on earth if they didn't have to focus on pleasing a spouse (1 Corinthians 7:33-34). In other words, through this passage of scripture, God makes it clear that a husband should be focused on pleasing his wife and a wife focused on pleasing her husband. Thinking of the interests of your spouse above your own and focusing on pleasing them is a vital part of the marital sexual relationship.

It is also important to look at who owns your body. Look at the wording. The wife's body *does not belong to her alone.* Same wording for the husband. In other words, *her body does belong to her.* This is a significant point, especially for women. The woman's body first and foremost belongs to her. Cliff and Joyce Penner, in their book *The Gift of Sex,* include a chapter on *By Invitation Only.* They discuss the fact that, when engaging in sex, women are opening up their bodies; they are allowing someone to enter them, and that this should only be done by the woman's permission. Without that permission, it is a violation. There are various ways to understand this idea. If someone just walked into your home and began going into your rooms, randomly opening up your drawers and going through them, you would definitely put a stop to that and consider that a violation. If a woman has her purse on a table and someone just randomly opens it and starts going through it, we would say, "Hey, what are you doing?" We understand that there are physical boundaries that would be inappropriate to cross without asking. How much more so with the physical body. When making choices about what to allow to happen to her body, it is vital that the choice, first and foremost, is the wife's to make. In marriage, God created us to be one flesh, to be unified in both body and soul (Genesis 2:24). Within the spiritual family, we are called to be unified (1 Corinthians 1:10). As the unity in the spiritual family would include considering one another as better than yourself (Philippians 2:3) and would not include forcing someone to do something they do not feel good about (1 Corinthians 8 and Romans 14), how much more so in the marriage relationship.

In a further look at this scripture, Paul points out that the wife and husband have the authority over each other's bodies. What does that mean? It has often been taught that this means a wife should never deny her husband sex. Though this is an important question to explore, the interpretation of 1 Corinthians 7:4 is much more nuanced than that. The wording in the Greek here is quite helpful. The term Paul uses here is *exousiazo*, which means: to exercise authority over. This is a term describing a delegated or conferred power or authority, which is much like the idea of stewardship, taught about throughout the Bible, especially in the New Testament. When someone is a steward, they are chosen by God, given authority by God, to care for something He has given them. And you are to do this for the benefit of others. We understand this when it comes to money. God gives us money, and we are but stewards of that money while in this life. We are to use that money as God sees fit. This is financial stewardship (Matthew 25:20-21, 23). There is also a common understanding that when you borrow something, you should return it in as good or better condition than when you received it. We know that God calls husbands to imitate Jesus and present their wives as radiant (Ephesians 5:27). These are the concepts reflected in 1 Corinthians 7:4. A wife is given her husband's body from God. He owns his body but God has also conferred power over that body to the wife, and she is to be a good steward of that handsome body and present his body back to God in as good or better condition than when it was given to her. The husband in the same way is given delegated authority from God over his wife's body. She is the owner of her body, but he has been commissioned to care for it as for his own body (Ephesians 5:28). God gave him stewardship over that beautiful body and he, the husband, is to return it to God in beautiful shape. When he seeks first to please his wife, he is then able to present her as radiant to God.

1 Corinthians 7 has been misused to demand or command sex. This is in opposition to the scriptures and to the overall use of authority in the Bible. If God has delegated to the wife authority over her husband's body, how is she supposed to use or wield that authority? If God has delegated to the husband authority over his wife's body, how is he supposed to use or wield that authority? Jesus taught that the disciples were not to lord it over others the way the Pharisees did (Matthew 20:25-26). Instead, a leader is to be a servant. So when we are given authority over each other's bodies, we are to use that authority as Jesus taught: as a servant, not making demands or being selfish (for a resource on changing selfish demands see Harley's "Selfish Demands" chapter in *Love Busters*). And so a woman's body is her own, and when she unites with her husband in marriage, she is deciding, just as the man is, that while her body remains her own, God is also giving her husband a delegated authority over her body. And he is called by God to use that authority well by, first and foremost, pleasing his wife.

For many couples, when they examine these scriptures, it puts the command not to deprive one another into a different perspective. If a husband or wife ends up using this scripture to say, "You are depriving me," they may be using the scriptures as a club or a weapon, much like a Pharisee would. If a wife or husband continues to "deprive" their spouse of sex out of selfishness, they are not being a good steward of their spouse's body. If both the husband and wife were focused on pleasing one another, holy sex can be the outcome, where the focus is mutual pleasure through giving and fun exploration that results in a "delightful convergence of duty and desire."[1]

Intoxication, Fire, and Duty

> *"May you rejoice in the wife of your youth. A loving doe,*
> *a graceful deer—may her breasts satisfy you always,*
> *may you ever be intoxicated with her love."*
> — Proverbs 5:18-19

So what else does the Bible say about sex? The above scripture says it so eloquently. We are to rejoice in our spouse and be intoxicated by our love for one another. We are to feel this intoxicated satisfaction about each other sexually. The word *satisfy* in the Hebrew here is *ravah*, which means to drink one's fill, to be saturated. The word *intoxicated* in the Hebrew here is *shagah*, which means to reel, as in reeling when drunk. It also means ravished, enraptured, captivated; to stray, reel, or swerve while intoxicated. That is how God portrays the effect the wife, and her love, and her breasts, have on the husband. That he drinks so thoroughly of her that he is completely intoxicated and cannot walk straight.

This is such a clear statement of God's intention for sexuality in the Bible. The passage right before this details how a man of God should drink only from his own cistern and not share his strength and wealth, the springs of water from his well, clearly his sexuality, with anyone else other than the wife of his youth. And then when they do share it, it should make him reel. This may be a passage directly written to the husband, perhaps because sexual temptation is such a challenge for men. However, it is a great illustration of the incredible emotional, physical, and ecstatic way that God describes the marital sexual relationship. In 1 Corinthians 7:9, Paul admonishes the unmarried to get married because they were burning with passion for another (*puroo* in the Greek, meaning *set on fire*). Sex sets us on fire, so God says the place for it is in the marital bed. In other words, our sexual life should set us on fire. It should make us reel like a drunkard. It should saturate us and captivate us. This should be true for BOTH the husband and wife.

Many commentaries on 1 Corinthians 7 talk about the duties of the marital sexual relationship. Duty has become such an awful word to describe the wonder of marital sex. The dictionary says duty is an obligation. The Greek word used in this scripture, however, is *opheile* meaning *debt* or *indebtedness*. This term is unique to the New Testament and only used two other times in the Bible. One is in Romans 13. There, Paul says give everyone what you owe him. If you owe him taxes, pay it. If you owe him honor, show honor. If you owe them respect, give them respect. Why would you pay that debt and show them respect and honor? Because they have earned it and are worthy of it. Taxes might be a bit of a stretch, but when you show someone genuine honor and respect, it is because they have done something that has earned that respect and honor, and you believe they are worthy of it. When you pay your debt to your spouse, when you do your "duty" and give to them sexually, you are not just "doing your duty." You are showing them that you consider them worthy and choose to show this by giving your love. When we say we feel indebted to someone, we feel grateful for something they have been or something they have done. So when a spouse fulfills their marital *duty*, this is an expression of indebtedness, an expression that *I am grateful to you* and *you are worth it. I am doing this for you because you are that important, of that high worth to me.* Yes, it is a duty. But it is not a compulsory obligation. It is not a dreaded must.

When our giving is out of duty, out of compulsion, that is not God's desire. "Each of you should give what you have decided in your heart to give, not reluctantly or under compulsion, for God loves a cheerful giver" (2 Corinthians 9:7). Yes, this passage in 2 Corinthians 9 is about giving money, but it lays out clearly the heart God desires from us when we give. How much more should this be true in the marital sexual relationship. God does not want us to fulfill our sexual duty in the sense that many of us think of that word today. He desires for us to enjoy, to be intoxicated by, to be set on fire by each other's love and our sexual relationship. He wants us to perform that duty, to fulfill that debt, because we are grateful and they are worth it, and therefore we want to make them feel radiant, saturate them with our love, make them reel, and set them on fire.

The Enjoyment of Her Body

One of the big cultural stereotypes is of men who ogle women. Unfortunately, it is a stereotype that has quite a bit of foundation behind it. It is commonly seen and portrayed, from what happens on the street to what it shown in movies and TV. And it is not in God's plan. Jesus clearly taught that looking at a woman in lust was the same as adultery (Matthew 5:28). However, put into biblical perspective, the male enjoyment of the female body can be both godly and enriching. Unfortunately, because of sin and sinful behaviors, it can be challenging to appreciate the rightness of a husband loving the view of his wife's body. We have often heard wives express that it really bothers them how their husband likes to touch them sensually and sexually ("All he touches is my butt and my boobs."). It may really bother them how easily their husbands become aroused when they see their wife naked or when they get into bed with their naked or lightly clothed wife. It has caused some women to stop dressing in front of their husbands. For others, they wear their pajamas like protective armor.

There can be many different things influencing the challenge women have with their husband's fascination with their wife's body. It may be that the only time the husband touches his wife is when he is sexually interested. It may be that the wife has a lower body image. The husband may have made derogatory comments about her body or about her weight. The wife may have a background of being objectified by men or may have seen poor examples of men who objectified women. If any of these things were true, it would be important to get help with them and to talk openly about them.

It is important to put the male interest in the female body into biblical perspective, for when it is right, it is very right. After God created Eve, "God saw all he had made, and it was very good" (Genesis 1:31). Not just good. Very Good. We see the Lover, in Song of Songs, speak about how he wants to hear his Beloved's voice and how he wants to see her form, her shape, her countenance, her appearance (according to different translations). Proverbs 5:19, as mentioned earlier, tells how captivating, intoxicating, and satisfying the wife's love and breasts are to her husband. God has created in men a love for the view of the female body and form. He even puts it in His holy Word. It is good and right for a husband to be drawn to looking at and touching his wife's body, both naked and clothed. Sam Laing, author of *Five Senses of Romantic Love*, says it so well:

"His [the Lover's] poetic, rhapsodic language expresses his fascination and arousal and gives honor to the entirety of her divinely given beauty without a hint of demeaning vulgarity ... The husband asks ... his beloved to let him see her 'form' ... Most men will readily identify with this statement, and with this sentiment. They long to see their wife unclothed. Wives, have you noticed that your husband will stop whatever he is doing to get a glimpse of your body? If you are having an argument and in the middle of it you happen to change your clothes, he will completely lose his train of thought. He will wander into the bathroom while you are bathing just to get a look at you. Rather than resenting this as juvenile and boorish, come to appreciate that the sight of your unclothed form is one of the greatest pleasures and joys your husband has in his life."[2]

For women, it is important to make the distinction between the objectification in the world of the female body and the genuine, godly appreciation of her body as seen in the Scriptures. A husband's enjoyment of his wife's body is from God. However, husbands, if the only time you touch her is to squeeze her breasts and butt, this will not feel like godly enjoyment. I, Jennifer, had a female client explain to me that when she was dressing, she would have loved it if her husband had come up to her from behind while she was naked, wrapped his arms around her, and told her what a good mom she was. Not that she was beautiful. Not that he loved her body. But that as he wrapped his arms around the body he so loved to see and touch, he told her how much he loved and appreciated the woman she was and what she gave to their family. This is such a delicate balance. Women love to feel admired by the men God has given to love them. They do love to feel beautiful. But if that beauty is not admired in the context of the whole beauty of the woman, it can lead to an unintended confirmation of that message she's been hearing from Satan and the world: that she is just another body; that she is only wanted for sex; that she, the woman, is not known and valued.

So husbands, imitate the Lover. Look at what he says about his Beloved. When he describes the body of his beloved, he talks about her eyes, hair, teeth, lips, mouth, temple, navel, waist, neck, and breasts (Song of Songs 4:1-15, 7:1-9). He even tells her that her breath smells good, that her legs are graceful, that her voice is sweet, that her feet are beautifully sandaled (yes, compliment her shoes), and that her face is lovely. If what she hears is a primary focus on her breasts and her butt, you have not followed this incredible example found in God's Word. You may be obeying God's Word in reading it daily, in reaching out to the lost, in being a loving, giving father, and a good provider. But if you wish to touch the heart and soul of your wife, your words to her must be full of Proverbs 31 (how faithful and hardworking she is, what a great hostess she is, what a great mother and wife) AND Song of Songs (her physical beauty in its entirety).

He Is Altogether Lovely!

In an amazingly similar way, in the book Song of Songs, the Beloved describes her Lover in intimate, bold, and admiring language (Song of Songs 1:16, 2:3-4, 5:10-16). She talks about his head, hair, eyes, cheeks, lips, arms, and legs. She calls him handsome, radiant, ruddy, and outstanding. She compliments his arms of gold and his body of polished ivory. She talks about the kisses of his mouth. She delights to be with him and talks in detail about his affection and care for her. She shares a very revealing phrase at the end of the book. "I have become in his eyes like one bringing contentment" (8:10). How does he come to view her in that way?

Hopefully, through reading this book, you will have the opportunity to work as a couple on your verbal and relational intimacy. We believe that will lead you to have victories in working through conflict. It is important as well that you get help with any long-term injuries, which we cover in chapter eleven. There may be some rather difficult things that have happened between you that make imitating the way the Beloved talks about her Lover seem impossible. It is incredibly important, however, that as you are in the midst of working at improving and repairing your intimate relationship, you examine the heart of God and His heart for you and have the same heart for your husband.

God is rich in mercy. While we were still His enemies, while we were still in sin, He looked at us with longing and affection (Romans 5:8; Isaiah 30:18). One of the greatest needs of the human condition is to feel loved and accepted. God does both of those things. For those of you who have children, we strive to do those things for our children, to love them and accept them even though they do things that are not OK, choose paths we do not support, or that are sinful. It is sometimes much harder to show that same kind of mercy, compassion, patience, and vision for someone who is not our child, but who is an adult who should know better. And yet God does call us to make sure our husbands are "respected at the city gates" (Proverbs 31:23) and that we, as wives, are the ones who bring contentment. The longer you are married, the more you see your spouse's faults and the weaknesses in their character. It is an opportunity for either mercy or for resentment. If we decide to imitate the heart of God, what we will offer is a love and admiration for an imperfect sinner.

As wives, we are called to imitate the example of the Beloved. She is so eloquent in her admiration of her lover. Your husband needs you to admire his beauty for "he is altogether lovely" (Song of Songs 5:16). Tell him what you like about how he looks. At the same time, he needs to know that you admire and appreciate what he does for you. It is not uncommon for husbands to share about how angry and frustrated they feel because they do not sense that their wife appreciates them. There may be a lot behind that. He may work longer hours than you feel good about. Or the opposite. He may not be the kind of hard worker you feel he should be. You may have had many arguments about how he uses his time. You may strongly disagree about what to prioritize. It is important, however, to keep our eyes on the cross. Our sins put Jesus on the cross, and God calls us to have the same kind of compassion toward others that He shows to us (2 Corinthians 1:3-4). Your acute awareness of his weaknesses can blind you from focusing on and telling him about his strengths. Wives need to view their husbands' weaknesses with honesty, wisdom, humility, compassion, and vision. When you reach that point, you will be able to genuinely speak of your husband with the heart of the Beloved, telling him his strengths from a place of honesty.

In Song of Songs, God shows how the Lover needs to be appreciated for his arms that are rods of gold (his strength, Song of Songs 5:14), his arms that embrace you (his love of touching you and holding you, Song of Songs 2:6), and his legs that are pillars of marble (again, his strength, beauty, and power, Song of Songs 5:15). Tell him about the beauty of his body, tell him what you admire about his lovemaking, and tell him what you appreciate about what he does for you. Tell him. *Tell him.*

The level of intimacy and closeness in marriage is hugely influenced by the quantity and quality of words, like those that the Beloved and the Lover share with each other. So check how much you admire your spouse. Check how much you tell them about their beauty and their strengths. See what happens to your overall intimacy when you decide to imitate the Lover and Beloved's vivid, sensual, enriching, life-giving language. As you do this, you will learn to enjoy, in a greater way, the unique blessing of marriage as God designed it, in all its fullness.

EXERCISES

Sexual Choices Exercise: What's Allowed

Use the following questions with the accompanying scriptures to explore together what you want to include on your sexual menu.

What's Allowed: Eight Questions to Guide Your Sexual Choices in Marriage

1) Is it prohibited by Scripture (i.e., lust, sexual immorality: Matthew 5:28, Galatians 5)?

2) Is it beneficial and constructive (1 Corinthians 10:23-24)? Does it build up? Does it benefit your relationship, and are you seeking your spouse's good?

3) Does it involve anyone else (including fantasizing – Hebrews 13:4, Matthew 5:28)?

4) What is the fruit (Matthew 7:16-20)? When you put it into practice, does it create intimate connection between you? Does it lead to anything detrimental?

5) Is it too contaminated by pollution of the world (James 1:27) or has Satan contaminated it but now it needs to be reclaimed (2 Peter 1:3-4)?

6) Is it pleasing to your spouse (1 Corinthians 7:33-34)?

7) Does it violate your or your spouse's conscience (Romans 14:5, 1 Corinthians 8:7-13)?

8) If you choose not to engage in this, is it truly about restraining or controlling sensual/sexual corruption in a God-given manner, or is it based on human teachings and self-imposed, false restrictions of the body (Colossians 2:21-23)?

3

Conflict That Creates Connection

When couples want to get help with sexual problems, it is common that they want to go straight to working on the sexual issues they are having. You may be in that category. You may be tempted to skip these chapters on conflict, communication, and relationship skills. We recommend that you don't. Check first to see if you have good verbal intimacy skills and good conflict resolution skills. Practice the conflict resolution skills in this chapter and the communication and empathy skills in later chapters. You will then be prepared to approach the sexual issues with greater confidence and unity.

Marriage and conflict often go hand-in-hand. Conflict can cause division, but conflict can also be a door that opens to deeper connection. But why focus on conflict that occurs outside of the bedroom in a book on sex? One of the primary reasons is that overall patterns of conflict in the marital relationship are often reflected in the sexual relationship as well. Your ability to share and respond to differing preferences, likes, and dislikes in others areas of your marriage affects how well you will do when talking about sex. This is good news! By strengthening your conflict resolution skills in other areas, you will be better equipped to navigate the issues in your sexual relationship. Research has shown that conflict can either lead to greater connection and intimacy or it can lead to withdrawal, disconnection, and/or problems with sexual intimacy.[1] Couples can also feel differently about how to interact sexually in the midst of conflict. When they have conflict in their relationship, some spouses feel that having sex helps them resolve the conflict and feel close.

Others feel they need to resolve conflict and feel close again emotionally before they can engage in sexual intimacy.[2] Overall, when couples have good skills in resolving conflict, this can have an important influence on how well they deal with their sexual issues.

But what level of conflict is problematic? Some couples have very high conflict and still maintain a healthy sexual relationship. Others say they don't fight, which sounds better on the surface. However, couples with low conflict can feel some of the same feelings as those in high conflict, and the level of avoidance can create distance and a lack of closeness. Other couples may have constant, low-grade conflict that destroys intimacy or high, aggressive conflict that results in multiple levels of damage. For couples at any of these levels, the desire to be understood in the midst of conflict is important. An assessment used by therapists to evaluate a couple's level of conflict includes statements such as: "My partner is able to put him/herself into my shoes," and "My partner has a hard time seeing things from my perspective."[3] Striving to see each other's perspective in the midst of conflict can help couples gain that closer connection.

Let's begin by focusing on a few skills that are crucial for healthy conflict resolution: seeking understanding, getting rid of the pointing finger, striving for empathy, and taking timeouts. In the next couple of chapters, we will then guide you through how to use these skills to work through conflict. As you progress, you will grow closer and have greater empathy for one another.

Seeking Understanding

Proverbs 4:7 says, "Though it cost all you have, get understanding." Before we discuss what true understanding entails, there is a caveat. We often confuse being understanding and validating our spouse's view with being a doormat or with just letting someone have their way. Rest assured, this is not what God had in mind when He called us to understand and have empathy for one another. Having clear boundaries is important in any relationship. It is healthy to know when to say "yes" and when to say "no" (Matthew 5:37), when and how to speak the truth (Ephesians 4:15), and how to deal with someone who is being hurtful with their words. Proverbs advises, "Do not answer a fool according to his folly, or you will be like him yourself" (26:4). The apostle Paul also advised, "Those who oppose him (The Lord's servant) he must gently instruct, in the hope that God will grant them repentance leading them to a knowledge of the truth, and that they will come to their senses and escape from the trap of the devil, who has taken them captive to do his will" (2 Timothy 2:25-26). The Scriptures also teach us, "Rebuke your neighbor frankly" (Leviticus 19:17). There are times in relationships when someone says and does things that are not from God. They may speak in a way contrary to the Scriptures, or they may be in need of coming to their senses. God says to deal with this kind of opposition with the firmness, frankness, and gentleness of Jesus, praying they will escape Satan's captivity. No doormats here.

So how about when your spouse comes to you bothered, hurt, or angry about something you have done? The Bible does call us to be humble and take correction (Proverbs 12:1). As mentioned, God calls us to seek understanding. The scripture mentioned above, Proverbs 4:7, says that in order to get understanding, it is going to cost all you have. It is expensive to understand someone, to truly grasp how they feel and what they experience. To do that, you may need to truly set your own self aside and consider your spouse as better than yourself: "In humility, consider others better than yourselves. Each of you should look not only to your own interests, but also to the interests of others" (Philippians 2:3-4).

When you strive to understand your spouse, to truly hear them when they come to you with how they feel about something you have done or not done, or something you have said, you will need to put yourself aside in order to hear them. Often, when someone speaks to us, our minds begin racing with explanations, corrections, and defenses. We want to do the following:

- Defend: "Excuse me!! You're the one who ...." "Yeah, but you ...."
- Explain: "That's not what happened." "Oh, I didn't mean ...."
- Fix it: "OK, so how do you want me to say it?" "Well, then, let's do this."
- Apologize or reassure before we truly understand: "Oh, I'm sorry. I didn't mean ...." "Oh, no, I don't think you are ...."

These responses are normal, but they get in the way of really being able to hear someone, of being able to understand. Your own hurt may also come up when your spouse comes to you with something they are feeling. It may be tempting to spend most of your time preparing your response while they are speaking. So what do you do with all those thoughts whirling through your head? Do not ignore them. Do not push them under the carpet or do the proverbial zipping your mouth shut. That will not be helpful. In fact, give those thoughts some room, honor them in a sense. Instead of blurting them out or shoving them down, we recommend putting them on a virtual shelf—one right in front of you. You set them aside, put them up there for safekeeping. After you are done focusing on your spouse, truly coming to an understanding of what they are feeling (*truly* being the key word), then you are ready to look back on that shelf and see what is still up there. We'll talk about what to do with whatever remains on that shelf later. However, this practice of putting your own feelings or thoughts up there and choosing to consider, think about, and put your focus on what your spouse has experienced makes room in your heart and brain for genuine understanding.

When you make this decision to put your spouse first, to consider them better, you are imitating the heart of Christ. The scripture continues, "Having the same mindset as Christ Jesus ... who made himself nothing, taking the very nature of a servant" (Philippians 2:5-7). When you decide to put your spouse first, to set your own stuff aside in order to understand them, you are imitating Jesus. You are putting the cross of Christ into practice in your marriage.

Dealing with Defensive Listening: Getting Rid of the Pointing Finger

> "If you **do away with the yoke of oppression, with the pointing finger** and malicious talk, and if you **spend yourselves in behalf of the hungry** and satisfy the needs of the oppressed, then your light will rise in the darkness, and your night will become like the noonday. The Lord will guide you always; **he will satisfy your needs** in a sun-scorched land and will strengthen your frame. **You will be like a well-watered garden, like a spring whose waters never fail.**" —Isaiah 58:9-11 (emphasis added)

A huge barrier in resolving conflict is the use of the pointing finger. It still amazes us that there is a scripture that actually uses these words. The pointing finger is the "yeah, but you" in a conflict. It may be verbal, it may be internal (the silent "but you"), or it may be in your body language. It is the blaming, the accusing, the attacking, and the assuming that permeates an argument. God says to get rid of it. Why? Because of the beautiful benefits God promises. Your light will shine. He will guide you and satisfy your needs. You will be able to walk on a well-lit path. It is one of those "give up everything for God and He will give you back a hundredfold" promises (see Mark 10:30). Humble yourself and He will lift you up (James 4:10). Get rid of the pointing finger, of defending yourself, of saying, "yeah, but you," and God takes care of you. He will satisfy *you*. And then, when you decide to stop finger pointing, you will be able to spend yourself on behalf of the hungry. All that energy you put toward defending yourself, all that energy you use trying to get the other person to see your view, or see what they need to change, or how they have wronged you, can be spent on behalf of your hungry spouse. Just like you, your spouse is hungry for understanding. We all long to be understood. Focus on satisfying your spouse's need for understanding, fill that need, and God will fill you up. Once again, this does not mean that you won't have the opportunity to share your own view or perspective. In fact, the opposite is true. "Speak the truth in love" (Ephesians 4:15). However, in order to have the marriage God intends, it is vital that we work really hard at putting ourselves in our spouse's shoes. In order to even get close to that, we must work very hard at getting rid of finger pointing.

And what is the outcome when you get rid of the pointing finger? "You will be like a well-watered garden, like a spring whose waters never fail" (Isaiah 58:11). This is what God wants to create in our marriages. Picture the most beautiful, green place you both have seen. Is it Hawaii, some botanical gardens, the beautiful green of the Pacific Northwest, or New Zealand? Conflict can cause our marriages to become empty wastelands. Finger pointing can be a significant part of causing that to happen. However, the lush beautiful garden that God desires for us is only possible when we get rid of the blaming, accusing, assuming, and attacking that can happen in our relationships, replacing those damaging interactions with understanding and empathy.

Striving for Empathy

Ultimately, the goal of each of the skills above is learning to be a good listener and genuinely understanding to the point of feeling empathy for your spouse. Empathy is the glue that makes intimate sexual relationships satisfying.[4] Look at the example God sets. "In all their distress, He too was distressed" (Isaiah 63:9). And then look at God's direction to us. "Mourn with those who mourn" (Romans 12:15). God is a God of compassion (2 Corinthians 1:3-4). He calls us to have compassion and empathy for others, which is especially important in our marriage. It can be quite hard to do that, especially when the person who wants our empathy is upset with us! And yet, this is God's heart, and this is God's call to each of us. "He is kind to the wicked and the ungrateful" (Luke 6:35). He calls us to imitate Him.

Jesus is the ultimate example of genuine empathy. Read Luke 7:12-15. Here we find Jesus in the town of Nain as He sees a funeral go by. The dead man is the son of a widow. When Jesus saw her, "His heart went out to her" (v.13). The term used here for His heart going out to her is *splagchnizomai*, which in Greek means movement of the inner parts, the gut. Jesus saw this widow walking down the street at the funeral for her son, and He was moved to the depth of His gut. His heart went out to her. This is the best example we could imitate in our marriage—that when we see our spouse's pain or hurt, our most inward parts, our heart, go out to them. The example of Jesus calls us to have empathy.

So how do we get there? In the literature and research on empathy,[5] this ability to look at things through someone else's eyes is sometimes called perspective-taking. Seeing things from another person's perspective undergirds the ability to have empathy and resolve conflict. However, in order to have empathy, we first have to be able to identify, understand, and allow ourselves to feel our *own* emotions. Research has found that when individuals are able to identify and articulate their own feelings, they have a greater ability to empathize with others.[6] One husband explained to

Jennifer his growing understanding of having empathy, of not dismissing emotion, in his marital relationship this way: "So you want me to sit in my crap. And you want her to sit in her crap. And then you want us to sit in our crap together, and then we'll feel closer and connected?" Yep!

When you are able to empathize with your spouse, you are then able to understand and validate them. Validation is not saying that you agree with someone or that they are right and you are wrong. When you tell your spouse that you understand how they feel, you may feel like you are saying, "You're right, I did do that," or "I agree with you and I'm wrong." When you are validating someone, what you are actually saying is, "That makes sense," "That's understandable," and "I can see how you would think that." Validating someone and having empathy for them is also saying, "You are important to me," "I care about you," and "I get you." Taking the time to genuinely listen and understand communicates to your spouse the value you place on them and that they are worth it.

In chapters four and five, we will take a deeper look into practical tools for building intimacy, including building understanding and responding with empathy.

Taking Timeouts

This all sounds lovely, listening and having empathy and all that, but what do you do when you are in the heat of a tense moment with your spouse? What do you do right in the middle of the conflict when understanding and empathy are the furthest things from your mind and that pointing finger is not backing down? The reality is, when conflict gets heated, our emotions and defenses can seem to take over our bodies. What do we do with those disruptive feelings and thoughts that can make reaching understanding and empathy difficult?

When someone approaches you in a way that feels conflictual, your body will often respond automatically with increased heart rate, perspiration, and respiration. This is the body's way of reacting to perceived danger. What is amazing is that the brain does not necessarily know the difference between the feeling of being *verbally* attacked and being *physically* attacked (like someone coming at you with a knife). The body has an automatic response system when danger is perceived, which sends the body into *fight or flight*, or in our experience, fight, flight, or freeze. Adrenaline floods the body and prepares the body to defend, flee, or go into lockdown. The amygdala, the emotion center of the brain, is said to hijack the brain at this point, almost taking the rational, executive part of the brain offline. It becomes very difficult to resolve conflict in any rational way when our senses are heightened or shut down. Couples may need to learn to take timeouts in order to gain some control over these responses before too much damage is done.

It is usually helpful to begin noticing how this happens in your body when you are upset with someone, or when someone approaches you in anger. Notice what your body does during an argument as you try talking with your spouse or as they are talking to you. If you notice a spike in your heart, breathing, or respiration rate, a tightening in your chest or your forehead, or a pit in your stomach sensation, it might be a good time to press the pause button. Take a break and get your body back under control. You may need to take some time to breathe and bring the prefrontal portion of your brain—the executive, planning part—back into gear. When emotion comes flooding in, this part of the brain shuts down. Taking low, deep breaths is one of the first practical skills to work on during conflict (see the breathing exercise at the end of this chapter).

If you decide to incorporate timeouts, it is important to think through how to talk about them. Communicate your need (to calm your response), not your spouse's need (i.e., "You need a timeout!"). Tell your spouse what you need, and then **put a time on it**. You could say something like, "I can feel myself becoming upset," or "I can feel myself having a hard time so I need to take a timeout. Can we talk about this in about an hour (or after dinner or when we get home from work tomorrow)?" It is vital that, if and when you use timeouts as a tool in your conflict resolution, you do not just say, "I need a timeout" and then abruptly leave. When a timeout is used this way, it can leave a spouse feeling abandoned or threatened. This is why it is important to let your spouse know how much time you need and when you will return to continue the conversation.

Though taking a timeout can be crucial, some feel that if you do not deal with it today, before the sun goes down, you are not following God's commands. The Scriptures teach to not let the sun go down when you are still angry (Ephesians 4:26). However, arguments often start after dark, or right before bed, and couples think that in order to obey the Scriptures, they cannot go to sleep until it is all worked out. But let's face it, the sun had already gone down before your argument even began. For some couples, it may be beneficial to push through and work it out so that they do not go to sleep angry. But for many of you, it may be necessary to put a hold on things and make a mutual commitment to return to the scene of the crime when you are in a better state of heart and mind. The point of the scripture in Ephesians 4:26 is to settle matters quickly (Matthew 5:25) and to not give the devil a foothold (Ephesians 4:27) where he can build the seeds of resentment (Hebrews 12:15). The point of this scripture is not to stay up late until the dark hours of the night, when you are exhausted and emotional, trying to work through things. However, if you do have a conflict that is unresolved as you head to bed, make sure you have a plan for when you are going to work it out. Put a time on it.

Talk with your spouse about how you could use timeouts. Talk about how you would both like to communicate your need (see the exercise below). Clarify that you will not leave the room or the house without sharing how much time you or they need to process things. Each of you needs to feel good about how a timeout is worded and how it is used. You do not want to use it as a weapon. If you just abruptly say, "I'm taking a timeout," and walk away without explaining why you need it and when you are going to return to the conversation, the timeout can feel like a rejection—like a slammed door or an angry retaliation. It can leave your spouse feeling anxious, scared, or angry. They may then feel the need to chase you down to work things out, which can set you up for a typical pursuer/withdrawer pattern, where one of you pursues and the other withdraws.

Next, whoever asks for the timeout then needs to be the one to initiate coming back together to talk about it. If you do not come back to reengage, it can trigger anxiety in your spouse, who may feel a strong need to resolve the conflict. Directly and respectfully ask for the timeout and tell them the time you need. Make sure to use the time to get yourself to a better, calmer place by doing things like breathing, praying, walking, writing, or talking. The goal is to get to a good place so that you can listen in order to understand (Proverbs 4:7) or speak the truth with love (Ephesians 4:15). When you get to that place of being able to speak in love (see chapter four on the Speaker) or to listen with empathy (see chapter five on the Validator), then initiate coming back together to talk.

It is also vital that the spouse receiving the timeout request honors that request. This is not time to run after your husband or wife to demand resolution.

When your spouse asks for a timeout, this is time for you to breathe as well, to get your reactive state under control, to go for a walk, pray, or call someone. Honor your spouse's request. Give them the room to work out their own response.

Finally, if you decide to put timeouts into practice in your marriage, remember, like any kind of communication, it can blow up. If asking for a timeout creates more conflict, agree together to stop and get help. Arrange to talk with someone else, another couple possibly, and go over what went wrong. Taking a timeout well can take practice but using timeouts with wisdom and care can revitalize the way you resolve conflict within your marriage relationship.

The exercises below give steps to practicing the skills of breathing and taking timeouts. Using these skills gives you the opportunity to calm the body's automatic response to conflict while giving both of you the space for self-reflection. When you implement these tools, you will be better equipped to speak truthfully and to hear, listen, understand, validate, and have empathy for our spouse when they share their concerns.

EXERCISES

Conflict Resolution Exercise 1: Breathing

Diaphragmatic breathing is intentionally used in singing, yoga, exercise, and in promoting physical and mental health.

Breathe in through your nostrils and take the breath deeply into your lungs. Think of your abdominal cavity, your stomach, as a balloon, and as you breathe in, fill that balloon up. As you do this, keep your shoulders relaxed. Exhale through your mouth, and go ahead and let all the air out, making some noise until the last bit of breath is out. Use that diaphragm muscle, which resides below your lungs, to press out all the air from your lungs. Now breathe in again through your nose, releasing and relaxing your stomach/diaphragm as you do, filling up your lower lungs. Do this when you can feel your heart rate and your respiration pick up when you are upset.

**If this is difficult to do while sitting or standing, practice it first while lying down. The body automatically breathes diaphragmatically when you lay down. Follow the same instructions and bring the air low into your lungs, keeping your shoulders relaxed.

Conflict Resolution Exercise 2: Practice Timeouts

*Remember: timeouts, when done correctly, can be very effective and helpful in working through conflict. You may have to practice them a number of times. You may need to fumble through several attempts. Get help if they are producing more conflict. It is vital that you use timeouts in order to help you speak the truth in love and to help you have the capacity to genuinely listen. "To answer before listening, that is folly and shame" (Proverbs 18:13).

Practice First:
1) Have a discussion with your spouse when you are not in conflict and decide the kind of words you would both like to say. Make sure you feel good about how each of you is going to ask for the timeout.

2) Make an agreement that when a timeout is requested, the other will honor the request.

3) Now practice. Face each other while sitting. Decide who is going to ask for the timeout first. The other should then respond with something like "Ok, sure" or "Of course." See how it feels when you say and hear the timeout request. Change the wording if it is problematic for your spouse.

4) Put a specific time on when you are going to return from the timeout.

5) Now switch and let your spouse practice asking for a timeout. Again, see how it feels and change the wording as needed.

Reminders on how to put timeouts into practice in a real conflict:

1) Word the timeout something like this: "I am feeling myself react to what we are talking about, and I need to take a timeout. Can we talk about this in an hour (after dinner, when we get home tonight)?"

2) Remember to ask for a timeout for yourself. This is not time to say, "I think you need a timeout." The timeout is for *you*.

After you ask for the timeout:

1) The one who asks for the timeout then needs to *USE* the timeout. Pray, call someone, sing, go for a walk, read the Scriptures, breathe/breathe/breathe. Get your heart rate down and get your heart and mind in a place to hear your spouse out or to speak in a way your spouse can hear. It also may give your spouse time to take his or her own timeout.

2) The one who asked for the timeout will initiate returning to the conversation. "Okay, can we continue talking about what we discussed earlier?"

4

Building Understanding: The Speaker

Approaching conflict in a way that builds understanding is important in the sexual relationship as well as in the overall marital relationship. In fact, if approaching conflict in your marriage is a problem in general, it probably is not going to go well when you have conflict regarding sexual issues.

When dealing with conflict, it is important to be an attentive listener (more in chapter five, *The Validator*). Being a considerate speaker is also extremely important. It is vital to pay attention to how we approach someone when we have a request or when we are hurt by, upset with, or angry with them. Researcher John Gottman calls this careful, thoughtful approach the *softened start up*. The Bible calls it "speaking the truth in love" (Ephesians 4:15). When dealing with conflict, it is important to be a good listener. It is also extremely important to be a good speaker.

The timing of when you choose to speak with your spouse is also imperative. Self-disclosure is most helpful when it happens at an appropriate time. If the disclosure is made in the middle of conflict, or with accusation, attacking, judgment, or criticism, the result will be counter-productive and may result in greater separation and distance rather than intimacy, closeness, connection, and resolution. You may wonder whether this incredibly controlled approach to talking is genuine. It is true that in order to have genuine intimacy, we have to be real, vulnerable, and direct. People will sometimes equate unfiltered venting with being sincere. "I was just being real." However, most of us do have the capability within ourselves to be authentic while leaving someone with their dignity and honoring them as a person.

You can "rebuke your neighbor frankly" (Leviticus 19:17) and still "speak the truth in love" (Ephesians 4:15). As Paul Tripp says in the *Age of Opportunity,*[1] "If you fail to speak the truth in love, it will cease to be the truth because it's polluted or corrupted by your frustration, impatience, and anger."

We recommend four steps to effective sharing for the Speaker:
1) **O**ne Issue, one moment : Share only one moment or one concern at a time.
2) **"I"** statements: Use "I" statements when sharing.
3) **N**o blaming, assuming, or accusing: Do not engage in finger pointing when sharing what is bothering you.
4) **K**eep it short: When you share, don't flood your spouse with too many words.

The Speaker: One Issue/One Moment, "I" Statements, No Blaming, Keep it Short (OINK)

One Issue, One Moment

When you share something that bothers you with your spouse, keep it to one issue that happened in one moment. In other words, don't *kitchen-sink it* by throwing in everything including the kitchen sink to make your point. When you are sharing with someone how you feel about something they did, keep it to one moment in time, not the other ten times it has happened. Often we feel the need to explain and justify (see below on *Keep It Short*), so we will bring up other examples to emphasize our point. If we feel like the other person is not getting it, we will just keep explaining and bringing up more and more examples. This will often cause the person listening to tune out (How effective is this with your teenager? Or when you were a teenager yourself?). Instead, keep your sharing to "last Friday, when you came in, you said... and I felt...." Don't use the example of the previous week when it happened as well, and don't give a litany of the number of times. Mention only *last Friday* and only that moment and that issue. Don't bring in other topics either. This is where you stay in the moment and actively choose to stay away from shaming words like "you always."

"I" Statements

Making an "I" statement allows you to be assertive with your feelings and perceptions while owning them as your own. Sharing something to promote active listening can be surprisingly hard. First of all, it can be difficult to figure out what we feel (more on that later). Plus, sticking to "I" when you want to say, "You did this," and "You made me feel ..." is quite difficult. When we are hurt or upset or angry, we often point the finger (see below). It is also hard to share our feelings using "I" because sometimes it can be hard to find words to describe our emotions beyond saying we feel angry. It can be easier to say, "I'm angry," because anger is a defensive emotion that keeps you safe and behind your walls. "I'm angry" is very similar to "I was frustrated," "I was annoyed," or "I was irritated." Each of these feelings can be accurate, but we recommend that you spend some time looking underneath these words to find the more vulnerable emotions that have been triggered.

For some of us who, though emotionally healthy, have a difficult time identifying those more vulnerable emotions, it may be helpful to use a poster or a worksheet with examples that label certain emotions. One such tool is the *Managing Your Anger* poster created by Aims International Books. Tools like this show how certain emotions might be underneath our anger—such as anxiety, embarrassment, hurt, and sadness. You might identify other emotion words such as feeling unheard, powerless, unappreciated, invisible, disrespected, unimportant, unloved, judged, or incompetent. See the list of words in *Appendix B* to help with identifying your feelings. Be aware that even these more vulnerable words can be used to make subtle accusations.

In general, saying, "I was hurt," or "I felt inferior, unappreciated, small, judged, alone, not good enough, or sad," are much more vulnerable words. These are considered more primary emotions. However, when you vulnerably share how you feel, it can be risky. You can't be sure how the other person will respond. Your spouse may use it against you in some way. They may get defensive and counter-attack or leave and abandon you to your hurt. This is the inherent danger in intimacy and in dealing with conflict. If you are vulnerable, it could be used against you, or they might not respond in a way that is reassuring.

However, when it is safe, and when you can have some assurance that they will take in what you are about to share, it works much better to share it from the "I" perspective. You may still end up using "you" in your sharing, but when you do, keep it descriptive: *When you said* (fill in the blank), *When your walked in*, or *When you didn't....* The challenge is to not assume what your spouse is feeling or thinking or what is happening inside of them (see "No Blaming, Accusing, or Assuming" below). Saying things like "I know you were angry," or "I know you thought ..." assumes you have the ability to get inside their head and read their emotions and thoughts. But you really can't. So telling them how they feel is just an assumption and usually shuts the conversation down. Keep it to what you saw, what you experienced, and what you felt.

Remember, there is a difference between saying, "I was attacked" and "I *felt* attacked." "I was attacked" has a clear finger pointing at the other, though the word "you" is not even used. "I *felt* attacked" says that this is what I experienced, even if that is not what was intended or even happened. Feelings are not always based on fact, and sharing what someone feels does not always have a connection to fact or accuracy. You may feel attacked even when your perception of the situation is completely inaccurate. Your spouse might feel attacked even when that was not your intention at all. Trying to convince someone they should not feel that way or that they are way off base is usually quite counter-productive. However, when you validate someone for how they feel, validate your spouse's feelings, or tell them that what they feel is understandable, this can go a long way toward making them feel heard and cared for.

No Blaming, Accusing, or Assuming

The concept of speaking from an "I" standpoint overlaps with this idea of not using blaming, accusing, or assuming language. We will reiterate a few points here to emphasize the importance of getting rid of blame and the pointing finger.

Often, when people share passionately or with anger, the person on the other side feels attacked and blamed, and their response may be to shut down or get defensive. One of the important parts of learning how to have conflict that creates intimate connection is figuring out how to share what you feel without attacking the other person. Earlier we mentioned Isaiah 58:9–11 and getting rid of the pointing finger. When we do that, there are great results. God can turn our marriages into that well-watered garden. We have all seen or been somewhere beautiful and green, lush and gorgeous. Take a moment and picture that and realize what God wants to create in your marriage.

It is crucial to remember God's perspective when you initiate a conversation. Remember the purpose of why you are sharing. Your ultimate goal is not to cast blame. It is not to get your spouse to see how wrong they are. Your goal is to invite your spouse in—to let them see who you are and how you feel. Casting blame, making sure your spouse sees clearly what they did that was wrong, and what upset you so much is the safer, yet more defensive way to communicate. It is much more dangerous to say, "When you said that, I felt hurt and I felt unloved," or "When you did that, I felt unappreciated and unimportant." So instead of making sure they see what they did that was wrong, work hard at staying vulnerable and share from the stance of "I felt."

When you share what you are feeling, watch out for making assumptions. Assumptions can be full of all kinds of land mines. They can also be very inaccurate. What looks like anger can often be someone feeling hurt. We can make incorrect interpretations, assume motivations, or misinterpret words and actions. Recall your own experience when someone came to you and told you they knew what you were feeling. It is very frustrating when someone takes something we say or the way we are acting and assumes what is going on inside of us. It is definitely not very productive to do that with your spouse. To say, "You were angry" just fuels the conflict. Instead, describe their body language and tone. This works much better. Descriptive phrases like *Your face was tense* or *Your arms were crossed* or *Your tone was short* can help your spouse understand how they are coming across. When you talk to your spouse, share what you are feeling without making any assumptions of what is going on inside of them internally.

Keep It Short

When we do not feel like someone understands what we are saying, or if we feel guilty, defensive, or uncomfortable about what we are sharing, we may start repeating ourselves or extending what we are sharing by adding explanations. The Bible states, "Where words are many, sin is not absent" (Proverbs 10:19). If you are in the habit of going into long explanations about why you feel something or what you experienced, this scripture may apply to you. Flooding your spouse with lengthy explanations about why you are bothered may shut them down or cause them to get defensive.

Have you ever been in a situation when goes on and on about something that bothers them? It feels like a fire hydrant is going off in your face! You want to run and take cover. It can be very hard to listen when we feel flooded. Learning how to express yourself succinctly can go a long way in getting someone to truly understand where you are coming from.

A good way to keep from flooding your spouse with too many words is to limit your sharing to two or three sentences at a time. This will give them the chance to take it in, to reflect on what you are saying, and to ask you some questions (see the next chapter).

Now, Put It All Together

When you approach your spouse with something that has bothered you, hurt you, or made you angry, it could look something like this: "Last Friday, when you came home, you came into the kitchen and you said_____. When you said that, I felt hurt and judged, and I felt really small." There it is. One moment, one issue (last Friday), said from the "I" perspective (hurt, judged, small), without an attack (no blaming) and shared succinctly (keep it short). Try it. If you blow it, apologize and try again.

You may have noticed that the mnemonic for the Speaker is OINK. In the next chapter, the mnemonic for the Validator is RACE. We love to tell people, and it is actually true, that this is our laughing nod to the hilarious pig races at the county fair every summer here in San Diego. Plus, you will never forget that when you want to communicate to create connection, you can do it with OINK and RACE.

Note to Avoiders: The "I" statement, and even attempting anything like this process, can be very difficult, especially if you have tried and gotten negative results before—during childhood or even with your spouse. If it has gone poorly for you when you have told your spouse what you feel and think, you may have good reason to avoid rocking the boat. However, the more you avoid, the more your spouse may pursue you, trying to work it out or get you to hear them. Although your spouse needs you to listen and truly validate what they are saying, they also need to hear what you are feeling as well. So we suggest you take the time to discover your "I" statements. Plumb what you are feeling. Then let your spouse in so that they can validate you. This builds reciprocal sharing. Knowing you came to them encourages them to come to you when they need to tell you something. You may feel uncomfortable spending time trying to identify your emotions. It may, in fact, feel like a waste of time.

Since you are reading this book in order to build greater relational and sexual intimacy, pushing through the ingrained response to avoid conflict could be a huge step in that direction.

Note to Pursuers: If you are married to an avoider, your anxiety may go through the roof when they tune you out or leave the room or disappear on you even while they remain standing right in front of you. It is important to get a good hold on your anxiety. This may mean taking a timeout before you approach your spouse or before you respond to them. This can be especially important if you share something with your spouse and they respond in a way that does not feel good to you. If you anxiously continue pursuing, your spouse may withdraw even further. For you to learn how to speak the truth in love, without attacking or blaming, you may need to get someone's assistance. Ask for help to learn a new way to approach your spouse. In the mean time, in order to have a better chance of getting your spouse to hear you, take a breath. Always breathe first before you approach. Then keep what you want to say short. If it does not go well, do not keep going at it. Take a break and either come back to it later or get someone to sit with both of you to help when you try again.

EXERCISES

(Pre-) Communication Exercise 1: Scriptural Exploration

1) Take some time to look up the scriptures in this section.
2) Journal about how these apply to you and to your marital relationship.
3) Look at each part of the rules (OINK) for the speaker here: one issue/one moment, "I" statements, no blaming/accusing/assuming, keep it short. Which part of this process would be hard for you and why?

Communication Exercise 2: "I" Messages

*This exercise is about exploring and identifying feeling and emotion. It is not about how to fix or work through a problem you have had with someone.

1) Using a journal, think and write about a challenging interaction you recently had with someone. The challenging interaction may have been with someone you are close to, with someone you work with, or with your spouse.

2) Spend some time thinking and writing out what bothered you about what happened. Make sure to use "I" language as you describe how you felt. Look hard at what you write down and explore it for any blaming, attacking, accusing, or assuming language. When you are trying to describe what your spouse did that was hard for you, use descriptive words such as "Your arms were crossed," "Your tone was short," or "Your facial expression looked angry." Read the words and think how you might feel if those words were said to you. Reword it until you have gotten rid of any attacking language.

3) As you write things down, strive to describe how you feel with words beyond "angry," "frustrated," "irritated," or "annoyed." Use the list of feelings in Appendix B to help with identifying what words apply to how you feel. Write down any of these words that fit: unappreciated, unloved, disrespected, small, hurt, embarrassed, disappointed, sad, guilty, scared, worried, anxious, alone, powerless, helpless, inadequate, inferior, not enough, judged, dismissed.

4) Practice saying this out loud to your spouse. As if speaking to your spouse, say something like, "When you came home, you said _____, and your face was _____, and I felt _____."

5

Responding with Empathy: The Validator

Conflict, when it leads to connection, can actually lead to a greater closeness. As we have mentioned, dealing with conflict well is one of the factors that can make a significant difference in the quality of your sexual relationship. In order for conflict to lead to closeness, it is important to feel and express empathy and understanding when your spouse shares something with you.

We discussed empathy in the chapter on conflict that creates connection. Both of you need to receive empathy. When your spouse approaches you with something they feel, truly listening to them and feeling genuine empathy and understanding will go a long way toward deepening your intimacy. Feeling connected and knowing that your spouse cares enough to know how you feel about things is one of the huge pieces that makes a difference between having sex with your spouse and having a sexually intimate relationship.

For example, let's look at Jesus in Luke 7:11-16. He is walking into town and there is a funeral passing by. When Jesus sees the mother of the dead young man, the Bible says, "His heart went out to her." This phrase actually means, in the Greek, "His guts were moved." God cares. Jesus cares. God calls *us* to care. He calls us to connect with one another on a gut level. When we have this kind of heart level response to our spouse, we are imitating Jesus in our marriage. To truly experience empathy for what someone else is sharing does require taking the other person's perspective, listening to them with the desire to have genuine understanding. We call this Validation.

How to Get There: Validation

Good listening includes several essentials. These are some we use: reflect what you heard; ask questions to seek true understanding; confirm with them what you're understanding; and then empathize with them. And while you're doing all that, make sure you are facing your spouse and looking at them.

Before explaining the process we use to coach couples, we want to further clarify one thing. Understanding someone and validating their hurts and concerns does not necessarily mean you agree with them. Something someone says can be valid and understandable, and you can still disagree with them.

Often, people feel that if they validate someone, it is as if they're saying the other person is right. Validating someone, however, is not saying, "You're right," or "I was wrong."

It's actually not about facts at all. It is about saying that their pain makes sense, that you can relate, and that what they are feeling is important to you. Now let's take a look at an easy-to-remember process you can implement in your relationship.

Before You Start

Pick an interaction that happened recently between you. Make it a small, unimportant one—something having to do with the trash, the laundry, or the dog poop in the back yard. It needs to be an interaction that was difficult for both of you in some small way—something that made you both feel uncomfortable, frustrated, or misunderstood. However, it needs to be relatively unimportant so that the level of emotional connection to the issue is not too high.

Remember, if things start to go sideways, breathe (see the chapter *Conflict that Creates Connection* and review timeouts and breathing). If you breathe, but things are still not going well, take a timeout. If it becomes too difficult to get things back on track, try again later with another person or couple there to support you. Now choose who is going to speak first. Whoever starts first will use the OINK mnemonic. And then, as the Validator, you will follow with this four-step process:

1) **R**eflect — Mirror back what you heard them say.
2) **A**sk Questions — Draw them out by asking about what they felt and experienced.
3) **C**onfirm — Share what you understand and see if you got it right.
4) **E**mpathize — Express your understanding by sharing your own experience.

The Validator: Reflect, Ask Questions, Confirm, Empathize (RACE)
Reflect

When someone shares how they feel with you, the first thing to do is tell them what you heard them say. Just simply say it back. Mirror it. "So, when I said _____, you felt_____." Don't interpret it or analyze it. Just let them know, *using their words*, what you heard.

Ask Questions

Asking questions can be challenging, especially when what we really feel is "I so totally disagree with what you said, and there is no way I am going to try to understand you." Asking questions won't work if you do not genuinely want to understand what the other has experienced. If you are stuck, and all your own feelings are hanging in front of your face, falling off your shelf (as explained in chapter three, *Conflict That Creates Connection*), and blocking any genuine desire to understand, STOP. Don't continue. Go take a timeout until you are in a better place to take in and respond to what your spouse has to say. Remember, validating confirms that your spouse is important to you—but it does not require agreeing.

When you've got your explaining, defending, fixing, apologizing, reassuring, etc. under some level of control, it is time to ask some questions. Proverbs 20:5 says:

> *"The purposes of a man's heart are deep waters;*
> *but a man of understanding draws them out."*

Darn. There's that understanding thing again. Isaiah 58:9-11 says you'll have to spend yourself. There's the cost again of Proverbs 4:7. The author of Proverbs 20:5 challenges us to draw others out. One of the best ways to do that is to ask questions. Put all those words swirling around your head up on that shelf, and ask some questions so that you can really understand. We always recommend asking on three different levels:

1) Ask for Facts—When did it happen, where? Also, what was it in your voice, your tone, your body language, words, or timing that was difficult?

2) Use their language—Ask them to further explain the words they chose to describe how they feel. "When you say hurt, can you tell me more what you mean?" "When you say disrespected, tell me what you mean by disrespected."

3) Draw them out. You probably know each other well. Ask things like, "Did it *seem* like___?" or "Did it *feel* like___?"

Ask questions until you truly feel you get a genuine, decent understanding of what they experienced.

*Reminder to the Speaker: when answering these questions, keep your responses to two to three sentences and, again, do your best not to use any blaming, accusing, or assuming language.

Confirm

Much like the first part, **Reflect**, *Confirming* is giving them their own words back, but now in an expanded, fuller form. You asked a number of questions to deepen your understanding. Now let your spouse fully know what you heard from those answers. "So, when I said that, you felt *unappreciated* and *disrespected*, and my tone was *strong*, and it seemed like I was not happy with you." Finish by asking, "Did I get that?" and "Is there anything you want to add?" This is a good time for the Speaker to let their spouse know, "Yes, that's it," or "Well, just about. I also said _____." The purpose of confirming at this point is to make sure you have the correct understanding.

Empathize

This is time for you to figuratively put yourself in your spouse's shoes. In order to go from cognitively understanding how they feel to getting it at a gut level, it often helps to remember when you have felt that way. If your spouse says, "I felt unappreciated," try to remember a time you felt unappreciated. If your spouse shares they felt dismissed, think about a time when someone—your mom, your boss, your friend—treated you in a dismissive way. How did it feel when they scolded you like a child or dismissed the incredible effort you put into something, and it twisted your gut? It might have made you feel angry, hurt, or unimportant. So, to empathize with your spouse and to understand how they felt unappreciated or dismissed, think about a time when you felt that way— not with them, but with someone else like your boss, a coworker, your sibling or friend, your mom/dad/grandma/grandad, someone in your ministry. What happened? Where were you? What did you feel? When you recall your own experience, you can say something like, "I think I can understand. Last month, when I finished that project, I met with my boss, and he just criticized each part, and I felt demeaned and unappreciated" or "When I was seventeen and my mom didn't show up for my graduation, I felt unimportant and unloved." Share that memory. Make sure to keep your sharing short, but connect what you experienced with what your spouse has shared.

This is a tough part of the process because we often think, "My situation was not the same." True. Your situation is never the same. However, what we often have in common is the *gut-level response* to situations. You might be concerned that sharing your own memory will derail the whole process because it moves the focus from your spouse's experience to your own experience. How can that help with feeling empathy for them? Or maybe you choose to relate an experience that you're afraid your spouse will feel doesn't relate at all. While it is true that it can feel like you have brought the focus back to you, you can keep it more about your spouse if you share your experience concisely, without lots of details or long descriptions. What we suggest is that you state your experience, of feeling hurt for instance, in just a few sentences, starting with "I think I can understand" and then briefly explain why. It doesn't have to be a perfect match but it does need to be specific: when did it happen, where were you, what was said, and how did you feel. You are looking for that gut-level emotion that helps you to relate and have empathy for your spouse.

Implementing the Process

There are a few important things to note in this process. While you were listening to your spouse share what hurt them or bothered them, if your internal reactions are making it difficult for you to genuinely empathize, initiate a timeout. Say, "I'm glad you shared this. I do want to talk about this but I can feel myself having a hard time, so I'm going to take a timeout. Let's talk about this in another hour, after dinner, or tomorrow when we get home from work." Then remember, after you have taken the timeout, you are the one responsible for initiating with your spouse to continue the conversation.

It is also important to realize that if you attempt this process on your own, without another person or another couple helping out or coaching, it may completely blow up. If you try this and it starts to go sideways, get someone you trust to sit in with you. You are not going to be successful every time. In fact, you will probably blow it a lot. What is important is that you tried, and that by trying the conflict will usually have slowed down significantly. That by itself is quite a victory. Many couples have to limp along, attempting this over and over, in order to change how they deal with conflict. It might take a while before your spouse can share without accusing or you can reflect and ask questions rather than defend or fix. Be patient and bear with one another. As in other things, with practice you get better at it, and it can become a very effective tool in your communication.

Lastly, you may have some big hurts that have occurred between you. Later, we will explore how to put this into practice around what some call the incredibly painful attachment injuries that occur in relationships (see chapter eleven, *Healing Relationship and Sexual Betrayals*). When you are facing what feels like big mountains of pain in your relationship, the process of validation may seem shallow, like throwing a pebble against the huge fortified wall of a city. What we have experienced, however, is that when couples learn to do this with small issues, they gain small moments of connection that build. It may begin with one small feeling of shared empathy. As you go through this process again and again, experiencing more and more of those little bits of empathy, you will begin to build a new foundation based on these accumulated small moments of connection. Little by little, you will both build and experience trust, bit by bit bringing the wall of pain and disconnection down. Take your time. Build slowly. Rejoice in each little victory. Maintain hope that a whole new relationship can arise out of your pain.

The Shelf

Another difficulty for the Validator is what to do with all of the challenges that surface in their own response, including the flood of thoughts running through their mind when their spouse is sharing. In the previous chapter, we talked about the shelf—that mental picture of a place where you can honor those thoughts and feelings whizzing through your head. Use the shelf for your defensiveness, your desire to fix the conflict, the desire to explain or reassure, or the impulse to say sorry too soon, before you really understand. Your own hurt may also get triggered as your spouse is sharing. Use that shelf.

But what do you do after you have worked all the way through RACE and arrived at empathy? After your spouse feels heard and understood, when they feel validated, you may then want to look at that shelf and see if there is anything left on it. Often, by the time someone has made the heartfelt effort to validate the other, the desire to defend and explain has disappeared from the shelf. The need is no longer there.

But sometimes, your own stuff that got triggered is still sitting there on the shelf, right where you put it while listening and asking questions. You may wonder if you should explain, or if this is the time to try to find a solution or to apologize. These are all legitimate wonderings. Each of these work a lot better after you have arrived at understanding and empathy.

When you have arrived there, look at that shelf and decide if it may be time to bring your own stuff down off the shelf and talk about it. This is not the same as finger-pointing. However, if it is going to destroy all the hard work you just did in validating your spouse, you may want to wait for a later time, such as later in the day or on another day completely.

When the timing is good, bring your own feelings down from the shelf and go through the validation process exactly as we have outlined, with your roles reversed.

It is especially important for those who tend to avoid conflict or those who tend to let it roll off their backs to check and see if there is anything on the shelf that needs to be discussed.

Making validation a reciprocal process can deepen the level of connection and leave no room for the seeds of resentment to take root.

Here, in a nutshell, is the process of the Speaker and the Validator:

The Validation Protocol

Speaker (OINK)	Validator (RACE)
One Issue, One Moment **"I"** statements **N**o assuming, blaming, accusing **K**eep it Short	**R**eflect **A**sk Questions **C**onfirm **E**mpathize

EXERCISES

Validation Exercise: OINK and RACE (We are off to the pig races!)

1) Give yourselves plenty of time to do this exercise. Especially when you try this for the first time, do not rush the process. Do not try to do it in five minutes, or as you are driving in the car, or right before you go to bed, or right before you have to walk out the door to go somewhere. Give yourselves time and a private space where you can talk openly.

2) Choose an interaction you had between you that created a slight amount of conflict. It is important that you choose something small that is not as loaded with the bigger issues of your relationship— something along the lines of a frustrated interaction around the trash, the gardening, the dogs, etc. This interaction needs to include something that was difficult for both of you.

3) Review the rules for both OINK and RACE. Place the rules in front of you. When you practice this way of talking through a problem or conflict, it is important that neither of you coach the other. Pay attention to the rules as they pertain to you. If it becomes frustrating or you feel your spouse is refusing to follow the directions for OINK and RACE, do not continue the exercise. It would be best to either talk about this together or get with someone you trust to get help and work through how you want to pursue using this tool.

4) Using the conflict chosen above, choose who will be the speaker first. This may be a struggle because you both want to be heard. If it is a struggle in your heart, this may be a good opportunity for a timeout in order to get your heart in a good place. The Speaker then—using OINK—shares their feelings about the conflict. The

Validator—using RACE—then responds, arriving at empathy.

5) If at all possible, sit with another couple who will then monitor and coach you through the process of using OINK and RACE. Ask them to interrupt and point out if a rule is not followed.

6) After the first speaker shares and the Validator reaches empathy, the spouses can switch. The Validator then becomes the Speaker, sharing their "one moment, one issue" during the conflict. The spouse then takes on the role of Validator, responding and arriving at empathy.

7) After you have finished, spend time talking about how you felt while engaging in this process. Did you feel understood? This is not about whether your spouse understands the bigger picture of your relationship, but simply—when you go back to that one issue, that one moment—whether they in some small way understand what you felt. Share with your spouse what it was that made you feel like they understood.

6

Talking About Sex

We share with couples that it is often easier just to have sex than it is to talk about sex. There is little that is more vulnerable than opening up and sharing what we think about, feel about, believe about, and have experienced about sex. A client once asked if it had always been easy for me (Jennifer) to talk so specifically and openly about sexual topics. This came after a thorough explanation of the physiology of sexual arousal and orgasm, where I used lots of terms (clitoris, penis, orgasm, anus, labia/lips, vagina, head, etc.), drew pictures, shared slides, and detailed the barriers and feelings that get in the way of experiencing fulfilling sexual intimacy. I laughed when my client asked this and shared that it is much easier for me to explain this kind of information with clients, or to get in front people and talk about the vivid details of sexuality, than it is for me to talk openly with my husband about our sexual life. Mind you, we do that. We talk openly and specifically, but truly, most of the time I just want to die when we have those conversations. It is like dragging and forcing the words out of my mouth, it is so deeply uncomfortable. For most of us, talking openly about sex with our spouse has its challenges.

Reciprocal sexual self-disclosure, when both partners talk openly about how they feel about their sex life, is especially important the longer a couple is together.[1] When partners tell their spouses what they prefer, it can help them have more understanding and allow them to choose what to do sexually that will please their partner, which in turn can lead to deeper intimacy. However, some people feel a bit of embarrassment about expressing things they like. This can be especially hard for women. Openly sharing how you feel about sex and what you do not like is also very risky. What if you receive a negative response when you tell your spouse something you don't like sexually? What if you tell your spouse what you would like and they still do not do anything to fulfill that? What if you tell them what you do not like and they keep doing it? What if they get angry about your requests or throw it back at you? Any of these negative responses can make talking about sex even harder. In fact, just the fear of these responses can keep the words from even coming out.

For many couples, it is important to be intentional in talking about their sex life. The research study Jennifer did was focused on how couples communicate about sex, probing those vulnerable places within and sharing them with your spouse. Building off of these findings, a goal of her model of sex therapy is to create greater relational, physical, emotional, and sexual intimacy. This is done by helping couples grow in their empathy for one another, helping them have genuine communication about their relationship and about sex, and increasing intimacy skills verbally, physically, sensually, and sexually. A primary focus of this kind of work is to help a couple learn how to take the risk of talking openly, honestly, specifically, and vulnerably about their relationship and about their sexual likes, dislikes, fears, hopes, turn-ons, turn-offs, feelings, needs, etc. What would it look like to talk openly about sex?

When to Talk About Sex: Pillow Talk Before, During, and After

When should you talk about sex? Any time. Often, the more you talk about sex, the more comfortable you will be in talking about sex. Sounds simple. However, it is important to gauge your spouse's level of discomfort in discussing sexual topics and to consider the atmosphere in which you have those conversations. If making sexual comments or sharing sexual innuendos about your spouse or your sex life in front of others makes your spouse uncomfortable, consider a more thoughtful way to make sexual communication more playful and normal without humiliating or embarrassing them. People sometimes make sexual jokes or unsuitable sexual comments because they are uncomfortable or because they have become used to speaking about sex in inappropriate ways. However, talking about sex in these ways can actually make intimate conversation more difficult. Also, it is not usually helpful to your intimate relationship if you talk about your sexual relationship when you are angry. If you have some resentful, angry, or hurt feelings about how sex is going, do your best to make sure you are not emotionally reactive when you do take the time to talk about it.

When discussing preferences or desires for your sexual relationship, take some special time to sit down and discuss it. Do not wait to do this until you are in the middle of sexual time together. Of course, it is helpful to learn how to talk openly about preferences, likes, and dislikes while you are engaging sexually, and these chapters contain a lot of direction and exercises on how to do that. However, it is also helpful to take the time to talk about what you prefer both before and after you have sex, rather than just in the middle of things. So, get a cup of coffee or a glass of wine, read one of these chapters, and then sit down and talk about it together. Pray about your sexual relationship. If things are challenging, you may want to pray before you have sex. God wants us to pray about everything (Philippians 4:6), and this includes our intimacy.

How about post-sex talk? Try engaging in pillow talk after you make love as well. As you hold each other or lie next to each other, share something you appreciated about what your spouse just gave to you. Tell them what you appreciate about them as a good lover ... *You have wonderful fingers* or *I love how willing you are to try things.* Tell them how they brought you pleasure ... *That felt wonderful* or *I love when you kiss me there.* Compliment your spouse on their lovemaking skills ... *You are very good at that.*

You can also talk about your time together the next day. Get that cup of coffee or a glass of wine, sit somewhere comfortable and intimate, and talk about how it went last night. You can bring it up as you are sitting on the porch, driving in the car, or getting ready for bed. Let your spouse know what you enjoyed and would like to do more or something you would like differently. Share what makes you feel wanted and loved and what helps you be sexually responsive. This kind of post-sex talk fosters ongoing refreshment in your sexual relationship.

The goal of deepening your communication about your sexual relationship is to increase sexual pleasure, improve sexual functioning, build relational and sexual intimacy, and learn to enjoy sex as God intended. There is a reason that the greatest concentration of nerve endings is in the sensitive erogenous zones of the genitalia. God intends for us to enjoy our sexuality. The first step we will take you through to get there is learning how to talk about it.

EXERCISES

Before beginning these exercises, and any of those in the rest of the chapters, consider the status of your relationship and whether you may need to first make sure you do the exercises in the chapters dedicated to conflict resolution, relationship intimacy, and touch and affection.

Depending on whether you are ready to speak about sexual matters, you may decide to start on the exercises below (exercises 1 and 2 in this chapter) but then wait to do the sexual language communication exercises (exercises 3, 4, and 5 in this chapter) when the work you have done in your relationship is further along.

So let's get started. As a couple, play the simple games described below to begin increasing your verbal intimacy and to get comfortable with using these basic sexual terms.

Intimate Communication Exercise 1: Prompt and Reflection

*Note: Prompt and Reflection Exercises are found throughout the book. Follow the directions below for each time you engage in these exercises.

This is a relatively simple communication exercise. In this exercise, each of the sentence prompts is about *how you are feeling about your intimacy and the process of working on improving your intimacy*. They are not necessarily about the sexual part of your relationship. Before you begin, sit in two chairs that can face each other. Husbands, sit with your knees spread. Wives, tuck your chair in so that your knees are touching your husband's chair. Get comfortable and then take each other's hands. When you share your sentence, look directly into your spouse's eyes.

Decide who will start first. Whoever goes first begins with the first prompt and finishes the sentence. The spouse then simply reflects the sentence (just mirror it back, not adding any interpretation or rewording Then the spouse who is second also begins with the first prompt and the spouse who went first reflects. Do this for each prompt. For some of these prompts, you may be sharing something from the history of your relationship. Begin.

1) "One thing I worry about is ...."
2) "One thing I fear is ...."
3) "Something I feel insecure about is ...."
4) "I feel guilty about ...."
5) "One thing I hope for is ...."
6) "Something that is difficult for me is ...."

After doing all of the above prompts, ask each other:

7) "Is there anything I've said that you want to ask me about or have me explain?"

Intimate Communication Exercise 2: Partner Interview about the Sexual Background

Read the directions below.

1) While facing each other, decide who is going to ask questions first.
2) For the spouse who goes first, ask each question and listen attentively. Gently reflect what you hear your spouse saying without adding much commentary. A reflection will sound

something like "So your mom didn't talk to you about how babies were made? OK."

3) Simply listen and reflect and then ask the next question.

4) After all questions have been asked and answered, switch who is asking and who is answering.

5) After reading the directions above, sit facing each other and begin:

    a) How did you learn about sex growing up?

    b) Did your family discuss sex at all?

    c) Did you experience anything negative sexually when you were a child or teenager?

    d) What kind of experiences have you had that made you feel shame about sex?

    e) Is there anything you have wanted to bring up about sex but haven't felt comfortable bringing up?

    f) Do you feel like we have friendships now where we can openly discuss sexual things?

6) After both of you answer each question, talk about what it was like to have this conversation.

Intimate Communication Exercise 3: Sexual Language

*The purpose of this exercise is to loosen up any discomfort and awkwardness you might feel about using sexual terms and discussing sexual topics. Have some fun with this one!

Make a printout of the terms at the bottom of this chapter. Gather some simple objects from around your home, such as a pencil, a rubber band, a paper clip, a marker, ChapStick, a small cup, a stapler, a small bottle of lotion, etc. Place the printout and the various objects in front of both of you. Follow these directions:

1) Choose who goes first.

2) Take an object and say to your spouse, "This is a pencil," and add one term from the printout. Your sentence would then be something like, "This is a pencil. Labia," or "This is a rubber band. Testicles."

3) Now your spouse does the same communication, such as, "This is a cup. Orgasm."

4) Do this back and forth for several minutes or until each of you has used most of the terms

5) Laugh!!

6) Talk about it afterwards: How uncomfortable, weird, or silly was this exercise?

7) Twister Version: Pull out or purchase the game Twister. Take the printout of terms and tape them to the wall. Play Twister, and each time you place your hand or foot, say one of the terms on the sheet. "Right Foot Red. Penis," "Left Hand Green. Vagina." Enjoy!

Terms: Vagina, Semen, Vulva, Shaft, Breast, Labia, Scrotum, Sex, Penis, Orgasm, Oral Sex, Clitoris, Testicles, Nipple, Pubic Hair, Head

7

My Lover, My Friend: Friendship in Marriage

"This is my lover, this is my friend."
(Song of Songs 5:16)

Roger and Marcie have been married eighteen years and have relatively low conflict. They make most decisions together and parent their three children effectively. Though they know how to do fun activities together, they both feel that they have become roommates who get along well but have little emotional connection. Their sexual relationship is rare and unfulfilling.

Chiyo and Kwan both work full-time and have two children with very busy, extra-curricular lives. They spend time together as a family but have little time for just the two of them. They continually interact with simmering irritation and frustration. They can't remember the last time they've been on a date and feel a lot of frustration and anger about their sexual relationship.

Eduardo and Rosalie were recently married and have busy lives in their ministry. When they do spend time together, they spend it talking about people they are helping. Their intimate physical relationship is minimal, and they have lost much of the emotional connection they had while dating.

Mark and Sylvia have been married twenty-seven years and have raised several children, who are now all out of the home. They argue frequently and loudly. They both express that they have no emotional or sexual intimacy. They don't do anything fun together and rarely talk beyond needs with their children and grandchildren and what things need to be done in the home.

There may be parts of these stories that seem familiar to you. Life is busy. Children take a lot of time. Conflict can make intimacy hard. Prioritizing time for the two of you can be difficult. It is also true that for many couples, the sexual part of their relationship is not mutually satisfying, mostly because the overall intimacy in their relationship has been neglected. Couples hear descriptions about what marital intimacy should look like and sometimes feel those words do not describe their marriage. Their friendship has become weak, and their level of emotional intimacy and fun is low or non-existent. But why is it important to have a chapter on relationship intimacy in marriage in a book focused on the sexual relationship? The truth is, sexual intimacy has a much better chance of going well and being mutually satisfying when there is a foundation of strong friendship and emotional connection.

What exactly is relational intimacy and what does it look like? In research, intimacy has been defined in many different ways: as verbal and nonverbal communication that makes people feel accepted and results in a commitment to one another; as reciprocal self-disclosure, a vulnerable sharing of the self with each other that leads to feeling intimate; or as a belongingness and togetherness that has developed from shared emotional interactions.[1] Intimacy usually involves intimate interactions (like touching and sex) and intimate conversations (sharing feelings and experiences). Some spouses define intimacy as self-disclosure, the face-to-face sharing of the self. Others define intimacy as the laughter and fun of doing adventuresome things together. All of these areas are vital.

The couples in Jennifer's sex therapy research[2] described intimacy in a variety of ways. Here are some of their *exact words*, captured during the research study:

> *Closeness and connection*: a close relationship between two people
> - Close physically, sexually, emotionally, and spiritually
> - Meeting each other's needs
> - Needing each other, wanting each other
> - Being on the same page
>
> *Intimate Knowing*: a sense of really knowing someone
> - How they feel, how they think, how they respond
> - That they know the same things about you
> - Trust that allows you to be comfortable in being who you are

- Trust that allows the other person to be who they are

Safety: having a safe relationship
- Confidence in one another
- Someone to lean on when times are difficult
- Feeling safe with your partner emotionally
- Being in a safe, loving, nurturing environment
- Feeling loved, supported, and cherished
- Giving your spouse the same feelings back

Vulnerable sharing: being close to someone, enough to share
- Able to share all of your past openly with no fear of judgment
- Emotionally vulnerable
- Trust, security
- Willingness to share yourself completely (emotionally, sexually, spiritually) with your spouse
- Communication on a deep, personal, soul-baring level
- An exchange of self/selves
- Being able to communicate deep feelings knowing those feelings will be affirmed

Being Real: when we allow ourselves to be seen
- Not trying to misdirect people from who we are or trying to sell them a 'better' version of us
- An honesty leading to vulnerability with our emotions

Empathy: emotional intimacy
- Feeling comfortable with someone
- Understanding and having empathy for their feelings

Fun together: sharing activities that both enjoy
- Watching romantic movies

Prioritizing the other: the mutual experience of love, caring, self-denial and self-sacrifice
- Putting the relationship before yourself
- Nurturing and honoring that relationship

Physical and sexual intimacy: kissing, cuddling, being in close proximity to each other
- Being held
- Laying down, resting my head on his lap
- Showing affection to your mate
- Smiling, touching, hugging, texting, calling, dating, and intercourse are all included
- Sexual intimacy, touching, kiss, holding hands, cuddling
- Sexual connection between a man and a woman

- It is more than just physical—it should bond the couple.

Spiritual connection: praying together, studying God's Word together

Unique, exclusive connection: knowing someone like you know yourself

- Relating to someone on a level that is deeper than a common relationship
- Connected in a special way
- Being very close to someone
- Talking with them about things that you would not talk to others about
- Sharing feelings and thoughts you would not easily share with just anyone

Almost all of the couples that gave these definitions had come into therapy longing for these things or for the return of these things in their marriage. It was amazing to watch these desires become much more of a reality as they began to work hard at the relational and sexual intimacy in their marriage. And they did have to work hard. As they did so, their scores on intimacy measures changed dramatically. The moral of these stories is that for most couples, when they make an intentional and purposeful effort to nurture the kind of relational intimacy in marriage that God intends, the results can be life-changing and encouraging.

Intimacy in Marriage

Harley, in *His Needs Her Needs*, uses the idea of a love bank and explains how the lack of intentional nurturing impacts relationships. When a literal financial bank account is full, car problems that cause a withdrawal from that account usually create minor anxiety. But if that bank account is already low, a car breaking down and needing new, crucial parts can create havoc and stress. In a relationship, when the emotional love bank account is full, a disagreement or hurtful comment will cause a withdrawal from the relationship account, but since there is so much capital in the account, so much cushion, the pain of that withdrawal is usually not difficult to overcome. When the love bank is already dangerously low, that same disagreement or hurtful comment can result in great distress and hopelessness.

If you are regularly contributing to the bank account of your relationship, you will have a foundation, a cushion, that provides a buffer from the pains and hurts that even close companions inflict on each other. The contributions may include talking through life, feelings, hopes and dreams, engaging in conflict in a way that builds closeness, spending fun time together, doing small acts of kindness for each other, and engaging in affectionate and intimate touch. If, however, there are not a lot of contributions being made to your relationship—if you do not talk openly and often, or share your hopes, dreams, and fears, or laugh and play together, prioritize time together, or work through conflict constructively—the emotional bank account in your relationship may be low and withdrawals may wreak havoc.

Ask yourselves, husbands, how are you doing at bringing happiness to your wife (Deuteronomy 24:5)? Ask yourselves, wives, how are you doing at bringing contentment to your husband (Song of Songs 8:10)? How are you doing at intentionally putting deposits into your marriage's emotional bank account? There is no question that a healthy, vibrant marriage takes work. It can be fun, rewarding work, but it is work. As John and Karen Louis explain in their book *I Choose Us,* mature love, in comparison to the infatuation early in a relationship, needs nurturing. So how should we do that? Let's start with how your humility is doing.

Humility

Improvement in the sexual relationship is usually quite dependent on the level of willingness to take ownership of our faults. It takes humility to recognize your mistakes, sins, and character flaws and to respond well when someone else points them out. Humility, or the lack thereof, strongly influences how much change happens for you as an individual and for both of you as a couple. This is all the more true when pursuing emotional intimacy in marriage. John Gottman, author of *The Seven Principles for Making Marriage Work,*[3] describes this type of humility as the ability to be influenced by your spouse. He found that a predictor for divorce was whether men allowed themselves to be influenced by their wives. However, this can be true in both directions. Les Greenberg, a therapist and researcher in Toronto, has written about couples that experienced infidelity.[4] He found that the ability to feel and express remorse, that humble response of taking full ownership, had a very strong association with whether the couple reached a point of forgiveness.[5] Even researchers have found that the ability for each spouse to humbly take ownership of their part in any problems in marriage can have a significant influence on the level of intimacy a couple is able to reach.

The concept of humility, though rarely discussed in the world of psychology, can be what truly creates genuine, lifelong change in your marriage. For the disciple of Jesus, this means truly understanding the sacrifice God made on the cross and the incredible love and mercy God gives to those who have been rescued by Him. As the apostle Paul wrote, truly understanding love from God can compel you to no longer live for yourself (2 Corinthians 5:15). Being humble and truly learning to consider your spouse as better than yourself (Philippians 2:3-5) and following the example of Jesus can have a significant impact on how well a couple is connected emotionally and relationally. Test yourself (2 Corinthians 13:5) and see how you are doing in your humility towards your spouse.

Nurturing Intimacy: Face-to-Face

Nurturing marital intimacy often means getting to know your spouse all over again. Gottman[6] talks about the importance of truly knowing your spouse, having an intimate map of the territory of their lives and knowing all the little things about their world. Having a clearer understanding of the map of your spouse's life can deepen your connection. Face-to-face intimacy is the reciprocal verbal sharing when a couple spends time together talking from the heart. It creates the safety, intimate knowing, and unique connection described by the couples quoted above. This kind of sharing, of learning what is on your spouse's map, might include learning what their day was like, what relationships are hard for them, what their favorite childhood memory is, what their hopes and dreams are, and what couple or individual they most admire and why.

How are you doing on knowing things like this about your spouse? How is your detailed map of their inner life? Really knowing your spouse's world is integral to genuine intimacy. The truth is that many married couples, after dating, engagement, or early marriage are past, put little time or effort into nurturing their emotional intimacy and their intimate knowledge of one another. As we have led our married ministries, I (Tim) have seen how many couples tend to coexist and morph into a "roommate" mentality, describing their relationship as a partnership rather than a marriage filled with emotional connection. We all need this kind of intimacy, but we do not always do the work to get there.

There are several things you can check to evaluate how well you are nurturing your face-to-face intimacy. How much do you engage in casual talk? How much are you engaging in more vulnerable discussions? Do you feel like your spouse truly understands you, and do they feel you understand them? Do you draw your spouse out and ask them questions, or do you merely ask, "How was your day?" and accept their "fine" as enough? Do you know what your spouse is worried about? Do you know how they feel about your marriage, their relationship with God, your jobs, your children, and their parents and siblings?

As a couple, we recommend reading a chapter like this and discussing how you each feel you are doing in this area. This conversation alone, when it is done in a way that is not in frustration and does not involve any attacking, can put you on a road to deeper intimacy. To continually nurture your knowledge of one another, work on increasing how much you talk together. You can do this in various ways, such as making sure you spend time together each day talking, going out on dates or going for walks to talk about life, and even by using communication cards like those we mention below. Ultimately, in the midst of busy lives, you have to intentionally change how much time you spend together talking and sharing.

Nurturing Intimacy: Shoulder-to-Shoulder

Building your emotional love bank in your marriage also includes spending fun time together, doing small acts of kindness for one another, and having simple moments of connection. Shoulder-to-shoulder intimacy is the friendship time and adventure part of marital intimacy. There are several things you can check to evaluate how well you are nurturing this shoulder-to-shoulder intimacy. Are you going on dates? How are you doing at getting time away, just the two of you? How often do you enjoy recreational activities together? When is the last time you did a service project together?

When we do workshops or when Jennifer sees couples in therapy, we give couples homework to go on dates. This seems elementary, but it is crucial to building intimacy. There is no substitute for time together. Prioritizing this kind of time together goes a long way in building relational intimacy and filling up the love bank.

Some couples need help in finding mutually enjoyable activities to do together. Harley has a section in *His Needs Her Needs* on recreational companionship that we recommend; it helps couples explore ways they can connect again in fun, enjoyable, creative time together. The companion workbook, *Five Steps to Romantic Love,* has a simple, detailed worksheet that takes about twenty minutes to fill out. It helps couples identify how they like to relax or have fun together and guides them in choosing new activities to engage in, ranging from card playing to sports, from gardening to dancing, or from rock climbing to museums.

We also give couples a *Cup Exercise* (described below) where both the husband and wife write requests, put them into a cup, and then do those things for their spouse that week. These requests might be simple things like a five-minute foot rub, sitting on the porch at night looking at the stars together, or putting a note in a lunch being taken to work. Fun together often starts in the small moments at home.

It is also important to note, as we are discussing how to get close, that couples sometimes have a difficult time figuring out the balance between how much time they spend together and how much room they allow in the relationship for individual pursuits. This balance of separateness and togetherness includes understanding how comfortable each of you are with independent activities (the separateness) and how you negotiate individual interests, time alone, or time with friends. This also includes how you both feel about the amount of time you spend together (the togetherness)—if you get anxious when you are apart, if you ever feel smothered, or how you respond when you feel like you do not have enough time together. Honestly evaluate your balance of togetherness and separateness. Like we've mentioned, a simple way you can evaluate this is to read this paragraph and ask each other about these different areas.

Spiritual Intimacy

> "Two are better than one. They have a good return for their work. If one falls down, his friend can help him up. If two lie down together, they will keep warm. Though one may be overpowered, two can defend themselves. A cord of three strands is not quickly broken." (Ecclesiastes 4:9-12)

Together. The cord of three strands, husband, wife and God, is strong. Together, a couple can win battles. What is amazing is that being in that battle together also has some perks. You get to keep each other warm. These are the definitions of friendship in this scripture: helping each other up when you fall, keeping each other warm, battling the enemy together. Psalms 34:3 says, "Glorify the Lord with me. Let us exalt His name **together**" (emphasis added). Spiritual intimacy can be nurtured in so many different ways. Praying together. Serving together. Sharing with each other what you learned in your quiet times. Teaching another couple the Bible together. Praying together when you have conflict between you. Going to the cross together and putting your eyes on Jesus. Together.

For some of you reading this, you were both disciples of Jesus when you got married, and you probably had some dreams of being a spiritual team. It can be very helpful to do a checkup and ask yourselves how that is going. How much have you nurtured that part of your relationship? How are you doing at laboring together spiritually? How is your partnership in the gospel? How are you doing being God's helper in getting your spouse to heaven? We all fall down. We all mess up. Do you pick each other up when you fall, or do you criticize each other? Do you know how your spouse is doing spiritually? We mentioned earlier how important it is to have a love map of your spouse. How good is your love map of your spouse spiritually? Do you know what they struggle with spiritually, what scriptures inspire them, what spiritual dreams they have? How well do you know their spiritual world?

The scripture quoted above teaches that two are better than one. We can help each other be better spiritually. The unique opportunity for a couple that follows God is to defend against Satan together. "Though one is overpowered, two can defend themselves" (Ecclesiastes 4:12). It is vital to remember the spiritual battle in which we are all engaged. Satan is the enemy, and as a couple we can fight against him. Talk about how your *together* is going spiritually. How can you as a couple more consciously and purposefully glorify God? Below we have included a list of questions to prompt a good spiritual conversation. Let this be a starting point or a booster to deepening your spiritual intimacy.

Strengthening Your Relational Intimacy

As you look at these different ways to strengthen friendship in your marriage, you may want to choose one thing and put it consistently into practice. That small, continual change can have a huge ripple effect. We recommend, if you do not do this already, start with praying together every night (or day depending on your schedule). Below we have included various exercises to start you along the path toward that ripple effect. Talk about this chapter together. Talk about it also with those you are close to. Remember, make sure the tone you use when talking about all this is open, genuine, and without attack. Then pursue some of the tasks below.

So What Happened?

How did the couples mentioned at the beginning of this chapter overcome their difficulties? Each of them came in for sex therapy. However, their overall relationship intimacy needed attention in order to improve their sexual relationship. Roger and Marcie (who felt like roommates with little emotional connection) learned how to work through the fears and risks that come with genuine vulnerability and began to be intentional about their time together both in and out of the home. This ended up making a huge difference when they worked on their sexual enjoyment. Chiyo and Kwan (who had a lot of irritation and anger and very little time together) had to do some hard work on how they attacked or withdrew during conflict. When they put regular, fun dates back into their schedule in order to intentionally prioritize time just for the two of them, and experienced some victory in feeling connection through conflict, their sexual intimacy improved dramatically. Eduardo and Rosalie (who spent time helping others but not much with each other) had to make a significant shift by prioritizing their relationship over their ministry responsibilities. They got back to laughing and genuine sharing that went a long way toward working on the difficulties they had been having in their sexual relationship. Finally, Mark and Sylvia (who argued a lot and had very little intimacy of any kind) worked hard on getting rid of harsh words and damaging interactions. When they did this, they were able to start enjoying one another again for the first time in years. As their friendship rebuilt, affection returned, and it was then that it became possible for them to work on their sexual relationship.

For each of these couples, as they grew in conflict resolution skills and rebuilt their friendship, they also worked on becoming more spiritually intimate and sharing what they were learning in their time with God. It goes without saying, but we will say it anyway—each of these steps in nurturing friendship in marriage will have a significant influence on how well your sexual intimacy improves.

EXERCISES

Relationship Intimacy Exercise 1: Building Intimate Communication Skills

Purchase: The Ungame (Couples Version), The Love Map (Gottman), and The Intimate Marriage cards: Decks 1 & 2 (Konzen - see back page for ordering information)

We often give out the decks recommended above in the order they are listed as couples work at deepening the levels of vulnerability and intimacy in their relationship. We recommend doing these types of card games *daily*. The daily use is very important. This simple addition to your day can create significant change. Determine a time of day that will work for both of you. Using the cards suggested can lead to months of healthy, encouraging, interesting, and much needed conversation.

*If conflict in your marriage is high, it may not be best to start with cards that ask about your relationship. You may instead want to start with the less personal *All Ages* version of *The Ungame* or another set of cards called *Chat Pack*.

Directions:
1) Using one of the card decks above, decide who goes first.
2) The spouse who goes first takes a card from the deck, reads the card, and answers it.
3) The spouse who is listening then reflects what their spouse has said.
4) Now the other spouse's turn. Take a card, read it, and answer. The spouse reflects.

5) Spend five minutes each day alternately answering and reflecting. If needed, set a timer to keep your time to five minutes. When the timer goes off, put the lid on the box. Keeping it to five minutes helps ensure that you will continue to do this on an ongoing basis.

6) For the person answering the card: keep your answer to two or three sentences. Too much information can flood your spouse and make it difficult for them to reflect.

7) During the five minutes of answering and reflecting, do not comment on your spouse's answers or have a conversation about the topic. It should go something like this: Your spouse picks a card, which says, "Tell your spouse your favorite holiday." Your spouse answers, "My favorite holiday is Christmas." You reflect your spouse's answer saying, "Your favorite holiday is Christmas." You now pick up a card and answer it, with your spouse reflecting.

*Note: This kind of rote reflection may seem empty and shallow. However, in our experience, learning to just reflect what your spouse says is an extremely important part of building better connection. Your spouse will thank you for becoming such a great listener.

8) When the five minutes are up (and your timer goes off), put the lid on the box. After the lid is on the box, you can talk further, ask your spouse questions, and discuss your answers as much as you want.

9) The most important part of the exercise is that you DO IT DAILY! If you are not consistent in daily participation, this could end up being just one more thing you try that has little impact.

Relationship Intimacy Exercise 2: Prompt and Reflection

*Recommendation: Before doing this exercise, make sure that you have a good handle on the Validation Protocol (found in the chapters on *The Speaker* and *The Validator*). Also, make sure you've been doing the card exercises above for long enough to have a good handle on answering simply, listening carefully, and reflecting.

Check your level of anxiety as you begin this exercise. If your anxiety is high, you may need to pause and breathe, share your anxiety with your spouse, or wait until a later time to do the exercise. Be patient and gracious with one another. We do not recommend forcing yourself to do these kinds of communication exercises or making your spouse feel coerced.

Each of the sentence prompts below are about *things you do or have done that make you feel close and connected.* As explained in the directions about the Prompt and Reflection exercises, before you begin, sit in two chairs that can face each other. Husbands, sit with your knees spread. Wives, tuck your chair in so that your knees are touching your husband's chair. Get comfortable and then take each other's hands. When you share your sentence, look directly into your spouse's eyes.

Decide who will start first. Whoever goes first begins with the first prompt and finishes the sentence. The spouse then simply reflects the sentence (just mirror it back, not adding any interpretation or rewording). Then the spouse who is second begins with the first prompt, and the spouse who went first reflects. Do this for each prompt. For some of these prompts, you may be sharing something from the history of your relationship. Begin.

1) "I feel close to you when_____."
2) "I really enjoy doing _____ with you."
3) "It is hard for me to feel close to you when you_____."
4) "Something you have done that made me feel connected to you was_____."
5) "Something you have done that has made me feel cherished was_____."
6) "You make it easy for me to talk to you when you_____."

After doing all of the above prompts, ask each other:

7) "Is there anything I've said that you want to ask me about or have me explain?"

Relationship Intimacy Exercise 3: Spiritual Intimacy

Using the questions below, sit down and have a genuine conversation about how you are doing spiritually and ways you can grow as a spiritually intimate team. You may decide to just use a couple of the questions to start and then do some more later. Decide who is going to go first answering each question. As your spouse shares, reflect what you have heard each time after they share.

*Remember to balance how much each of you is speaking. Think of the Validation Exercise and the *Keep it Short* rule. If you are the spouse who uses more words to explain yourself, be more concise so that you do not flood your spouse with too many words. If you are the spouse less likely to share much, your spouse may be hungry to hear your thoughts and feelings. Stretch yourself and *share*.

1) What concerns do you have about your own spiritual walk?
2) What was your toughest spiritual decision?
3) Who is your favorite character in the Bible and why?
4) What would you go backwards in time and change spiritually if you could?
5) What are areas of strength in your marriage spiritually?
6) What do you believe and think about heaven?
7) Where would you like to be at spiritually as an individual?
8) What is a spiritual doubt you have?
9) What characteristic of God's character amazes you the most?
10) What do you believe is your greatest spiritual strength as an individual?
11) What is an area you feel you need spiritual accountability?
12) What is an area you feel you need to grow the most in your spiritual intimacy as a couple?
13) How do you feel you are doing in living out your discipleship in your marriage?
14) Who is a couple you admire spiritually and what do you admire about them?

After having this time together, share about what is was like to talk about these things and about any discomfort or encouragement you felt. Discuss ways you can continue to do this. Allow this exercise to spur more conversations over time.

Relationship Intimacy Exercise 4: The Cup Exercise

Both of you take two small slips of paper and write a small request for your spouse on each one. Make your requests small and simple—something that can be done around the house in five to fifteen minutes. It may be a head massage, cuddling outside on the hammock together, watching the stars on the porch, or writing a small note to put into a lunch or briefcase. Choose two cups, and each of you puts your two slips into your cup. Sometime in the next week, take out your spouse's slips from their cup and do them. Refill your cups each week.

Relationship Intimacy Exercise 5: "Dwell on These Things"
(Philippians 4:8)

This is an exercise many of us have heard about when we go to marriage retreats. Writing out a list of what we are grateful for in our spouse is a great recommendation for any couple. It is important that as you do this, make it genuine. A couple who taught this once admitted that there was a point in their relationship where all they could put on their list was that they were grateful their spouse brushed their teeth. Hopefully your list will be longer!

1) Read Philippians 4:8—read this in several versions and feel free to use the words we have suggested below (we have used the NIV and Holman versions) and any from other versions you would like.

2) On a blank piece of paper, write out the word "true." Next to that word, write out what is encouraging and *true* about your spouse.

3) Write out the words "noble" and "honorable." Next to those words, write out what you have seen in your spouse that is *noble* and *honorable*.

4) Write out the words "just" and "right." Next to those words, write out what you have seen in your spouse that is *just* and *right*.

5) Write out the word "pure." Next to that word, write out what you have seen in your spouse that is *pure*. Continue with the words *lovely, commendable, admirable, morally excellent, praiseworthy*.

6) Write the word "strengths." Add any other characteristics, abilities, actions, attitudes, strengths, talents, etc. that you see in your spouse.

7) Remember—be real. Be genuine. If your list starts small, that's OK.

8) With God: Now spend time praying about each of these things, telling God the good things you see in your spouse.

9) With Others: Throughout the next week, share these things with multiple people. Talk about your spouse this week with others— when you are at church, with friends, at work, or with our kids. Without mentioning this exercise, tell them about your spouse. It is especially important that this part of the exercise is genuine. Share the things you can say from your heart that you truly believe about your spouse.

10) With Your Spouse: When appropriate, share this list with your spouse. You can also share simply, "I was talking about you at

work today. I was telling my friend that I really appreciate how talented, kind, hardworking, (fill in the blank) you are."

Relationship Intimacy Exercise 6: Recreational Companionship

Purchase Harley's *His Needs Her Needs* and the workbook *The Five Steps to Romantic Love*. Read the chapter on Recreational Companionship. Then fill out the Recreational Companionship worksheet in the workbook. Identify two or three activities with the highest scores. Of those, choose one to put into your schedule now. You can make plans for putting the other ideas into practice in the future.

8

Touch and Affection

Raoul and Rachel engage in sex rarely, and Rachel has never experienced an orgasm with Raoul. They share that there is little touch or affection between them since they have been having sexual problems. However, affection and touch have been a source of conflict between them for most of their relationship. Rachel says she loves affection but that the only time Raoul touches her is when he wants to have sex.

Rob and Stacy say they have been having sexual problems throughout their marriage. They are also not happy with their overall intimacy in marriage. Other than the few times they have sex, they rarely touch. They do not express affection when they say goodbye leaving for work or when they greet one another as they come home. They do not hold hands as they walk together and have never kissed each other in public other than the kiss at their wedding.

Ingrid and Malcolm have sex regularly, though they are not happy with how things are going in general. Ingrid feels claustrophobic with Malcolm at times, especially because of how much he likes to constantly touch her. Malcolm experiences feeling rejected by Ingrid when she pulls away so quickly from his touch.

Touch can be such a sensitive area in a relationship. Couples often express that they want to have a warm, loving relationship, but that it is hard to talk about touch and it is even harder to sustain any changes to their overall affection. Addressing problems with touch and affection can mean working on them directly in marriage, but it can also mean looking at how each man or woman has or has not experienced touch throughout their life. This chapter aims to address experiences of affection and touch throughout life and to explore the challenges with touch in marriage and ways in which to improve this sensitive area of intimacy.

The Importance of Touch

Touch was important to Jesus. Though He could heal people without touching them (Matthew 8:13; Matthew 12:13), He still touched the leper (Matthew 8:3), touched Peter's mother-in-law (Matthew 8:15), held a girl's hand as He brought her back from the dead (Matthew 9:25), touched an attacker as He healed his ear (Luke 22:51), and touched a deaf man's tongue and the inside of his ears (Mark 7:33). He touched or even wanted to touch His enemies, desiring to gather and enfold under His wings those who wanted to stone Him (Luke 22:51, Matthew 23:37). He held children, took them *in his arms,* and put His hands on them (Mark 9:36, 10:16).

Jesus was so personal about His touch. When a woman was healed by touching His garment in the midst of a large, moving crowd, He stopped everything to find out who had touched Him (Luke 8:45). He held the smelly, dirty feet of His disciples, washing them with water (John 13:5). He firmly grasped Peter's hand after he got scared walking on water (Matthew 14:31). And how amazing it must have been for the boy who had been possessed by a shrieking, violent demon, to look up and see the hand of Jesus reaching out to lift him up (Mark 9:27). What a claim the scriptures make—that all who touched Jesus were healed (Matthew 14:36). Yes, His touch brought physical healing, but He also touched people just to reassure them, hold them, help them be safe, and serve them. There is no doubt that these kinds of touches brought healing in other ways. As followers of Jesus, our touch can reflect His, showing kindness, reassurance, and compassion. A simple hug can make others feel safe and show them their worth to us. Our warm touch to those in distress can bring about emotional healing. Giving in this way also gives us the opportunity to receive touch from others in a way that makes us feel loved, safe, healed, and believed in.

In the field of mental and physical health today, there is a considerable amount of research on touch. Warm touch, such as massages, cuddling, hugging, and hand-holding, is connected to increased oxytocin (i.e., the cuddle hormone), decreased blood pressure and heart rate, improved cardiovascular circulation, and reduced stress hormone levels in the cortisol activation response to stress.[1] When they are held, babies cry less and when they receive warm touch, deep coma patients have improved heart rates.[2] Warm and loving touch lowers anxiety and improves health. Healthy touch improves work and athletic performance. Touch has a therapeutic effect on ADHD, diabetes, migraines, asthma, and immune functioning. And yes, waitresses who lightly and briefly touch the hands or shoulders of customers get higher tips.[3] People who experience lower levels of affectionate touch have lower self-esteem.[4] In fact, those who go without physical touch often experience a kind of skin hunger—that strong desire and need for human physical connection. We definitely need touch.

There has been some important research on how touch influences the quality of marriage and the marital sexual relationship. For couples, touch not only arouses, but it also soothes and comforts.[5] Partners feel like touch is an expression of warmth and support, especially in the midst of conflict.[6] In fact, the more a couple continually gives and receives affectionate touch, the deeper their intimate connection.[7] On the other hand, couples who are less affectionate are often less satisfied in their marriage.[8]

In the sexual relationship, ongoing affectionate touch can make a couple feel more satisfied with their sex life and more at ease when they are discussing sexuality.[9] Couples who cuddle, fondle each other, and kiss and caress more have higher marital and sexual satisfaction.[10] Warm touch can also help couples become more resilient in the wake of sexual dysfunction or sexual pain.[11] On the other hand, when husbands or wives say they are uncomfortable with affectionate touch, they also experience additional roadblocks to their relational and sexual intimacy.[12] If touch has so many benefits, how can touch become problematic?

Problematic Touch

Though we need touch, it is not uncommon for someone to dislike certain types of touch. This response could be tied to a number of different things: the emotional state someone is in at the time; negative experiences someone has as a child or adolescent involving touch; physical or chronic pain or illness; or unresolved conflict in marriage. For some individuals, as they grew up, relatives and friends of the family demanded hugs and kisses. Others have experienced physical or sexual abuse in those formative years, which may have had a significant effect on how they feel about touch as an adult. If they then continue to experience touch as intrusive or violating in their adult intimate relationships, this can have a strong influence on how someone feels even when touch is positive.

You may remember disliking touch even as a child. Perhaps you quickly shrugged off hugs and avoided or quickly ended any affection initiated by others. As an adult, you may have experienced an increase in the enjoyment of touch in romantic relationships, though this may have faded with time. The enjoyment of giving and receiving touch may have increased strongly after you had children. Parents experience pleasure in holding their infant, cuddling with their toddler, and receiving hugs from their child. However, some of us still find it hard to desire to hold or touch our children, even though we desire to be more affectionate. If you have young children, especially more affectionate children, you may feel annoyed (and then guilty) when your child demands touch or continually clings to you. If you are the primary caretakers for your children, you may also struggle to accept frequent touch from your spouse. "I am with the kids all day, and the kids are constantly touching me and holding onto me. And when my spouse walks in and tries to hug me and kiss me, I just want to push him/her away. Somebody is always touching me, and sometimes it just makes me crazy." This can be a very natural struggle for parents of young children and especially mothers who feel they no longer own their own bodies.

There are a number of other issues that affect how we experience touch. The need for touch can change according to our emotional state. During emotional distress, we may dislike certain kinds of touch or not want any touch at all. Some of us want to be held when we are upset or sad. Others of us do not want to be touched while we are feeling that vulnerable, though we still might want someone to stay with us as a supportive presence. We may be open to a light hand on the shoulder or the knee at the appropriate time that might say, "I am here." More than that might be difficult.

Physical pain also influences how much we desire touch. This is especially true for those who experience neuropathy associated with lupus, diabetes, kidney disorders, surgeries and chemotherapy, chronic pain, or infections. When battling these kinds of chronic illnesses, it can literally hurt to be touched, which can be challenging for both spouses. Sometimes spouses of individuals with chronic illness or pain can feel rejected even while they are trying to be understanding and compassionate.

Touch is also problematic when couples have chronic conflict. Some of us want more touch when there is conflict. Others do not want touch of any kind during conflict. In fact, warm and reaffirming affection often disappears due to a lack of safety and the increased disengagement, resentment, and anger that come with chronic conflict.

For some couples, it is not the lack of touch that is the problem; it is the excess of touch. Some spouses feel that the amount and frequency that their spouse touches them makes them feel smothered or irritated. They may have always acknowledged that their partner is the more affectionate one, but over time they may have begun avoiding touch or pushing their spouse away. Others dislike constantly being touched, but they either do not voice how they feel or the only time they do is when they become angry or irritated. For some couples, differing preferences for touch can become an area of conflict; a hidden, undealt-with source of frustration that causes division but is often not discussed.

For any of you who experience these responses to touch in your relationship, it can be very healing to start discussing the feelings you have when your spouse touches you or how you feel when there is little affection between you. This could be an important step in improving the physical connection in your marriage. If these passages describe you or your spouse, spend some time talking about this chapter. Make sure that you speak and listen without judgment. Touch can be a very touchy subject (pun intended).

Touch and Affection in Marriage and Sexuality

It is not uncommon for couples to share that their level of affection has slowly died off as time has passed. You and your spouse may have experienced free, exciting, fun, and easy affection throughout dating and engagement. Later, however, that simple, playful, non-sexual touch disappeared gradually, beginning early in marriage or with the birth of children. It is not uncommon for couples to intentionally limit touch and affection before they married, either because of concerns with becoming sexual, or because they become aware early in their relationship of the differing likes and dislikes they have around affection. As a couple, it may be helpful to talk about how much affection you had while you were dating, engaged, or early in your marriage and what may have caused it to change.

Feelings about touch can also become very connected to sexuality in marriage. For some women, they would like more touch, but they sometimes feel that touch has become connected only to sexuality. "You only touch me when you want sex," is a common expression. Research has shown that when physical affection is expressed primarily in the context of sex, relationship and sexual satisfaction is lower.[13] On the other hand, husbands whose wives have withdrawn from touch because sex has become problematic often share that they feel lonely and isolated.

It is also common for men and women to have different interpretations and responses to touch. For many men, touch from their partner that communicates sexual desire and arousal makes them feel loved.[14] However, for many women, if their partner primarily touches them when they want sex, then touch does not make them feel loved. Sometimes, though, it is the husband who feels this way. Men sometimes feel that their wives rarely touch them unless they are engaging sexually. There are also wives who feel hurt and angry that since their husband has not been initiating sex, all other touch has also disappeared in their relationship. It is usually helpful to untangle the expression of affection from being associated only with having sex (more below). Healing this vital connection requires communicating more about your needs and wants for touch and affection.

87

These kinds of changes are critical to experiencing and renewing the joy of physical affection in marriage.

Expressing Preferences

Husbands or wives often do not tell their spouses what they do not like about touch or, if they do, they often say it when they are irritated and in a tone that shows distaste. Some couples have been kissing and holding hands for years and have not told each other, "I really don't enjoy kissing like that," or "It bothers me to hold hands like that and I'd rather do it like this."

You may wish your spouse held your hand more, or stroked or played with your hair, or came up behind you to give you a spontaneous hug. You may want your spouse to sit closer to you when you are at church, or to reach across and put their hand on your thigh while driving in the car. You may like your spouse to hold you when you are stressed or to randomly kiss you as they walk by you at home. Have you told them that? Do they know? Is it embarrassing to verbalize that and to ask for it? Does it feel like you're being needy if you tell them you wished for more affection? Does asking for that directly feel unmanly or like a clingy female? Do you wish they loved you enough to just know? I mean, they should know! This is what couples who love each other do, right? Were they more affectionate earlier in your relationship and you're hurt that they no longer are? Have you brought it up too many times to count and it still hasn't changed? Have you begun to feel like it is just too painful to bring it up again?

How much do you talk about touch in your marriage? You may need to find a way to start. It may be hard, painful, and embarrassing, but it is vital. Talk to each other about your feelings regarding holding hands in public and private. Do you kiss each other in greeting or when you say goodbye? Talk about the type of kiss you would prefer at those times. Tell your spouse what type of light caresses you would like as you pass one another in the house. Would you prefer a shoulder squeeze or a light touch on the curve of your back? Communicate with your spouse how long and in what positions you prefer to hug, cuddle, or spoon. Openly talking about your affection preferences, rather than just assuming your spouse knows, is often the first step to changing how you both feel about touch. Some of the exercises below can help you move in that direction.

Working on Touch and Affection

You may find that when you and your spouse start working on touch, many of your underlying conflicts, hurts, and frustrations come to the surface. This is not always negative or unexpected. That is why we always recommend working first on building quality verbal and emotional intimacy alongside working on conflict resolution skills that lead to empathy, understanding, and connection. If you have already been working on these skills, and they are going well, you will now have the opportunity to put these very skills into practice when conflict arises around affectionate touch.

If you have been deeply disconnected up to this point, working on touch can be very tricky. Serious, unresolved conflicts may require additional healing before you begin working on improving the affection in your relationship. Trying to improve physical affection without addressing these can be quite damaging, stalling improvement in the relationship. When a couple is still emotionally disconnected, doing touch exercises can feel mechanical. If you get stuck while trying to work through issues on touch, slow down or stop. Get some help, either from a couple you are close to, or from a professional.

So what kind of touch is usually enjoyable in marriage? Typically, people enjoy touches to the hair and head, light caresses to the cheeks and chin, a simple running of the thumbs over the knuckles, warm touch of the hands to the legs and arms, light scratches to the back, or hugs that last enough to say something. Some enjoy draping a leg over their partner's leg, sitting or lying in their lap, gentling being wrapped in their spouse's arms from behind, or receiving a warm massage to the feet. Since preferences for touch are unique to each individual, you may need to ask your spouse what they like and tell your spouse what you enjoy.

It is also important to identify the types of touch that are not enjoyable or even irritating. Repeated touch that is done again and again to the same spot on the body can cause irritation. Pinching, though enjoyable for some during sexual play, may be unpleasant at other times. Some women feel startled or feel unappreciated when their spouse gropes them, grabs them in the buttocks or breasts, or gives them hugs that feel aggressive. If your hands are rough from work, you may want to use a strong moisturizer to soften your fingers. This is especially relevant during sensual and sexual touch, when lotions and oils can go a long way to increasing the enjoyment of touch during sex. Making sure to communicate about the kinds of touch you find unappealing in a way that does not shame your spouse or make them feel hurt or defensive is important. And if you or your mate have experienced physical or sexual abuse, you may need to relearn touch and how to talk about touch within the safety of your relationship (see the recommendation for *Additional Touch Exercises* below by Wendy Maltz).

The exercises below may be helpful both in talking about preferences in affection and touch as well as in practicing the little behaviors that make touch uniquely enjoyable for a married couple.

The Sexual Vacation

You may wonder what this term *sexual vacation* means and why there is a section on this in a chapter on affectionate touch. When couples decide to work on improving things in their sexual relationship, they often tend to go straight to working just on sex—talking about it, doing it, trying different things. Often, however, it is important to work on all the other types of intimate touch first. For some couples, all forms of touch may have become strongly associated with sex. Spouses can become reactive to simple touch, or to working on simple touch, if they think that exploring these things means that sex, orgasm, or sexual intercourse is an automatic expectation.

For some couples, reactivity to touch has become so strong that in order to improve the sexual, sensual, and affectionate part of the relationship, the couple needs to take a sexual vacation. During a sexual vacation, couples decide not to have sex or engage in anything leading to orgasm until they have reached a certain point of healing, connection, openness, and safety. Though it may be difficult, it is important for couples to have an open discussion and make a mutual decision as to whether they may need to forego intercourse and orgasm for a time in order to improve their intimate relationship. If you desire this and your spouse is not in agreement, draw in another couple to help you make this decision in a way that honors both of you.

So how does this apply to couples who decide to continue having sex while working on the things found in this book? It is *vital* that the exercises done in this chapter and in the chapters on sensual and sexual touch are done without being followed by sex. We cannot emphasize strongly enough the essential value of learning to enjoy touch when it is not connected to orgasm. This can be quite challenging for some and can bring up a great amount of anxiety for those who feel like sex has already not been happening very much. However, please believe us when we say that taking a time out from sex or delaying orgasm, intercourse, and sexual release in order to learn how to *take in* the incredible pleasure of affectionate and sensual touch will have an immeasurable long-term impact on the quality of your sexual relationship.

So What Happened?

What happened with the couples we shared about in the beginning of the chapter? Raoul and Rachel and Rob and Stacy (who each had not been experiencing much touch and affection in their relationships) had to first work on their verbal intimacy and going on dates regularly. Working on becoming affectionate was very awkward at first. It was very important for each of them to learn to be genuine with their spouse about their feelings, their fears, and their dislikes around simple touch. When affectionate touch became genuinely enjoyable for each couple, they were then able to begin working on the enjoyment of sensual and sexual touch. Through the process of therapy, each couple had to periodically come back and check on the areas of verbal and relational intimacy and affectionate touch to see if any of those areas needed strengthening before continuing. After things improved in their relationship and in their affectionate, sensual, and sexual touch, Rachel experienced her first orgasm.

For Ingrid and Malcolm (who had so much affection in their relationship that Ingrid felt smothered), they had to work through some of the traumatic reactions Ingrid had to touch. She had been raped as a young woman, and although she knew Malcolm loved her and would never harm her, some of his touch felt overpowering. As she became more verbal and assertive, and as Malcolm became more sensitive rather than taking her reaction personally, they were able to reach a healthy level of mutually enjoyable affectionate touch. Working through their challenges with touch went a long way in bringing their sexual relationship to a new and exciting place.

EXERCISES

AFFECTIONATE TOUCH EXERCISES

*Before doing any of the exercises below, make sure that it is a mutual decision to do so. These exercises are appropriate when conflict resolution and relational intimacy are going well. Also, check in with each other on the level of anxiety you have during these exercises. If at any time it becomes problematic, stop, take a break, and come back later. If you need to, seek some help before beginning.

**Reminder: These exercises are to be conducted without having sex either before or after the exercise.

***At the end of each exercise, talk about how you felt while doing the exercise.

Affectionate Touch Exercise 1: The Hand Cradle

Before you start this exercise, read the directions all the way through. Then begin.

1) Decide who is going first. Whoever goes first takes the hand of their spouse palm down and then holds it and cradles it within their two hands.

2) After holding it for a short time, tell your spouse what their hand feels like physically (something like: "Your hand is warm. It is soft. It is dry.")

3) Now take your upper hand and gently caress the back of your spouse's hand as you continue cradling it with your other hand (only the hand and not the forearm). Use the tips of your fingers to lightly explore their fingers, and the backside of their hand. Now turn their hand over and explore their palm. Notice the different textures of their skin. Describe to your spouse what their hand feels like as you continue gently caressing.

4) Go back to gently cradling their hand, palm down, in both of yours.

5) As you hold their hand in yours, describe to your spouse what you know of this hand. Tell them what you have seen this hand do. Share what memories you have of this hand. This will be something like, "When I think of this hand, I think of _____," or "I have seen this hand_____" (explain what you have seen this hand do through the years in tasks, touch, with children, etc.) Take some time with this part.

6) End the Hand Cradle with a final gentle caress.

7) Continue the exercise with the other spouse providing the cradle, the caress, and the description and memories of their spouse's hand.

8) Share with each other afterwards what the exercise was like for you.

Affectionate Touch Exercise 2: The Hand-to-Hand, Hand-to-Head, Hand-to-Face Caress

Read the directions below first, all the way through, so that you understand what you are going to do and can do the exercise without continually referring to the directions. Then, follow the directions as specified:

1) Sitting comfortably, face each other and then decide who is going first (who is the first giver).

2) **Hand-to-Hand/Forearm:** Whoever goes first, take your spouse's hand with one of your hands; with the other hand, lightly caress your spouse's hand and forearm.

3) Describe what physical sensations you notice as you caress their hand and forearm.

4) For the spouse who is receiving the caress, describe how the caress feels and what emotions you are experiencing as you receive the caress.

5) Now switch and follow the above directions. After both have taken time to be the giver, do the next caress exercise.

6) **Hand-to-Head/Scalp:** After the hand and forearm caress is completed by both spouses, the spouse who went first is the giver once again.

7) Facing each other, take both of your hands and gently begin exploring your spouse's scalp and head (but not yet the face).

8) For the spouse who is receiving the caress, describe how the caress on the head and scalp feels and what emotions you are experiencing as you receive the caress.

9) Now switch and follow the directions above. After both have taken time to be the giver for the hand-to-head/scalp, do the next caress exercise.

10) **Hand-to-Face:** After the head and scalp caress is completed by both spouses, the spouse who went first is the giver once again.

11) Facing each other, take one or both of your hands and gently, after asking permission, begin exploring your spouse's face. Using gentle fingers, explore the forehead, cheeks, chin, nose, eyebrows, and lips.

12) For the spouse who is receiving the caress, tell the spouse where on the face you prefer not to be touched and the level of the pressure you desire for the touch.

13) Describe how the caress on the face feels to you and what emotions you are experiencing as you receive the caress.

14) Now switch and follow the directions above.

Affection Touch Exercise 3: Hugging and Spooning

Level 1: While standing upright, take turns hugging each other until you are relaxed; until you experience an inward sigh.

Level 2: At another time, choose a place, either in your room or on a couch. Taking turns with who lies behind the other, find a comfortable spooning position, with each of you lying together with one spouse's back curled into the other spouse's chest and stomach, arms enfolding the other.

1) Spoon until you experience an inward sigh of enjoyment and contentment.

2) Switch who is lying in front of the other and shift positions until you are comfortable. Spoon again until you are relaxed.

3) At different times, ask each other, "Would you like to stop or continue?" If you choose to stop, add, "What I would rather do is_____."

Affection Touch Exercise 4: Brush and Caress

1) Find a comfortable place to sit with your partner where both of you can face the same direction.

2) Decide who will sit behind the other, with their partner's back to them.

3) The partner sitting behind then gently strokes the hair, arms, back, and shoulders of their partner.

4) The receiving partner then tells their spouse what they would prefer (i.e., the type of pressure, whether they would like them to use their fingers). Remember, this exercise is a caress exercise, not a massage.

5) Using a comb or a brush, or fingers if preferred, brush and comb through your spouse's hair.

6) Do this for ten minutes, and then gently pat your spouse on the hair to let them know you are done.

7) Now switch who is sitting behind, and the other spouse then gives the same touches to the hair, arms, back and shoulders of their partner, with the partner sharing their preferences. Continue the directions above using the comb, brush, or fingers to comb through your spouse's hair.

8) Do this as well for ten minutes, ending with a pat to the hair.

Affectionate Touch Exercise 5: Hand and Forearm Massage

Before beginning this exercise, read the directions below completely. Begin.

1) Choose a lotion for this exercise. Decide who is going to give first. For the spouse that gives first, take your spouse's hand in both of yours. Begin to massage their hand and forearm using the lotion.

2) For the receiving spouse, tell your spouse what you like about the touch they are giving. "I like it when you_____."

3) Tell your spouse verbally what you would like them to do differently, where you would like them to massage. Tell them the type of pressure you want. Use words like firmer, softer, faster, slower. "That is good there. Go ahead and do it firmer."

4) Now take your spouse's hand and guide their hand to where you want them to massage and with your hand (without words) show them the type of pressure and movement you want.

5) Tell your spouse what you like about the way they are massaging your hand and forearm and what it feels like. "That is very____," and "I like how you____."

6) Stop/Continue: For the giving spouse, ask, "Would you like to stop or continue?" For the receiving spouse, answer saying, "I would like to continue," or "I would like to stop, and what I'd rather do is____."

7) Now switch and continue.

Additional Touch Exercises: Wendy Maltz

For those of you who have a background in sexual abuse, or if touch has become quite problematic in your relationship for other reasons, we *highly recommend* some additional touch exercises to bring about healing. You can purchase Wendy Maltz's video on *Relearning Touch* and practice the pen exercise, the hand-clapping exercise, the back-writing exercise, the nesting exercise, and others.

TOUCH AND AFFECTION COMMUNICATION EXERCISES

Touch and Affection Communication Exercise 1: Prompt and Reflection

Each of the sentence prompts are about *touch and affection*. As explained before, sit in two chairs that can face each other. Husbands, sit with your knees spread. Wives, tuck your chair in so that your knees are touching your husband's chair. Get comfortable and then take each other's hands. When you share your sentence, look directly into your spouse's eyes.

Decide who will start first. Whoever goes first begins with the first prompt and finishes the sentence. The spouse then simply reflects the sentence. Then the spouse who is second begins with the first prompt, and the spouse who went first reflects. Do this for each prompt. Also as before, for some of these prompts, you may be sharing something from the history of your relationship. Begin.

Remember, each of these prompts are about touch and affection:

1) "One of my favorite memories was when we _____."
2) "I really enjoy it when you _____."
3) "One way I like to touch you is _____."
4) "One way I like to be touched is_____."
5) "You are very good at _____."
6) "The type of touch I don't like as much is _____."
7) "One thing about touch and affection that I feel insecure about is _____."
8) "The type of affectionate touch I would like more of is _____."

After doing these prompts, ask each other:

9) "Is there anything I've said that you want to ask me about or have me explain?"

Touch and Affection Communication Exercise 2: Preferences

Take time to *show* each other your preferences for touch. This is not so much a talking exercise. Each part of this exercise is a show-and-tell. Do this when you are not pressed for time and when you have privacy. Begin by saying:

1) "The way I like to hold hands when we are walking is like this."

Take your spouse's hand and show them. Now your spouse says and does the same. Then continue with each of the following, showing each other what you prefer:

2) "The way I like to holds hands while sitting is like this."
3) "The way I like to sit together in public is like this."
4) "The way I like to sit together when we're alone is like this."
5) "The way I like to be hugged is like this."
6) "The way I like to kiss when we greet each other or say goodbye is like this."
7) "Other ways I like to kiss are like this."

Touch and Affection Communication Exercise 3: Adding Affectionate Behaviors

1) Consider the answers from the Touch and Affection Communication Exercises 1 and 2 immediately above.
2) Choose one affectionate behavior your spouse would like more of.
3) Without telling your spouse, engage in that affectionate behavior regularly for three weeks.
4) As you put that choice into practice, make sure you do so without any mockery, sarcasm, or teasing. Making changes in affection can be surprisingly vulnerable. Do so with thoughtfulness and care.

Touch and Affection Communication Exercise 4: Intimate Marriage Cards

Purchase *The Intimate Marriage* cards, Deck 3 (see back page for ordering information). Use only the cards up to the *Sensual Touch* card. Play this daily, and follow these directions:

1) Determine a time every day when you can spend five minutes playing this.
2) When you sit down to play, decide who is going to go first and then set the timer for five minutes.
3) The spouse to go first then takes a card from the pile, reads the card, and then answers the card.
4) The spouse listening simply reflects what their spouse has said. The card may say, "Tell your spouse which of these areas you find touch arousing: inner thigh, neck, stomach, butt, feet, lower back." The spouse going first shares their answer, and the other spouse reflects.
5) Now the spouse going second takes their turn. Take a card from the pile, read, and answer. The spouse reflects.
6) Continue until the timer goes off at five minutes, snap the lid on the box, and finish.
7) During the five minutes, only read, answer, and reflect. After the lid is on the box and you return to your day or evening plans, feel free to talk more about the questions and answers.

9

Influences on Sexual Challenges in Marriage

For many reading this book, you are looking for some direction on enhancing your sexual relationship. Things are going well, but you'd like to make them better. For others of you studying these chapters, there are various things that have happened, or are happening, in your life—medically, relationally, or sexually—that influence how sex is going for you. That is what we are addressing in this chapter.

God has the ability to create incredible beauty in our marital sexual intimacy. As you have been reading and using the exercises found here, hopefully you have had some growth in your thinking and in your relationship. For some of us, it can be difficult to untangle certain challenges to building lasting, fulfilling intimacy. There may be physical issues creating problems in the sexual relationship that need medical attention. Sexual sin, either from the past or more recent, may have magnified the problems. Past sexual abuse or molestation may be affecting your relationship now. In this chapter, we will explore each of these issues. Some of this material can be a bit technical at times due to the subject matter, but hopefully it will provide a way to get help and to talk about the challenges you face.

Physiological and Medical Issues Complicating Sex
Medical Challenges with Sex. One of the areas that often goes unexplored for Christian couples is the possibility of medical problems or physiological/biological issues that create sexual difficulties.[1] Some of these may need a medical diagnosis along with medical care. We always

99

recommend that if someone is experiencing erection, ejaculation, orgasm, or pain symptoms, they should seek out a sexual medicine specialist. Though those in general medicine are often the first point of contact for questions about sexual problems, many in the medical field receive only limited training or experience with sexual dysfunction, sexual pain, and sexual disorder diagnoses or treatment. Though treatment in these areas is better focused in the fields of gynecology and urology, sexual medicine specialists often have more up-to-date training with treatments that may not be offered by other professionals. Practitioners may utilize quick and simple solutions such as prescribing a pill or cream for the issue, but often the sexual problem is not quite that simple. If these are challenges you face, speak with a sexual medicine specialist who has a greater understanding of the specific issues involved in the sexual dysfunction you are facing, or go see your primary care physician and get a recommendation for a specialist.

For men, it is important to find out if there are problems with blood flow (remembering that problems with erection can be the first indication of cardiovascular problems), with testosterone levels (blood tests should check *free testosterone* levels, not just *total testosterone*), or with the pelvic floor (pain, nerves, and musculoskeletal problems). For women, it is important to assess if there are any problems with pain (vaginal, internal, external), lubrication and elasticity of tissues, or achieving orgasm. Medical problems that affect desire and arousal and sexual functioning include chronic illness (i.e., lupus, renal disease, diabetes), chronic pain, back problems, hypertension and cardiovascular problems, surgeries (i.e., prostate surgeries, hysterectomy, vaginal and cervical surgeries), cancer and cancer treatment, hormone levels, traumatic brain injury, or neurological disorders (i.e., multiple sclerosis). All of these can also affect desire, erection, ejaculation, the ability to achieve orgasm, and sexual pain. Certain medical issues also cause other problems such as urinary difficulties, yeast infections, and hormonal changes that, in turn, affect sexuality.

Medications, Drugs, and Sex. Both prescribed and over-the-counter medications (i.e., blood pressure medications, SSRIs, antihistamines, pain relievers) can have a significant effect on sexual functioning.[2] Antianxiety medications can influence desire and the ability to orgasm in men and women, as well as cause delayed ejaculation in men. Antidepressants (especially SSRI antidepressants) and certain anticonvulsants can affect desire in men and women and erectile functioning in men. Antidepressants are also associated with delayed ejaculation in men and challenges reaching orgasm for women. Anti-hypertensives may cause decreased desire, vaginal dryness, difficulty reaching orgasm, and erection and ejaculation difficulties.

Over-the-counter medications can also affect sexual difficulties. Antihistamines can cause vaginal dryness for women, and hair loss treatments are associated with decreased desire, erectile dysfunction, and delayed ejaculation in men. Pain relievers such as ibuprofen or naproxen can cause erectile difficulties and vaginal dryness. Heartburn medications and opiate pain relievers (i.e., codeine and hydrocodone) affect desire, erectile dysfunction, and vaginal dryness. The effects of these medications on sexuality may not necessarily be a good enough reason to discontinue a medication. However, being aware of these side effects can explain some of the challenges you could be having in your sexual response. This knowledge can also help you speak with your medical provider about possible alternatives.

Both legal (i.e., alcohol and tobacco) and recreational or illegal drugs have an effect on sexual functioning. Tobacco use influences erectile dysfunction and sexual desire. With alcohol, it is common for people to drink to get *in the mood*. Though the initial use of alcohol may lower inhibition, which some feel helps them overcome their anxiety or reservations about having sex, it is also important to understand that alcohol is a depressant that can impair orgasm functioning for men and women as well as delay ejaculation for men. Men who regularly use alcohol to increase the amount of time before they ejaculate can then develop problems with erection and ejaculation. Women who use alcohol to help them enjoy sex more can begin to have problems with reaching orgasm. Regular or daily consumption of alcohol also eventually lowers sexual desire.

Finally, though most illegal or recreational drugs are used to intensify the sexual experience, most illicit drug use eventually causes problems with erection, ejaculation, and desire. These drugs have often been used to compensate for sexual difficulties. For instance, heroin has been used to increase penile rigidity, but continued use leads to problems with reaching orgasm. These drugs are used initially to enhance sexuality but end up inhibiting sexual functioning.

Age and sex. Aging brings a unique set of challenges to sexuality for both men and women. The most common question women have asked is how menopause affects sexuality. Sexual challenges can be associated with natural menopause, surgically induced menopause (i.e., hysterectomy), or chemically induced menopause and ovarian failure from cancer treatment. The hormonal changes in estrogen, progestin, and testosterone connected to menopause do have an effect on the elasticity of vaginal tissues, clitoral atrophy, atrophy of the vulvar tissues, the amount of lubrication (vaginal mucosa) in the vagina, and vaginal dryness. These hormonally induced changes that lead to loss of elasticity or increased dryness can further irritate the labia and the vestibule of the vagina. The glands at the vestibule (see *The Physiology of Sexuality* for more information) can become red and irritated, and women may experience a burning and tearing sensation common to experiences of vaginal pain during intercourse.

For women, these hormonal changes can also influence levels of sexual desire and arousal, challenges in reaching orgasm, and the intensity of orgasm. Treatment of these issues would be very similar to the treatment of sexual pain found in the *Female Sexual Challenges* chapter. Older women who are experiencing dryness and discomfort or pain during intercourse have benefitted from using sexual lubricants or moisturizers such as Replens. Some women have also benefitted from estrogen replacement. However, the tissues of the vestibule are testosterone fed, and the elasticity and atrophy of those and other surrounding tissues may benefit from testosterone replacement. Most women have only been treated with estrogen, which may fail to address the problems that are due to low testosterone. A thorough sexual medicine assessment would be necessary to determine the best course of medical treatment. When older women experience vaginal dryness, lower lubrication and elasticity, and the associated vaginal pain, this can have an effect on how much they desire and enjoy sex. This makes seeking specialized sexual medicine care for these issues vital.

As men age, most will experience a decrease in sexual desire, an increase in erectile difficulties, and an increase in the amount of time to reach full erection or achieve ejaculation. Although this is often influenced by the significant drop in levels of testosterone that occurs as men age, testosterone replacement has had inconclusive results in research. The introduction of Viagra in 1998 was revolutionary in the treatment of many of these issues. However, there can be a number of factors influencing aging men that may also need to be addressed, including the quality of overall marital intimacy, nutrition, and health. For instance, increased body fat is associated with cardiovascular issues that affect erectile functioning. Enjoyable physical activity, exercise, and nutritious eating cannot only improve overall health but can also improve sexual functioning. Having a flexible and adaptive approach to these sexual changes can also be vital for sexual satisfaction. This may include having a more accepting attitude toward the ebb and flow of erection (versus reacting negatively), adjusting sexual positions to increase stimulation, changing the time of day for sexual activity to maximize energy, and focusing more on the enjoyment of non-intercourse sexuality such as sensual touch.

Treatment for medical issues that affect sexual functioning for both men and women as they age can include the use of wedge pillows to help with back problems and sex swings that aid in challenges with thrusting due to various disabilities. In further chapters, we will discuss in more detail sexual dysfunction specifically related to erection, premature or early ejaculation, vaginal pain and pain during penetration, low desire and arousal, and difficulties with or lack of orgasm. Ultimately, when looking at sexual challenges, it is important to consider and treat any medical factors that may be influencing sexual functioning and sexual satisfaction.

Sexual Abuse and Trauma

Addressing the challenges that individuals with a background in sexual trauma have in their married sexual lives deserves an entire book of its own. We recommend Robin Weidner's *Grace Calls* for women who are looking for help and support with spiritual recovery through these kinds of traumas. This section is intended to briefly highlight some of the primary challenges that sexual abuse and trauma have on marital sexuality and to help couples begin to find a direction in working through these issues.

Sexual Trauma. Sexual trauma can come in many forms, including inappropriate touch (i.e., an older individual touching the buttocks of a younger child), exposure to sexually explicit materials or experiences (pornography, having watched individuals engage in sex or masturbation), exploitative sexual comments (sexual jokes, comments about the body, or harsh and negative responses to sexual exploration), or sexual molestation and rape (including penetrative and non-penetrative sexual violations). If you have experienced sexual or physical trauma in your past, you may benefit from individual therapy. The process of healing from sexual trauma can help a survivor to release themselves from blame, to recognize that the perpetrator was responsible for the sexual violation, and to experience sexual activity without fear.[3]

Sexual trauma can result in challenges in adult sexual relationships such as flashbacks during sexual activities, problems with sexual functioning (i.e., vaginal pain, low sexual desire and arousal, problems with orgasm, erectile dysfunction), *numbing out* during sexual activity leading to a lack of sexual enjoyment, and sexual avoidance. Survivors of sexual abuse may have a number of other challenges, such as sexual anxiety and distress about sexuality, negative feelings about sex (i.e., feelings that sex is dirty; guilt about sexual preferences and sexual desire; suppressed anger about sexuality in general), and unwanted sexual fantasies or disturbing sexual thoughts.[4] They may also feel powerless during sex, lack sexual assertiveness, have difficulty communicating about sex, and experience emotional withdrawal during sex. Sexual abuse can result in conflicted feelings about having sex, such as experiencing a desire for sex and not wanting sex at the same time. Survivors can sometimes feel they do not have a right to sexual enjoyment and often think they just need to learn to endure sex. For some individuals, these various symptoms show up immediately after a sexual violation and for others, they do not show until years later.

Treatment. Reclaiming God's view of sexuality can be an incredibly important part of a sexual abuse survivor's journey. Sexual abuse treatment might also include understanding the effects of sexual abuse, learning how to reclaim the right to enjoy sex, reexamining sexual beliefs, learning how to stay emotionally connected during sex, and finding ways to deal with intrusive images and thoughts. Also, if someone with a background in sexual abuse experiences sexual pain or erectile dysfunction, they may benefit from a combination of medical, psychological, and spiritual interventions to address the physiological problems that may be associated with the sexual abuse.

Part of the journey of sexual healing for a married individual may also include healing for the couple. When someone has received needed individual healing from sexual trauma, it could be important to address how these issues are influencing the current marital sexual relationship. Good treatment should include both individual recovery and couple's work. For instance, when someone has experienced sexual trauma, touch, even non-sexual touch, can be very difficult. If a couple seeks sex therapy to help with these issues, therapy might include a gradual approach to intimate touch that is safe, comforting, and eventually, sensually and sexually enjoyable. The process, timing, and length of treatment may need to be adjusted to include addressing these elements.

Whether or not you seek out a professional, you may need, both individually and as a couple, to assess and reevaluate the views and beliefs you have of sexuality that could have been tainted by any sexual exploitation. There might also be times when what is happening in your marital relationship or in the sexual relationship re-triggers a past sexual trauma. Your spouse may also need to hear what they are doing that triggers painful feelings or negative responses. Finding ways to communicate about these things and building a new safety in the sexual relationship can be very healing both for the individual and for the couple. When couples pursue treatment for sexual trauma, as an individual and as a couple, this can help alleviate or manage the symptoms of sexual pain, low sexual desire, and the ability to reach orgasm.

Spouses of those who have gone through sexual abuse often benefit from counseling as well, for they may feel confused, rejected, abandoned, inadequate, and unattractive. Because of the effects on both spouses, couples need to commit time and resources to overcoming the challenges associated with sexual abuse. For some, this might mean putting a hold on sexual relations until some relearning can happen sexually. It can be helpful to understand that "sexual healing is rarely as fast as survivors and intimate partners would wish."[5]

Being and Staying Present During Sex. After sexual trauma and its impact on the current sexual relationship has received some help and attention, building or returning to sexual intimacy may need to include learning how to stay present in your body during sexual time with your spouse. Separating yourself from your own body may have been a way of keeping yourself safe during the abuse. Learning to be present with your spouse, and learning to feel safe while they touch and caress you, is usually a process. Many times, when memories of sexual abuse are triggered during sex, the survivor will continue to engage sexually, ignoring the traumatic trigger and disconnecting from their own body and from their spouse in the middle of sexual activity. It may be helpful to learn how to express what you are feeling and what is happening internally when you get triggered during sex. This may be necessary in order to truly remain in the body so that you can experience sexual pleasure to the fullest extent.

When I (Jennifer) work with individuals who disconnect, or disassociate, during sex due to sexual trauma, I begin with helping the individual learn how to stay in their body first while talking about sex, then during simple touch exercises to the hand and forearm. Gradually this technique is applied to each level of touch and then to sexual touch and orgasm. During both sexual healing and during sexual interactions, it is also vital that each man and woman feels they have the choice whether to engage sexually. It is especially critical for sexual abuse survivors to feel like they are the ones driving the car, that they have control of their own body and rights over their sexual selves.

Here are some resources we recommend while working with couples where one or both of them have experienced sexual abuse or molestation:

Grace Calls, Robin Weidner

The Sexual Healing Journey, Wendy Maltz

Relearning Touch, Wendy Maltz Video (found at http://healthysex. com/booksdvdsposters/dvds/relearning-touch/)

Sexual Sin

Often couples become Christians, disciples of Jesus, after they have experienced sex in ways God never intended. Some individuals carry a number of scars from previous sexual relationships, or have feelings of guilt about past sexual choices. Some have engaged in patterns of sexual behavior that were, or later become, problematic. God has a great plan for sex. He intends the sexual relationship to be mutually enjoyable and satisfying. However, past sexual choices and experiences can influence God's intention for the marital sexual relationship.

These choices might include pre-marital or extra-marital sexual relationships, past sexual practices with masturbation or pornography, participating in sexual entertainment venues (strip clubs, massage parlors that provide sexual services, etc.), same-sex sexual relationships, cybersexual involvement, etc. These experiences may be associated with both positive and negative sexual feelings, such as memories of sexual pleasure, guilt about sexual choices, or guilt about arousal during past sexual interactions that are now viewed as wrong.

The reality is that we were not created to be involved in sexuality outside of marriage. "The body was not meant for sexual immorality" (1 Corinthians 6:13). What a simple but powerful phrase. It is not in the nature of how God created our bodies that we be involved in sexuality outside of God's plan. So when we are, even when we have repented, there are consequences and after-effects. Our experiences can taint our views and beliefs about sexuality, and they can affect how we live out our sexuality within our marriage. We can have expectations influenced by these experiences (levels of sexual pleasure or types of sexual activities or positions, etc.) or strong negative responses to sexual interactions associated with those memories.

It is also true that sexual relationships that occurred before a couple marries often influence the couple's current relationship in various ways. It would be great to be able to say that a Christian spouse never makes comparisons, negative or positive, with past sexual relationships, but that would be a very naive assumption. At times, a wife or husband may compare their spouse sexually to a previous partner and find the spouse lacking in some way sexually. Perhaps they had orgasms with those past partners but do not have orgasms with their spouse or the quality, intensity, or type of orgasm was greater with a past partner. It is possible that previous partners were more fun or paid more attention to giving pleasure than a spouse does currently.

Other individuals might have experienced some serious negative interactions sexually with past partners. They may have been ridiculed for their sexual performance or felt forced to engage in sexual practices they did not want to engage in. They may have had a partner who was sexually disengaged or a partner who was sexually demanding. They may have been sexually betrayed in a past relationship.

All of these kinds of experiences have an effect on the current marital relationship, but they are often not discussed—either because of guilt, embarrassment, shame, or due to a lack of awareness. People sometimes feel there will be no benefit in bringing these things up as it may cause an incredible amount of pain, disruption, hurt, or anger. The challenge is that if these things are not discussed and worked through, these interactions go on having a negative impact on the couple, often in unacknowledged ways.

Other sexual sins that affect the marital sexual relationship are affairs that happened earlier in the marriage or use of pornography and other cybersexual activities during marriage. If you are a couple with this experience or you work with couples, it is important to not assume that past unfaithfulness has been completely resolved. At times, sexual sin is revealed when a husband and wife study the Bible and become Christians. Or the affair may have happened after they became Christians, yet the couple decided to remain together and work through the damage caused by the betrayal. The betrayed spouse may have been commended for how they forgave their spouse and worked diligently to move on. Sometimes this leads to a glossing over of the problems and hurts that then remain unresolved. Couples often need to work through injuries that have occurred in their relationship in the past, both sexual and overall relationship injuries, in order to have a truly fulfilling sex life. This is covered more in chapter eleven, *Healing Relational and Sexual Betrayals.*

As we mentioned earlier, research has shown that when sex is good, it has little association with satisfaction in a relationship (15–20 percent) but when sex is not going well, it has a significant association with overall relationship satisfaction (50–70 percent).[6] This could explain how when things are going well in a marital sexual relationship, those past sexual experiences and relationships—positive or negative—might not have as much influence on a couple's current relationship. However, when things are not going well sexually, couples may engage in remembering or comparing. They might project past hurtful experiences onto the current relationship or be resentful about how their spouse's past sexual relationships are affecting their marriage. They might also recall greater sexual pleasure they experienced in the past and wonder why it is not happening now. These internal comparisons might come out primarily in arguments or hurtful comments. However, couples often don't verbalize what they are struggling with even though it is slowly eating away at how they feel about their marital sexual relationship. Unspoken wonderings and comparisons can also influence a partner's level of confidence.

So what do you do with all this baggage? If you are concerned that your past sexual experiences or your spouse's past experiences may be causing some challenges in your marriage, you may benefit by finding a way to talk about these issues. You may need to talk to someone individually first. You can often find this help through your support system or with a minister or elder, or you could seek out someone professionally. If these experiences are affecting your marriage and your sex life, it may be beneficial to get some help in finding ways to bring it out into the open in a way that will not cause further damage. This should be done carefully and delicately. The reward of bringing these things out into the open could be quite significant, and it may help your marriage be more genuinely close and connected than ever before. To guide talking about any of these challenges between you, see the exercise below.

Current Sexual Sin. Many times the sexual sin is happening currently in the marriage. One or both spouses may have recently revealed using pornography or having had an extra-marital affair. Sexual unfaithfulness and pornography use clearly have a significant influence on marital and sexual relationships. If any of these challenges have occurred in your relationship, get help dealing with the level of pain and devastation and rebuilding trust that is essential for healing. For more on this, see chapter eleven on *Sexual Betrayals.*

EXERCISES

Sexual Challenges Communication Exercise: Healing Conversations

Medical challenges may be affecting your sexual relationship. Past sexual experiences may be causing challenges in your marriage (experiences such as past sexual abuse). The steps below can help you communicate with your spouse about these things or help you with how to respond to your spouse when they share their thoughts with you.

*This exercise is especially helpful if a couple has become comfortable using the Validation Exercises found in chapters three, four, and five.

**This exercise is not for conversations about sexual betrayals in your marriage that get triggered. See instead the exercise in chapter eleven.

1) **Reflect**. Merely say back to your spouse what they shared with you. Tell them what you heard.
2) **Validate**. "It makes sense that that would come up for you" or "That was so hard and I can see how that would come up now" or "That is so challenging."
3) **Ask.** If appropriate, draw out from your spouse how they are feeling about this. "How is that making you feel?" or "How has that been affecting things between us?" or "In what ways does that make things difficult for you in our sexual relationship?"
4) **Gratitude**. "I am really glad you shared this with me. I want you to tell me when it comes up for you."
5) **Find the Need.** After your spouse is feeling understood and validated, if appropriate, ask them what they need at this time. Do they need to share more? Is there anything you are doing that brings this challenge up for them? Do they need anything from you to work through this? Do they need some reassurance? Do they need you to hold them? Or do they just need you to be in the room listening?

10

Body Image and Sexuality

"I walked all the way around the whole school to avoid a group of kids that would call me fatso."

"My parents always talked about my big butt... My mom would always say, 'so round, so firm, so fully packed.'"

"They would say things like if you stood sideways and stuck out your tongue, you would look like a zipper."

"I had a boyfriend that dedicated the song [to me], 'Fat Bottom Girls make this Rocking World Go Round.'"

"I didn't ever feel very pretty. Definitely did not feel very pretty."

"[My dad] put my older sister on a scale in front of all of us [so] I wanted nothing curvy, and any body part that was attractive I would try to hide it."

"My mom, she would just never eat at the table. She'd put all the food on the table and then always talk about what she shouldn't eat. 'I shouldn't eat this, I shouldn't eat that.' She still does that."

"The whole body image thing, like I always want it under the covers in the dark, pretty much."

Why discuss body image in a book on intimacy and the sexual relationship? The words above are quotes from women in a research study exploring their experiences of shame in connection to sexuality.[1] Most of the women in the study had associations between feelings of shame about their body and shameful feelings about sex. Each of these women spoke about how these early comments about or experiences with their bodies affected how they viewed themselves sexually as an adult. They described how they wanted to cover up their bodies during sex, how difficult it was to be naked in front of their spouse, and how they preferred sex with the lights low or off so that their spouse could not see their body.

Women Jennifer has worked with in therapy share that they sometimes prefer to be partially dressed during sex for fear that the fat around their waists will be seen. Some express that when they picture themselves in the midst of orgasm, they feel deep levels of embarrassment and discomfort at the thought of what their body must look like in such an unrestrained state. They flinch when the body parts they do not like are touched during sex. They prefer not to be hugged or held if it means that their husband's hands might touch their body fat or the parts of their body they are insecure about.

Women often express the desire to feel pretty but share that no one had ever told them they were pretty, they did not perceive themselves as pretty, or their parents or spouse rarely or never told them they were pretty. Where women rank themselves in the spectrum of beauty and attractiveness (though these concepts are strongly influenced by society and media) can have a significant influence on how they feel about sexuality. This can be especially true if their spouse has made negative comments about their body or level of attractiveness. This can also be true of the more sexual parts of their body. For instance, if their breasts developed early, having large breasts might have made them feel unattractive or embarrassed. They might have experienced a desire to cover up their breasts and sometimes share that they do not want their husbands looking at or touching their breasts.

These are just some of the many different ways that body image affects the marital sexual relationship for women. When men talk about body image challenges, they express things like feeling small, feeling like they do not have enough muscle tone or enough muscle mass, or being concerned with weight and body fat. Some men have shared that they only look at their faces in the mirror because they feel that the lack of musculature in the rest of their body makes their body unattractive. Men sometimes wonder if being "skinny" or not having an attractive, muscular physique might be the reason why their wives are not attracted to them or why they don't initiate sexually. Men also talk about being overweight and wonder if their wife's lack of interest in sex is due to a lack of attraction.

When sharing about the parts of their body they do not like, men have expressed that they feel insecure about the amount of hair on their body, especially on their backs, the lack of broad shoulders, the facial and chest hair, extra weight on their torso, and other specific body features (feet, ears, etc.). Men share about denigrating comments made by their spouses about their body, their weight, or how they were disparaged by past sexual partners or others for the size of their penis. Some men express an overall negative view of their penis due to its perceived smaller size. Others, who are larger, more muscular, and are perceived as more overtly masculine, feel their wives expect them to be more accomplished lovers. This can be especially problematic when a man is perceived as sexually attractive (due to size and features) but does not have a high level of sexual drive.

These concerns about the body are reflected in research on sexuality. Internalized body objectification and body self-consciousness have been associated with sexual dysfunction and a negative view of the sexual self, the adult sexual self-schema.[2] Christian women who received negative messages about sexuality from their families or their churches often have a history of both sexual abuse and objectified body image.[3] Body image for both men and women has been connected to challenges with sexual desire, initiation, frequency, enjoyment, sexual satisfaction, the ability to achieve orgasm, and feeling sexually unattractive.[4] When someone has a negative body image, this can cause an aversion to sex and a greater self-consciousness during sexual activities that makes it more difficult to relax and allow arousal to build.

On the other hand, women who have a positive sexual self-esteem do not usually have the same level of concern with the appearance of their body during sexual intimacy. In general, the concerns with body image for women are usually centered around the stomach, hips, thighs, legs, and increased fat in the upper back.[5] Men who have experienced body shame and objectification in connection to the lean, muscular body image ideal in the media may have experienced problems with sexual arousal, pleasure, erectile functioning and orgasm.[6] Both men and women who feel their bodies have been disfigured by surgery or illness tend to be more sexually inhibited.[7]

General shame about the body has been known to cause emotional and physical withdrawal, decreased eye contact, slumped posture, negative self-comments, and inappropriate emotional responses.[8] Versions of these responses also occur during sexual interactions. This can cause people to hide their body, to cover up, or to have strong emotional responses when sensual and sexual touch happens. It can also lead to internal negative dialogues during sexual interplay or to withdrawal from genuine emotional or physical contact during sex. Sometimes this leads to spectatoring, when someone goes into a third-person perspective as if seeing themselves from above, becoming preoccupied with and watching how they are performing sexually. Men and women may engage in wondering and worrying, with almost hypervigilant attention, how they are performing sexually and how they look to their partner. Low body image can also lead to avoidance of romantic or intimate interactions. All these worries are reflected in plastic surgery statistics.[9] The number of plastic surgeries have doubled in the last fifteen years and Americans spent almost $13 billion in 2014 on plastic surgery, with the greatest procedures being breast augmentation, nose surgery (rhinoplasty), liposuction, eyelid surgery, and facelifts.

Understanding these overlapping challenges with body image and the sexual self-image is important when helping couples who are working on improving their sexual relationship. Women with poor body image have a more difficult time with doing sensual touch exercises that might be recommended or are found in books. In order to improve the sexual relationship, it may be necessary to improve their overall body image before exploring sexual intimacy. One of the first steps may be to understand how God views the human body. Most of us have heard of the scriptures about the body being a temple and that gluttony is a sin. We are often unaware, however, of other scriptures explaining how God views our bodies. It can also be helpful to reevaluate what influences our view of the human body and how media has a significant impact on those views. Couples can also learn to openly discuss body image concerns and explore how these concerns affect the marital sexual relationship.

The Back Pew – Jeff Larson

Be honest Adam .. do these fig leaves make me look fat?

In the beginning Eve was with child and asked Adam that age old question... and we all know the correct answer by now. "NO DEAR."

God's View of The Body

"You created my inmost being; you knit me together in my mother's womb." — Psalm 139:13

How does God see the human body? According to the author of Genesis, when God created the world, at the end of each day He declared, "It was good." The day He created Adam and Eve, "male and female He created them" (Genesis 1:27), He said, "It was *very* good" (Genesis 1:31; emphasis added). According to the psalmist, when God knit us in our mother's womb, He did a wonderful work. "I praise you because I am fearfully and wonderfully made" (Psalm 139:14). The Hebrew word, fearfully, or *yare*, means *afright*, to cause awe and astonishment. The Geneva Study Bible states it well. "Considering your wonderful work in forming me, I cannot but praise you and fear your mighty power." When we look at the pinnacle of God's creation, the forming of the male and female body, it should produce reverence and awe when we see the awesome majesty of God as portrayed in our body. We look at majestic mountains and at the vast and powerful ocean and we praise the amazing power of the Almighty God. Yet do we do the same when we look at the human body?

When you look at another person's body or when you look in the mirror at your own, do you focus on the appearance or are you amazed by the Creator? For most of us, it is probably the former. Just as the above research shows, as a society we tend to focus on weight, fat, and muscles rather than on the intricacy of God's handiwork. The apostle Paul speaks a bit about the body. He calls our body a temple (1 Corinthians 6:19). Many have said that people need to stop doing certain things in order to treat the temple of God's Spirit

with honor (1 Corinthians 6:20). However, we often fail to say, "Wow, my body IS a temple." That one shift in thinking can completely change how someone approaches his or her body. Not "I should be treating my body as a temple of the Spirit" but "My body IS a temple of the Holy Spirit."

So how are we supposed to view the body? What does the Bible teach about health, eating, and fitness? We know we are supposed to be filled with awe when we contemplate God's creation of the human body, but where does self-control of the flesh fit in? The scriptures shed some light on these questions. We are to honor God with how we use the body (1 Corinthians 6:20). We should not be gluttons or riotous eaters (Proverbs 23:2, 20). We are called to be wise and self-controlled in how much we eat and the type of food we eat (Proverbs 25:16). When we do eat and drink, or do anything else for that matter, we should do it in a way that glorifies

God (1 Corinthians 10:31).

Jesus grew in both wisdom and stature (mature, bodily strength) (Luke 2:52) and the wife of noble character worked vigorously and had strong arms (Proverbs 31:17). We need to control our body in a way that is holy and honorable (1 Thessalonians 4:4) and are called to subdue our bodily passions (i.e., sexual immorality, 1 Corinthians 9:27, 1 Corinthians 6:13-18) in order to receive our reward in heaven. We should use our body in such a way as to help others get there as well (Philippians 1:20-22). We are to love God with all of our strength (Mark 12:30) and to offer our bodies as living sacrifices to God (Romans 12:1). When we fear the Lord and shun evil, there are health benefits (Proverbs 3:7-8). The apostle John even prayed for Gaius' health (3 John 1:2).

Our society has continually changing trends in physical health, fitness, weight loss, and diet fads. Some trends focus on nutrition, health, and overcoming illness. Many of these trends are more like idolatry of the body and are focused on appearance. Some people completely ignore health and medical findings and live in ways that damage their health or harm their bodies. Whatever our personal view, as a culture, we clearly have a fascination with health, fitness, and the body. Biblically, it is clear that controlling our flesh, using our body for God, and being strong are good and godly things. The danger for many disciples of Jesus, however, is that we can buy into and focus on the worldly view of the body (thinness and muscularity) rather than on feeding the spirit. Paul warned Timothy of this. He explained that physical training of the body could yield some benefit (i.e., in order to pray), but that there was a more lasting, eternal benefit to be found by training in godliness (1 Timothy 4:8). What is important to understand is that the term *physical training* in this scripture refers to refraining from sex and certain foods. This is not a reference to exercising, such as working out or running. Paul also warned the Colossians that human rules, such as do not eat or do not touch, would have no value in restraining sensual indulgence (Colossians 2:23). These kinds of rules look wise and humble, but are mere human teachings, and in the end, even research shows that they do not work very well in attaining a healthy body.[10]

In our current culture, with the intense focus on outward appearance, it is important to reclaim what the bible does say about our bodies. Ask yourself, are you looking at your body as a tool and means to give to others, to promote the gospel of Jesus? Are you aware of how much you have bought into the world's focus on weight, dieting, and the body ideal? You are fearfully and wonderfully made. Your body is amazing. When you fail to see your body this way, you may fail to grasp the awesome power of God that is at work in you.

Your Spouse's Body

How do you feel about, think about, and talk about your spouse's body? This is a loaded question. The world presents a constantly shifting standard of what makes up attractiveness. None of us (even models, actors and actresses) can measure up. A look at how the Lover and Beloved talk about each other in Song of Songs can be very instructive and challenging.

For husbands, the Lover says of his Beloved, "You are altogether beautiful my love, there is no flaw in you" (Song of Songs 4:7). What woman would not like to have her spouse say this to her? Look at the words he uses to describe her (4:1-15 and 7:1-9): lovely, delightful, pleasing. And when he speaks of her body, he talks in detail about her eyes, hair, teeth, lips, mouth, temples, neck, breast, navel, and waist. He even compliments her on her breath and her voice. He tells her she has graceful legs, beautiful sandaled feet, and a lovely face. He says she is like the dawn, as fair as the moon, as bright as the sun, and as majestic as the stars. He sees her as totally unique and special. "My dove, my perfect one, is unique" (6:9). Consider these words and ask yourself when was the last time you told your wife how she is uniquely beautiful; how she had lovely feet, beautiful eyes, or a pretty face. Do you tell her about the beauty of her neck, her hair, and her mouth? God has included these words in His writings to us to model for us how a loving husband should speak about his wife's body.

For wives, the Beloved says of her Lover, "Oh how handsome you are my beloved! Oh, how charming ... My beloved is radiant and ruddy, outstanding among ten thousand" (Song of Songs 1:16 and 5:10). What man would not love to have his wife speak about him this way? Look at the words she uses to describe her response to him (2:3-4 and 5:10-16): she delights to sit in his shade, he is sweet to taste, and she loves kisses from his mouth. When she speaks of his body, she in turn describes his head, hair, eyes, cheeks, lips, and arms. She talks about how his body is polished ivory (his protection, 5:14), how his arms are rods of gold (his strength, 5:14), and how his legs are like pillars of marble (again, his strength, beauty, and power, 5:15). When is the last time you described your husband with these kinds of admiring terms, telling him about his physical strength, his bodily protection, and the wonder of his mouth? How long has it been since you have told him how much you love his cheeks, his smile, his expressive eyes, and how he does his hair? Do you caress his muscles and admire his legs? God has allowed these descriptive words to be included in His inspired scriptures to call women higher on how they view and talk about their husband's body.

You may ask, "Where does attraction fit in then? What if you are not actually attracted to your spouse's body? What if you feel like your spouse's body does not reflect the kinds of words mentioned above?" Your husband may have extra weight on his body or he may not have arms of gold and legs of marble. You may feel that your sexual desire is lower due to the fact that your wife does not have the body you are attracted to. Our challenge to both of you would be to examine how the Lover and Beloved speak about each other's bodies. Do you view your spouse's body **the way God does**? You *can* be both honest and honoring.

One of our favorite examples of this is the relationship between Guy and Cathy Hammond, founders of the Strength and Weakness ministry. Guy is a same-sex attracted man who lived a homosexual lifestyle for over ten years, and who has now been a faithful disciple of Jesus for over three decades. Guy and his wife Cathy have been married for over twenty-five years and have four children. Guy openly shares that, even now, though he has not engaged in homosexual acts since he became a Christian, he is still not attracted to the female body. Many who have heard him share this have wondered, "Wow. How does that work between you and your wife?" His response to those bold enough to ask this question out loud is to share in detail how he sees his wife as an amazing rose that is a wonder to behold—a rose that has a long fragile stem and rich, beautiful, soft red petals that release a wonderful scent. What woman would not like to be described in this way?

Cathy also shares very openly when she is asked what it is like for her to know that she does not have the type of body her husband finds sexually attractive. Her response is that she knows, and he knows, that her body will never be able to live up to her husband's sexual fantasy. Still, they regularly compliment each other, telling each other how they find one another attractive. They have made their physical relationship about giving and honoring each other. What an incredible example these two are!

Husbands and wives, ask yourselves this: do your thoughts and words reflect a godly appreciation for your spouse's body as found in God's Word? We can all grow and change in this area. When we do, we will honor our spouse in a way that creates a lasting and loving intimacy and that fosters a confident, godly view of one's body.

The exercises on the following pages have a number of different purposes. They may expose how media influences your view of your body. They may help you regain a biblical view of your body. They may help you communicate as a couple how you feel about your bodies. These are just a couple of steps that can start you in the direction of reclaiming how fearfully and wonderfully made you are.

*Cartoons from The Back Pew by Jeff Larson, used by permission.

EXERCISES

Body Image Exercise 1: Videos in the Media

Watch both of the following videos together:

1) Women: "Watch Photoshop Transform Your Favorite Celebrities" on BuzzFeed

2) Men: "Before and After Fitness Transformation" on YouTube (Warning: There is bad language used in this video.

Take some time to talk about what you each think about these videos

---

Body Image Exercise 2: Fearfully and Wonderfully Made

*This is an individual exercise, though you can share your experience with your spouse.

1) Find a comfortable, safe place in your home

2) Read all of Psalm 139, and then focus on verse 13

3) While sitting comfortably, place your hands on different parts of your body, reciting Psalm 139:13, "I am fearfully and wonderfully made." Example: place your hands at your waist and consider the internal parts of your body below your hands (your kidneys, stomach, lungs, etc.) and the external parts of your body your hands are directly touching (your waist, hips, etc.) and share with God how they are fearfully and wonderfully made.

4) Speak and pray with God about the intricacies and wonders about each part of your body and how it works with the other parts of your body.

Body Image Exercise 3: Song of Songs

1) Read all of Song of Songs.

2) Highlight or underline all of the phrases where the Beloved and Lover describe each other.

3) Make a list of things you could say to your spouse about their body

and their overall attractiveness to you.

4) Make a decision to begin complimenting your spouse as the Lover and Beloved do in Song of Songs.

Body Image Exercise 4: Pre-mirror and Mirror Prompt and Reflection

Below is a body image communication exercise. Read the directions for each level before beginning. Do each level on subsequent days or weeks, at a rate decided according to your comfort level. Each of the sentence prompts are about how you view your body and your spouse's body.

Level 1: As explained before, take the same sitting position in two chairs facing each other, holding each other's hands, looking at each other as you speak. Decide who will start first. Whoever goes first begins with the first prompt and finishes the sentence. The spouse reflects. Then the spouse who is second begins with the first prompt and their spouse reflects. Do this for each prompt.

1) "One part of my body I like is…."
2) "Another part of my body I like is…."
3) "What I think is attractive about my body is …."
4) "One part of my body I am not fond of is …."
5) "Something about my body I'm insecure about is …."
6) "One thing I like about your body is …."
7) "Another thing I like about your body is …."

Level 2: Do the exact same exercise above. However, this time, while fully clothed, do it standing side-by-side facing the mirror. As you speak about the parts of your body, take your spouse's hand and place it on that part of your body. As you speak about the parts of your spouse's body that you like, ask permission to place your hand there.

Level 3: Repeat the exercise as described in Level 2. However, this time do it while partially clothed in front of the mirror.

Level 4: Repeat the exercise as described in Level 2. However, this time do it unclothed in front of the mirror.

Level 5: Repeat the exercise as described in Level 2. However, this time do it unclothed, lying in bed, facing each other (no mirror involved).

*After each exercise, sit together and talk about what the exercise was like for each of you.

Healing Relational and Sexual Betrayals

What do you think about when you look at me
I know we're not the fairytale you dreamed we'd be
You wore the veil, you walked the aisle, you took my hand
And we dove into a mystery

How I wish we could go back to simpler times
Before all our scars and all our secrets were in the light
Now on this hallowed ground, we've drawn the battle lines
Will we make it through the night?

It's going to take much more than promises this time
Only God can change our minds

Maybe you and I were never meant to be complete
Could we just be broken together
If you can bring your shattered dreams and I'll bring mine
Could healing still be spoken and save us
The only way we'll last forever is broken together

How it must have been so lonely by my side
We were building kingdoms and chasing dreams and left love behind
I'm praying God will help our broken hearts align
And we won't give up the fight

Maybe you and I were never meant to be complete
Could we just be broken together
If you can bring your shattered dreams and I'll bring mine
Could healing still be spoken and save us
The only way we'll last forever is broken together

—"Broken Together," lyrics by Casting Crowns

You didn't get married planning on betraying each other. You didn't say, "With this ring, I pledge to dishonor you." And yet, for that couple that walked down the aisle together, there can be things that happen that cause great hurt and devastation. The words of this song describe so well the shattering of dreams that can happen when there are betrayals in marriage. God's plan has always been to heal the brokenhearted (Psalm 147:3). Often as God's children, we either bring brokenness into our marriage or we do things that cause one another to be brokenhearted. His promise is to bring healing to our marriages in the midst of our brokenness.

"I was actually going to call a year ago to get some help, but I ended up not pursuing it. And now, here we are." This statement is not uncommon to hear from couples that come into therapy or from those coming in to get help from their ministry leaders. They knew they were having trouble in their sexual relationship and thought about seeing someone to get some help, but for various reasons, it did not get any further than that. What eventually may force them to reach out for help is when one or both of them got involved in pornography, in an affair, or in some kind of relationship or sexual betrayal. For some, the revelation of involvement in pornography, in an emotional affair, or in a sexual betrayal comes out of the blue. The spouse had no idea anything was going on. For others, they suspected that something was going on for quite some time, and may have even investigated until their suspicions were confirmed. There are many different circumstances and stories.

Sexual sin or sexual and relational betrayals can be extremely destructive to the marital and sexual relationship. There can be many levels of pain and many emotional expressions of anger and hurt. The revelation of the betrayal usually involves lies and deceit that further complicate the picture and create additional levels of the loss of trust. The focus of this chapter is not recovery from sexual betrayals. Help with recovery can be found in various ways, and we have included resources at the end of this section to aid in that. However, because these issues have a strong influence on a couple's sexual relationship, we will address some components that may be needed in order to work through the betrayal toward a fulfilling marital and sexual relationship.

Get Help

If there have been sexual betrayals in your relationship, and you have decided to work through it and stay together, make sure to get whatever level of help you need to genuinely come out on the other side stronger. However, in order to do that, most couples need an increased amount of support. It is crucial to have close friendships that provide the encouragement, comfort, and the right amount of challenge when needed. It is important to get with other mature couples that can provide couple-to-couple counseling. You also might benefit from a support group for one or both of you, or from professional counseling. The key ingredient in recovering from betrayal as a couple is not to attempt this in isolation. A great combination of care would be to have professional help, to also get with a strong spiritual couple in your ministry to work on things spiritually and relationally, and then to also have close personal male and female friends and mentors for both of you to talk to.

Our hope is that this chapter will be one of your sources of help through the process of healing in the midst of brokenness. However, we do want to caution all who read here—make sure that you use these passages for your own process of healing. Shoving this book under your spouse's nose and saying, "Read this—this is exactly what I've been trying to tell you," will probably not go very far in bringing about change. If there are things you read here that you long for your spouse to understand, get help with finding how to speak the truth in love when you share it with them. Your spouse does need to hear your pain. It is actually vital for their own process of repentance and growth. However, there is a significant difference between attacking someone with your pain and asking them to step into it with you. Perhaps some of the passages below can guide you in how to accomplish that.

But This Is Old Stuff

The sexual sin or betrayals in your marriage may have happened a long time ago. We have found, though, that couples often have not actually worked completely through the damage. Yes, it may be old stuff, but it may be that there are some unhealed injuries that need to be addressed in order to truly achieve a genuine, life-giving intimacy. So how does a couple work through the hard stuff that is still there from ages ago? First, get with someone who will support you through the process. There are times when well-meaning Christians, disciples of Jesus, shame someone or challenge them if they continue to experience pain, traumatic memories, sadness, or hurt over a betrayal that happened "in the past." Make sure you get with someone you can trust spiritually. That person can help you discern if there is growth you need to experience spiritually, emotionally, and relationally, sin you need to face, and/or coping skills you need to learn.

Are You Keeping a Record of Wrongs?

"You still haven't forgiven." This may be something someone has shared with you about your response to your spouse that, yes, your spouse sinned, but you are still struggling (or in sin) because you have not forgiven them yet and are keeping a record of wrongs. This may be true. Discerning between a trauma response with its associated triggers and the sin of resentment can be challenging. You may be holding a record of wrongs, and you may be resentful (Hebrews 12:15). That is important to explore. However, there is a difference between being resentful (i.e., keeping a record of wrongs in 1 Corinthians 13:5) and experiencing triggers that cause painful feelings to resurface. It can be hard to tell between the two. The reality is that even for the most spiritual disciple who is close to Jesus, certain things will happen that bring them right back to the pain they experienced. Memories with strong emotional attachments can remain throughout someone's lifetime, even when they have forgiven and been merciful toward the one who harmed them. And this may have absolutely nothing to do with sin. The revelation of betrayals, and especially sexual betrayals, is often a very traumatic experience and the effects of those revelations can literally linger in your body, heart, and mind the same way that other kinds of trauma do. The pain of these kinds of betrayals can create a serious injury to the attachment in the relationship.[1] Couples can engage in a very careful process to gain healing from these traumatic injuries (see exercises below).

It is crucial, first of all, to realize that it is understandable and normal for pain to resurface when the trauma of a betrayal is triggered. The challenge is sometimes where to go from there. If someone becomes triggered, and all the hurt and pain come flooding in, you would be able to share it with your spouse in the best-case scenario, when your relationship is safe. If you do decide to share, this is not the time for an attack but it may be time to honestly and genuinely share what is happening for you (Ephesians 4:15, speak the truth in love). If you find that your heart rate went up as the feelings came flooding in, you may need to take a moment to practice some deep breaths in order to begin calming your increased heart rate. If things are safe between you, you can even share with your spouse that you are having a hard time and ask them if they can sit and breathe with you. Then, your conversation can go something like this: "When I saw your phone in your hand, I just had this immediate overwhelming flood of pain and hurt, and I felt instantly sad and angry. Everything I've felt came back. And I started to worry about what you were doing on your phone and if you were trying to hide it from me."

Notice that this sharing is specific, genuine, and not assuming anything about your spouse. It is just a very real expression of what is happening inside of you. It is vital to get to the point that you can share this in a way that is genuine, gut-level honest, and not an attack. If you cannot share it in that way, get some help until you can. Also, get some help as a couple until your spouse can hear it and respond in a way that is healing. Communication like this can ultimately lead to great closeness and intimacy in the middle of pain. However, this works best when you are confident that your spouse's response will be supportive, safe, and humble. So, spouse, how do you get there?

The Spouse's Response to the Re-Triggered Pain of a Betrayal

If you are the spouse who committed a betrayal and are reading this, how should you respond when your partner shares when their pain is triggered? You may feel like you will always be in the doghouse. You may have said or felt things like, "Are we ever going to get over this?" or "Do you want me to grovel? How many times do we need to go back to this?" Your spouse may have responded at times to your betrayal in ways that have also caused you some damage. Your spouse may need to pursue help regarding how they communicate when their pain is triggered. In the meantime, how can you respond in a way that would mirror the heart of Jesus?

Here are a few recommendations. First, watch your initial response. A response of "When will you ever give that up?" can actually cause greater damage than the original violation or trauma. So if your spouse shares with you that they are experiencing a flooding of pain about a past betrayal you committed, and if you feel yourself wanting to respond with anything close to, "How many times do I need to say sorry?"—stop. Then, before you answer, take a calming breath. Maybe pray, go for a walk, and call someone who is a wise counselor. You may need to take a timeout to get yourself into a spot where you can respond with humility, love, compassion, and patience, rather than anger, judgment, hurt, and frustration.

So, now, how do you respond when your spouse shares about the flood of emotions that may at times come over them? Before you even answer them, tell them you are glad they told you. If you're not, spend time with God and talk with those in your life to help you get there. Satan only wins if your spouse keeps hidden in the dark what is happening inside of them. Your spouse, who just shared their pain with you, has just made a strong stance against Satan by bringing their pain into the light. They need you to see that and be glad for it, to actually want it. Let's look at how to respond.

First, reflect what you just heard. Don't elaborate. Just say back to them what they shared with you. Second, validate them. Let them know that it is understandable they had those feelings, that it makes sense considering what has happened. Third, take responsibility and own it. Choices you made, even if they were long ago, put them there, where they could get triggered in that way. Taking ownership, no matter how long after a betrayal, conveys love and trustworthiness. Finally, let them know again that you are glad they shared it with you. Reflect. Validate. Ownership. Gratitude. This kind of response is healing, trust-building, and connecting.

The whole conversation might sound something like this: "When I saw you pick up your phone, all these feelings came rushing through me and I'm just having such a hard time."

"I am so glad you told me. So, when you saw me pick up my phone, it brought all that pain and hurt back. (pause) I can see how it would, and that must be so very hard. I did some terrible things against you, and I know I really hurt you. I'm so sorry that what I did still comes up for you, that it continues to hurt sometimes. I am glad you told me, and I do want you to tell me whenever that comes up for you."

When it is appropriate, some reassurance can also help build trust. You might be able to ask something like, "Would it help for me to tell you where things are at for me? OK. I haven't looked at anything inappropriate or pornographic on my phone since the last time I shared with you how I have been doing. When I feel the pull at all to look at something, I have been talking with (close friend/accountability partner) in order to be open about it so that things don't go any further than that." This kind of gracious, understanding, humble response can go an incredibly long way toward healing in your relationship. It also goes a long way toward rebuilding trust. No explanations, no *What did you think I was doing? Why can't you just forgive me?*

A continuing high level of openness and repentance will also have a significant influence on the rebuilding of trust after a betrayal, even long after a betrayal. Ask yourself if you have continued to be radically open and repentant. This is especially important for those whose betrayal is recent. Have you have continued to seek out reliable men or women to guide you? Do you have relationships in which you are comfortable asking for help with any other ways you may struggle or are tempted? This level of continual repentance and openness will go a long way toward reassuring your spouse and building trust. Continue learning, reading, and studying about how you got where you did. Share what you are learning with your spouse, when and if that is appropriate, in order to continue rebuilding trust.

How Much to Tell

Everything. Not everyone agrees with this direction, but in our work with couples, we have found that complete honesty is necessary for complete healing. We recommend that the spouse who committed the betrayal share any details their spouse asks for. However, it is *essential* that the offended spouse, the one who was betrayed, realize that though they have the right to ask any questions, they are going to have to live with those answers. If you are the spouse asking questions, consider if the questions you want to ask could reveal specific details that will leave pictures in your mind that actually make the trauma more difficult to overcome. This level of detail may not be helpful to your own process of recovery. Everything is permissible, but not everything is beneficial (1 Corinthians 10:23). If there is any conflict on how much to tell, get with someone reliable to help navigate these waters.

Accountability

It is crucial for anyone who has gotten involved in addictive or compulsive behaviors—such as sexual, drug or alcohol, or behavioral addictions—to have some place to go (i.e., support groups, etc.) or some person to talk to that will hold them accountable to their process of recovery. This would be someone to specifically support the process as a mentor/discipleship partner, an accountability partner, or a sponsor. The recovery process is best supported when a person finds accountability in both a group and an individual setting. It is also important for the offended spouse to get this kind of support, both through a support group and through an individual mentor or sponsor.

1 John 1:5 says that God is light. If we walk in that light, He washes us clean. Walking in that light also results in fellowship with one another. God's command to confess our sins (James 5:16) comes with many benefits, both personal and relational. So find someone to trust who will speak the truth in love (Ephesians 4:15), rebuke you frankly when you need it (Leviticus 19:17), and know when you need encouragement, comfort, or challenge (1 Thessalonians 2:12). If you are specifically working at overcoming pornography use, remember that when you sweep out your house to get rid of the junk (Luke 11:25), it is vital that you replace the junk with good stuff. That is how you make sure that nothing else harmful comes to live there. Get the support you need to fill up your house with good things.

Like we mentioned, this kind of support and accountability is not just for the offender. Both the wife and husband need to have someone they trust to provide teaching, counseling, and accountability for how they are managing through this difficult time. Also, one of the major benefits of the offender having someone they are regularly talking with and being accountable to is how reassuring this is to their spouse. As mentioned, this can go a long way in rebuilding trust.

Initiate Openness Regularly

It can be very difficult for couples to know how to talk about their concerns and struggles in the aftermath of a sexual betrayal. If you are wondering if your spouse is still struggling, do you ask? If you are struggling, do you tell? When and how is this kind of openness between spouses beneficial, helpful, and healing, if ever?

There are a number of communication needs that should be addressed when a couple first experiences a sexual betrayal, some of which have been mentioned above. Another practical tool is the Daily Trust Conversation from Timothy O'Farrell's workbook *Behavioral Couples Therapy for Alcoholism*.[2] Each day, the offender initiates with their spouse and says something like, "For the last twenty-four hours, I have not _____ and I will not _____ for the next twenty-four hours. Thank you for supporting my recovery." The spouse's response is simply, "Thank you for sharing with me. Let me know if there is any way I can be helpful." This simple, daily (sometimes couples choose weekly) conversation may be a little weird and awkward at first, but it can be quite supportive during the process of healing.

As a couple, decide if this would be beneficial for you. The offender would then initiate the conversation each time. Make sure you to continue speaking with the couple or individuals who are helping you navigate this particular part of your rebuilding and how it is working for you.

The Impact on the Sexual Relationship

A big question that comes up is "When and how should we resume our sexual relationship?" The revelation of a sexual betrayal often leads to a complete stop in sexual interactions, sexual intercourse, and sexual, sensual, and affectionate touch. There is no easy answer to the question of where to go from there. Some spouses are able to genuinely engage sexually soon after a confession or discovery. This may be prompted by the desire to communicate mercy and forgiveness. Some might initially engage sexually out of fear that they may lose their spouse if they do not. Others may engage sexually in order to keep their spouse from seeking sexual gratification elsewhere. The second two of these possible reasons can be quite problematic to genuine recovery. It is incredibly important to get the help and guidance from wise individuals in your life to examine the reasons for and appropriateness of immediately engaging in sex soon after discovery.

Most offended spouses have the need and right to work through the pain and grief of a betrayal before they can entrust their body to their spouse again. For most, this will be important before they can experience the joy of sexuality. There is no one-size-fits-all answer for how long this takes. However, the offending spouse's response should always be one of humility. Ultimately, sexual betrayals have a strong impact on the sexual relationship. The offended spouse of someone involved in pornography may wonder during sex: *Is he seeing those pictures in his mind, Is she wishing I were him,* or *Is he asking me to do this because he saw this in something he watched?* The offended spouse of someone involved in an affair may wonder if their partner is comparing them to others they had sex with. Their anger may suddenly rise up even in the middle of sex.

There is also the reality that some couples—those who have not had sex in a long time even *before* the sexual betrayal was discovered—may find restarting the sexual relationship particularly difficult with the added pain of betrayal. If you have not yet talked about these things and have either already reengaged sexually or are contemplating how to get back to having sex, we recommend that you read this chapter together and talk through the feelings that you have. You may need to speak with a close adviser first and then talk about it together as a couple, either alone or with someone to help you. However you go about this, it is important to remember that reengaging sexually without working through the emotions attached to the injuries will often just bury those injuries deeper, where they can continue to do considerable unseen damage.

So what do you do if the pain and grief come up right when you are in the middle of sex? Pain may wash over you while you are having sex together. Thoughts and pictures and wonderings may start filling your mind. Do you just go on and push through, ignoring what is happening inside of you? Do you tell your spouse, or do you just shut down, turn off, or turn away?

In general, it can be quite beneficial to slow things down sexually right then and share what you are feeling. It is important at this point that you have gotten comfortable having the type of conversations mentioned in the above section on "Are you Keeping a Record of Wrongs?" during non-sexual time together. Reflect. Validate. Ownership. Gratitude. If you have had some safe, healing conversations during your regular day when you get triggered, then you can apply these same principles to triggers that come up during sex. There may be times where praying internally and taking your thoughts captive may work. But for most, this is not helpful until you have had a few honest, healing conversations in the middle of engaging sexually. So when you notice that you are reactive, let your spouse know. "Honey, I'm starting to have a hard time." Yes, they are probably aroused and it might bring about disappointment, maybe even frustration. But continuing to engage sexually when you become flooded can be very counterproductive to genuine intimacy. So, share what is happening for you with your spouse. Hopefully they have done the work of practicing their responses to you when you have shared these triggers at other times; those practiced responses are especially helpful in the heat of the moment.

For the offending spouse, if your husband or wife has to put a halt to things sexually because they are triggered right in the middle of the act, it is important that you respond with humility and understanding, even in the midst of sexual frustration. Continuing sexually when someone is triggered can be a further violation in your relationship. The sexual release is not worth the damage. Take the time, step back (literally), and give your spouse the right and the space to express themselves. Do nothing out of selfish ambition but consider your spouse as better than yourself (Philippians 2:3-4). This is the basis of genuine, sexual intimacy. This is how you can get the real thing back.

After you both share, and you validate one another, you may need to do something healing but nonsexual. Check inside yourself and with each other and see what you need. You may want to just hold each other, spooning or cuddling. You may want to pray together. You may want to return to light affection, playing a game, watching a show, or giving each other a massage. This kind of genuine, real sharing can be an important step in building or rebuilding your intimacy on a true, solid foundation.

Sexual Desire

For some, involvement in sex outside of the marital relationship may affect levels of sexual desire. A person whose spouse became involved in extramarital sex may need to take some time to rebuild desire. Some couples reengage sexually because they desire the sexual release, but they have not yet returned to an actual desire for their spouse. Our experience is that as you pursue some of the things found in these chapters, couples can rebuild desire. However, if this continues to be a challenge, it may be helpful to seek some professional guidance. Give yourself time and when the time is right, put some strategies into practice on building desire, found in other chapters (especially chapter seventeen, *Low Sexual Desire and Arousal*).

We also get questions about the effect on desire when someone has a background specifically in pornography.

- Can masturbation and pornography influence whether someone will have a sexual desire for their spouse (who does not physically look like, sound like, or act like someone in a pornographic picture, video, or online sexual chatroom)?
- Has their pornography usage permanently affected their sexual desire and sexual expectations?
- Will pornography affect erectile functioning and sexual desire (either by making their sexual desire higher or making them have a lower desire)?

These are painful, difficult questions. Those who have a background in pornographic use ask these questions, as do their spouses. Although there are no definite answers, we will briefly explore some possibilities.

We do get asked whether pornography affects erectile functioning and sexual desire. As I (Jennifer) have worked with individuals involved in pornographic addiction, I have seen a number of probable factors that affect levels of sexual desire when someone has used pornography:

- The spiritual convictions of the individual and the level of solid repentance and remorse (Matthew 18:9; 2 Corinthians 7:10-11)
- The age when an individual began viewing pornography
- The amount and length of time or years involved in pornography
- The type and intensity of pornographic images
- Any previous challenges with erectile dysfunction and low sexual desire that may have led to using pornography and engaging in masturbation
- The degree to which someone actively and intentionally works at improving their intimate relationship with their spouse

Pornography introduces and reinforces sexual expectations that are formatted around unrealistic scenes, unreal sexual scenarios, seemingly perfect bodies, self-stimulation while watching pornography, or the thrill of pursuing the forbidden. This can produce an environment where some individuals have a difficult time becoming physically aroused while being with their spouse sexually.

Retraining the heart and mind is often a part of the process of changing desire and arousal patterns. The process needed for this kind of retraining is beyond the scope of this book. However, for some, this may be possible through sex therapy, sexual addiction counseling, or biblical discipling. For others, it may be helpful to begin anew and build a new kind of attraction, desire, and arousal. Some of this is addressed in the chapter on desire and arousal and in the chapter about body image.

What Do You Need

For all couples who are impacted by sexual betrayal, this section is primarily included to prompt you to get the support and help you need to work through:

1) The actual betrayal
2) How to reengage sexually when the time is right
3) Communicating the feelings and thoughts that come up when reengaging sexually
4) The challenges to the sexual relationship that are unique to couples recovering from sexual betrayal

After you read through this chapter, talk together about it. Share your feelings with those close to you. If you see that you need more help, get it.

Below are some further resources to aid in your recovery, both individually and as a couple.

RESOURCES

It is often necessary to focus on dealing with sexual betrayals before beginning work on the sexual relationship. For those who have been involved in an affair, we recommend reading and using *Torn Asunder* and the accompanying workbook by Dave Carder, or Harley's *His Needs Her Needs* and *The Five Steps to Romantic Love* book and workbook. For those involved with pornography, we recommend books by Mark and Debbie Laaser and websites and seminars by Dave and Robin Weidner (see below). We also recommend that, in order to work through sexual issues, those involved in pornography attend support groups, have a sponsor, and/or engage in online teaching, accountability, and support through various online resources.

Further Resources

Covenant Eyes - Internet filtering program
Dave and Robin Weidner - *Building a Pure Marriage: In an Impure World* (Purchase the audio of the conference by Dave and Robin Weidner at ipibooks.net.)
Robin Weidner: *Grace Calls: Spiritual Recovery after Abandonment, Addiction or Abuse*
Dr. Mark and Debra Laaser website: https://www.faithfulandtrue.com/
Dr. Mark Laaser: *Healing the Wounds of Sexual Addiction* and other books
Debra Laaser: *Shattered Vows* and other books
Patrick Carnes, PhD: *Out of the Shadows: Understanding Sexual Addiction*
Dave Carder: *Torn Asunder* (book and workbook)
William F. Harley, Jr.: *His Needs/Her Needs*
Linda Brumley: *Hand in Hand with God: Finding Your Path to Forgiveness*

EXERCISES

Betrayal Communication Exercise: Steps to Healing the Attachment Injury

*Betrayals can cause an injury to the attachment in a relationship. These injuries can be quite traumatic. When the trauma connected to the attachment injury is triggered, remember these steps in responding to your spouse when they share the trigger with you.
**This exercise is especially helpful if a couple has become comfortable using the Validation Exercise found in chapters three, four, and five.

1) **Reflect**. Merely say back to your spouse what they shared with you. Even if they attack or say it in anger, take a breath and tell them what you heard.
2) **Validate**. "I know that what I did really hurt you. And it is completely understandable that this would bring it up."
3) **Ownership**. "I did things then that caused so much damage to our relationship and that hurt you tremendously. I am so sorry that the things I did then still come up and cause pain for you now."
4) **Gratitude**. "I am really glad you shared this with me. I want you to tell me whenever it comes up for you."

5) Ask your spouse what they need at this time. Do they need some reassurance? Do they need you to share with them how you are doing in guarding yourself from further sin (i.e., pornography use, etc.)? Do they need you to hold them? Do they have any questions for you? Or do they just need you to be in the room listening?

12

The Physiology of Sex

*"So God created man in His own image, in the image of God
He created him; male and female He created them."*
(Genesis 1:27)

God created man. And yes, that means that He created the penis. God created woman. And yes, that means that He created the vagina. When you look at the genitals closely, you may wonder just what He was up to. It is a question to ask Him one day. There are many different artistic representations of the male and female genitalia in paintings and sculpture throughout history and the focus on the sexual organs historically has been primarily procreation. Anatomically, it is significant that the greatest number of nerves are found in the genital organs. However, it is also important to understand that God created the entire body, not just the genitals, to experience the incredible pleasure of sex. All parts of the body have the potential to be involved in sexual pleasure and arousal. Sexual pleasure is much more than just stimulation to the penis and the vagina. And of course, the most important sexual organ is the brain. The brain receives all the signals and sends out all of the instructions involved in sex (including communication to the nerves and all of our senses of smell, taste, touch, etc.). The brain also regulates all of the sexual chemicals, increases the blood flow, sweating, and heavy breathing involved, and organizes all the emotions and memories associated with sex.

In the last several decades, there has been a growing understanding of exactly how the sexual parts of the body work and what kind of biological processes are going on during sex. This chapter is devoted to understanding the physiology of sex and is divided into four sections: male sexuality, female sexuality, the sexual response cycle, and medical complications in sexuality.

The following, rather technical section will involve a number of anatomical and medical terminologies. It is included here to answer some of the detailed questions we receive about how the body functions during sex, especially when medical complications, illness, pain, and age have caused problems with sexual arousal and desire, erection, ejaculation, and orgasm. In particular, the section on medical complications and brain injury is especially technical, with many medical and neurological terms unfamiliar to most of us. This section may be particularly important for those dealing with medical and biological challenges and those who are affected by neurological complications or brain injuries that are consequently affecting their sexuality. For those hardy souls who decide to delve below, our hats are off to you. We recommend you keep a dictionary or your laptop on hand. Enter if you dare. For the rest of you that would become cross-eyed, feel free to skip this entire passage. All you may care to know is this:

"God saw all that He had made, and it was very good." — Genesis 1:31

Male Sexual Anatomy

Male external genitals are primarily made up of the scrotum, the shaft, and the head of the penis. Within the shaft are the three erectile columns providing blood to the penis: the corpus cavernosum (two columns) and the corpus spongiosum (one column). The corpus spongiosum is the tube of erectile tissue that surrounds and protects the urethra. The head of the penis includes the most sensitive part of the penis, the glans, and the coronal ridge, which circles the head of the penis at the base of the glans (in the diagram, you can see the coronal ridge beneath the glans). Along the underside of the glans,

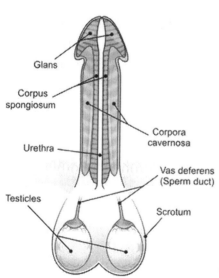

Glans

Corpus spongiosum

Urethra

Testicles

Corpora cavernosa

Vas deferens (Sperm duct)

Scrotum

perpendicular to and crossing the coronal ridge, is another sensitive part of the penis, the ridge of tissue called the frenulum (not shown). An elastic skin structure in the circumcised penis as well as the foreskin in the uncircumcised penis surrounds the entire shaft. The tissue at the base of the penis between the testicles and the anus is the perineum (not shown). Stroking and rubbing this sensitive area can be very arousing, especially when done concurrently with stroking the penis. The scrotum is a suspended sack of skin that holds the testicles, where sperm is produced. After leaving the testicles, sperm travels through the pelvic cavity via the vas deferens. Each vas deferens narrows and passes through the ejaculatory duct. The vas deferens then joins with the urethra as it passes through the prostate. Semen, the milky fluid that is ejaculated during orgasm, is produced by the prostate gland and the seminal vesicles and is combined with sperm as it passes through the prostate (not shown). The sperm and semen mixture is then sent to the penis via the urethra for ejaculation. The penile and scrotal structures are anchored, supported, and innervated by various muscles, ligaments, and nerves within the pelvic floor.

Female Sexual Anatomy

The vulva. The female vulva surrounds the entrance to the vagina and consists of the vestibule (the *vaginal entrance*), the minor and major labia (the lips or labium majus and minus), the clitoris, the mons pubis, which is the fatty tissue usually covered in pubic hair that protects the clitoris, and the anterior perineum (perineal raphe), which includes the tissue between the vagina and the anus. Within the vestibule, above and below the vagina, are two sets of glands, the Bartholin's and Skene's glands. The Bartholin's glands release lubrication for the vagina, and lubrication is also released within the vaginal walls. The vagina is an elastic tube that begins at the vestibule and ends at the cervix. Most nerve sensation is felt only in the outer third of the vagina.

Female erectile tissue is located around the head and shaft of the clitoris (see diagram next page), underneath the labia (the vestibular bulbs that surround the legs, or crura, of the clitoris), around the

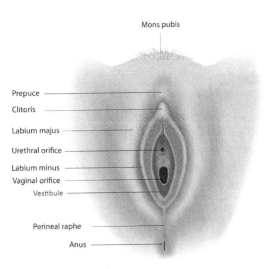

135

urethra (the urethral sponge), and in the perineum. Like the erectile tissue in the penis, erectile tissue in the vulva fills with blood during arousal. During sexual stimulation, the engorgement of the erectile tissue that is the most apparent is that of the vestibular bulbs. These surround the vulva and vagina and are underneath the external skin structure of the lips. The labia, or lips, will actually swell and turn a deeper shade of pink or even purple during high stimulation and engorgement.

The clitoris. The clitoris is more than just the head that sticks out

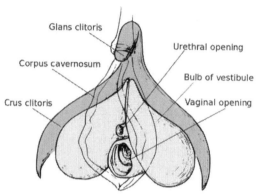

from beneath the mons pubis. The clitoris is made up of the head (the glans), the shaft, and the crura (the legs) which extend around the vagina under the labia. When the erectile tissue of the vulva is stimulated and engorged with blood, this in turn stimulates the clitoris, leading to orgasm. Therefore, touch to the labia, the mons pubis, the perineum, the urethral sponge (the G spot), and directly to the clitoris can lead to orgasm. Because the clitoral legs and the surrounding vestibular bulbs of erectile tissue lie on either side of the vagina, vaginal intercourse and the friction caused by the thrusting of the penis during intercourse, can cause enough stimulation leading to orgasm for some women. However, only about one-third of women reach orgasm through intercourse without additional direct clitoral stimulation. The majority of women need additional stimulation to the other erectile tissues of the labia, perineum, and G spot, and direct stimulation of the clitoris, in order to reach orgasm. This is important to understand, because many women and men have an expectation that vaginal sex is what leads to orgasm for women. Some women also find that breast stimulation, especially in combination with clitoral stimulation, is what they need in order to orgasm.

It is important to note a major difference between these primary structures between men and women. The male penis has a number of jobs. It sends the sperm on a journey to the female eggs via the vagina, which can result in pregnancy. The penis holds the spongy bodies that protect the urethra where toxins are expelled through urination. The penis is also the location of the majority of erectile tissue in the male, leading to arousal, sexual pleasure, and orgasm. The female clitoris, however, has only one job. Sexual pleasure. The clitoris has no other purpose in the female body than to be stimulated, give pleasure, and facilitate orgasm. The tongue

Human Sexual Response Cycle

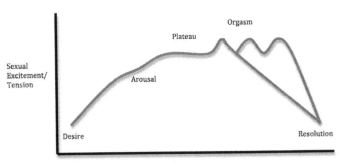

and fingertips have some of the highest number of nerve endings in the human body. However, in comparison, the clitoris has 6,000–8,000 nerve endings, much more than any other part of the female body (the tongue has half that, the finger much less). God created the sexual organs of the body, including the female clitoris. Throughout history and even in the world today, sexual pleasure has tended to be focused on men. It is interesting to note here, however, that women are the only ones God made with a body part, the clitoris, exclusively dedicated to sexual pleasure. God created the female body to enjoy sexuality in an amazing way.

The Sexual Response Cycle

The traditional sexual response cycle that has been commonly used in sex therapy, illustrated at right, is divided into desire, excitement/arousal, orgasm (preceded by a brief plateau), and resolution, a combination of the Kaplan (1974)[1] and Masters and Johnson's (1966)[2] models of sexual response. The more circular definition of sexual response, in which desire is more of a response to arousal and sexual stimuli within an appropriate context, is covered in chapter seventeen.

In her formulation on sexual response, Kaplan (1974) identified two physiological phases that occur during sexual response: vasocongestion, which is the blood flow into the genitals that causes the dilation of blood vessels leading to penile erection and vaginal lubrication and swelling; and rhythmic muscle contractions that occur specifically in the genitals during sexual activity and orgasm. Let's look at each of the stages of this cycle and the associated physiology.

Desire. During this stage, desire is often activated by a mental excitement, which then leads to a motivation to engage in sex.[3] Though desire is considered the more psychological component of sexual response, there are a number of biological factors that affect desire, such as illness, surgeries, hormones, stress, and fatigue. Relationship factors, such as great talks and fun time together, or high conflict and high disconnection, also influence desire. Desire is also affected by anxiety, depression, and other mental health challenges. Because low sexual desire is the most frequent sexual concern reported by both men and women, we have devoted an entire chapter to this topic (see chapter seventeen, *Low Sexual Arousal and Desire*).

Excitement/Arousal. During the excitement/arousal stage, when the erotic zones are stimulated or caressed (i.e., the penis, vagina, pelvic area, breasts, neck, thighs, scrotum, buttocks), the receptor neurons in those regions—the end of the nerves that perceive the touch—are activated and send a message either to the spinal cord or the brain where the message is received and interpreted. From the reception site of the brain or spinal cord, effector neurons receive the signal and respond to the stimulation signal by sending messages to the muscles, telling them to contract, or to the glands, telling them to secrete hormones that help with the sexual response. For both men and women, the vasocongestive response is when the neural signals from the spinal cord and the brain cause the engorgement of blood to the spongy, erectile tissues of the corpora cavernosa and corpus spongiosum in the penis and the corpora or erectile tissue of the vulva, urethra, perineum, and the clitoral shaft.

It is important to understand that penile erection is principally a spinal reflex.[4] The receptor neuron that perceives the touch in the penile region sends a message to the reflex center in the lower (sacral) section of the spinal cord. This reflex center then responds by way of the parasympathetic division of autonomic system (which regulates the unconscious actions of the body) to the muscles found in the walls of the penile arteries. This causes vasodilation, the relaxation and expansion of the smooth muscle of these arteries that allows the increased blood flow into the erectile tissue of the corpora. The penile arterial valves that lead out of the corpora close and the arteries become compressed, which causes a restriction in the outflow of blood leading to erection. Erection is an involuntary, cardiovascular reflexive response,[5] whereas ejaculation, in contrast, is a muscular response that involves some voluntary control by the brain.

Vasocongestion in the female, the engorgement of the erectile tissue in the vulva, results in vaginal lubrication.[6] The tiny capillaries in the vaginal wall dilate, similar to the process during erection, the blood flow to the tissues of the vulva increases, and the lubrication seeps through the membranes of the vaginal wall. During excitement, the outer third of the vagina swells and tightens, the inner two-thirds inflate, or balloon (tenting), and the inner lips (labia minora) and outer lips (labia majora) swell. At the same time, the glans of the clitoris swells, like the engorgement of the penis, and the cervix and uterus pull up, contracting and releasing. The legs of the clitoris, which lay deeper in the body and surround the vagina, and the vestibular bulbs that rest beneath the labia, also swell. Several other parts of the body respond during the excitement stage. For both the male and female, nipples become erect, the breasts swell, the skin of the body becomes covered with a sex flush, and the pulse rate, breathing rate, and blood pressure increase. Muscle contractions occur throughout the body, including in the feet, face, fingers, hands, arms, thighs, legs and buttocks, which leads to an increased, pleasurable tension and then to orgasmic release.

The excitement stage can plateau, leading up to the brink of orgasm, while respiration, heart, and breathing rates continue to remain high. With a well-functioning bladder and urethra, the urethral sphincter will contract to prevent urine from being released and to prevent retrograde ejaculation (when semen reverses direction, entering the bladder). Men may also emit pre-ejaculate from the tip of the penis. At this stage, the skin of the scrotum thickens and the vas deferens tightens, pulling the scrotum up into the pelvic cavity. For women, the clitoris may become very sensitive and withdraw under the clitoral hood.

Orgasm. During orgasm, the pulse rate, breathing rate, and heart rate continue to increase. In general, orgasm is the shortest phase, lasting for several seconds. For the male, orgasm occurs with rhythmic contractions in the pelvis.[7] Ejaculate is forced into the base of the urethra through contractions in the vas deferens, the seminal vesicles, and the prostate. This results in ejaculatory inevitability. At this point, ejaculation is inevitable and cannot be stopped. The penis and urethral bulb containing the ejaculate contract rhythmically, the semen is propelled out the tip of the penis, and there is a dramatic release of sexual tension. For the female, identifying orgasm can be a bit more elusive. Physiologically, the muscles of the vagina contract and the pulse rate sharply increases. Orgasms have been described by women as a spreading sensation starting in the clitoris that then spreads through the entire pelvic and vaginal region, ending in an explosive release. The warm glow and tingling sensations that women sometimes label orgasm may actually be those associated with pre-orgasmic intense arousal. Women have described orgasm with terms such as falling off a cliff, the top of their head blowing off, or an almost out of body experience. Some women have reported experiencing ejaculation, which is believed to involve fluid secreted from the G-spot, which is believed by some to be the female prostate.[8] The amount of fluid ranges from a small teaspoon to what feels like a flood or gush of fluid.

Resolution. During the resolution phase, the body returns to an unaroused state and releases the muscular tension and the congested blood in the erectile tissues that peaked during orgasm.[9] Breast swelling reduces, the clitoris returns to normal size, and the penis loses its erection as the spongy bodies of the corpora cavernosa and the corpus spongiosum and the glans of the penis empty. Men then experience a refractory period in which orgasm is not possible, which might last several minutes to more than twenty-four hours. Women do not experience a refractory phase, which allows for multiple returns to orgasm. During resolution, couples experience feelings of well-being and enhanced intimacy (the afterglow), as well as fatigue. We recommend that couples prioritize the afterglow in the same way they prioritize foreplay, with talking, complimenting, and holding one another.

Medical Complications

Research studies on sexuality have explored the influence of medical factors on sexual functioning—factors such as chronic disease, cancer, and neurological disorders.[10] Erectile dysfunction has been associated with multiple sclerosis, diabetes, hypertension, prostatectomy, and vascular and nerve damage after radiotherapy for prostate cancer. Chemotherapy has caused vaginal atrophy and decreased vaginal lubrication, which may also be associated with testosterone loss. Premature ejaculation is associated with illness, medication, and surgery; erectile dysfunction is correlated to cardiovascular disease and endocrine illnesses. Sexual pain has been correlated to yeast infections, urinary tract infections, early contraceptive use, decreased lubrication, various surgeries (episiotomy, hysterectomy, prostate surgeries), and inflammatory disorders.[11] Medical complications leading to reduced sexual desire and arousal are discussed in chapter seventeen. Other biological factors that affect sexuality also include fatigue, weight, eating disorders, and sleep disorders. Medical complications are also covered in chapter nine.

Sex and Injury to the Brain. Traumatic brain injury (TBI) and other neurological diseases and congenital defects that result in injury to the brain can affect sex and the sexual response. Unfortunately, neuropsychological assessment and treatment rarely include addressing sexual concerns, even though patients who have experienced brain injury report a high level of sexual dysfunction and sexual concerns. Patients with brain abnormalities and both non-impact and impact brain injuries experience sexual dysfunctions at rates ranging from 4 percent to 71 percent,[12] and sexual dysfunction in connection specifically with TBI (traumatic brain injury) ranges from 34 percent to 68 percent. These challenges have been known to cause a significant degree of distress.[13] We will share a very small amount of information here on these challenges, principally to prompt further exploring for those who experience sexual challenges due to trauma, injury to the brain, or neuropsychological and neuromuscular illnesses.

Other than the spinal reflex of erection, the brain controls most of the muscular responses to sexual stimulation.[14] The cerebellum, the cauliflower-looking part at the base of the brain, receives signals from the brain's neurons and then modulates the muscle tension associated with the sexual response.[15] Damage to the cerebellum is believed to cause problems in maintaining control of this muscle tension that is necessary for peak levels of sensory pleasure during orgasm.

TBI has been associated with erectile dysfunction, difficulty reaching orgasm, decreased sex drive,[16] and increased sex drive,[17] depending on the areas of the brain that have received injury. Men with TBI also experience a lower level of satisfaction due to fatigue, decreased mobility leading to problems with certain positions or during thrusting, and pain and loss of sensitivity during sexual stimulation.[18] Women with TBI have had similar challenges with sexual drive, initiation, and orgasm as well as additional problems with sexual arousal, pain, and lubrication.[19]

Lesions in the middle of the brain, at the nuclei of the medulla, have been specifically associated with hypersexuality and disinhibition, or loss of control, of sexual behavior.[20] On the other hand, when the MPA (the medial preoptic area) of the hypothalamus (in another area of the middle of the brain) is damaged, male sexual behavior decreases significantly; if someone has lesions on the MPA, this can lead to serious sexual deficits.[21] Damage to the orbitofrontal cortex (the front of the brain which helps maintain inhibitory control) has also been linked to hypersexuality, or over-sexualized behavior.[22] Those who have experienced neuropsychological damage due to a stroke or traumatic brain injury, or who have multiple sclerosis, epilepsy, or muscular dystrophy, or who have had a shunt placed in the septal region of their brain, may end up with injuries to these areas of the brain that control sexual functioning. This damage can lead to problems in sexual functioning, such as low or absent sexual desire, hypersexuality, paraphilias, and inappropriate sexual comments and touch.[23]

Sometimes one of the most important steps an individual or couple can make in working on their sexual problems is to seek the help of a medical professional who specializes in sexual medicine and can explore the possibility of medical complications affecting sexual functioning.

So there you have it. Your Sexual Physiology 101 class. Go forth and spread the news of the wonder of God's creation in all its glory.

13

Exploring Sensual Touch

*The Beloved: "Your lips ... your neck ... your navel ...
How beautiful you are, my darling."*

*The Lover: "His arms ... his legs ... his mouth ...
He is altogether lovely."*

(Song of Songs)

Listen to the words of the Lover and the Beloved from Song of Songs. Notice the sensual parts of the body being described and the beauty each finds in the other. This is God's plan for the intimate kinds of touch that greatly enhance the joy a couple can find in each other and in their physical relationship. However, many couples share that though they might regularly express affection in various ways, such as hand-holding, they rarely engage in other more private, intimate touches, such as cuddling, spooning, or caressing. When they do engage in sex, they quickly move to touching genitals and proceeding to orgasm. "We hold hands, kiss hello and goodbye, and hug. We have sex. Not much in between." The area of touch for couples that is often the most neglected is sensual touch.

Erogenous zones of the body are typically divided into three areas. Erogenous zone one would include whole body touch such as touches to the arms and the head, the shoulders, the back, and the back of the feet and hands. Erogenous zone two is typically the areas of the body that are both more private and more sensitive and might include warm intimate caresses to the face, legs, stomach, butt, small of the back, inner thighs, behind knees, neck, bottom of feet, palms of hands, inside of the arms, lips, and eyelids. Erogenous zone three includes the sexual areas of the body, such as the breasts, nipples, penis, vulva and vagina, anus, and scrotum. When speaking of sensual touch, this typically means touches in erogenous zone two, those sensual and sensitive areas that do not include the genitals.

Research has shown that sensual touch has an impact on how couples feel about the quality of the marital and sexual relationship and that couples who engage in physical affection, including frequent kissing, cuddling, touching, fondling, and caressing during foreplay, usually have higher levels of sexual satisfaction.[1] Couples share that when they intentionally increase how much they engage in sensual foreplay, the level of overall enjoyment of sex increases dramatically, where the focus of enjoyment is no longer just the orgasm, but the arousing pleasure of giving and receiving increasingly intimate touches.[2]

Sexual desire and arousal is also involved in how men and women perceive touch, specifically sensual and sexual touch. Men and women have different interpretations of what certain types of touch mean, especially whether the touch indicated an interest in sexual contact or was a simple expression of caring and appreciation for the other.[3] When touch was associated with sexual desire and arousal, men view touch as more enjoyable and indicative of love. However, for women, when touch becomes regularly associated with sexual interest, touch may actually feel less pleasurable, as it may begin to feel like those affectionate touches are less about love and warm affection. Making sensual touch about giving and loving, and not relegating it to use only when sex is desired, can greatly enhance the level of sensual enjoyment in a relationship. It is also important to realize that for some, any form of touch may feel sensual and be arousing.

There are many different reasons that couples do not engage in sensual touch. Some are more interested in reaching orgasm and forget—or have not considered—that their partner might want more. For others, they just want to get the sexual time done and over with, so sensual touch is left out. Some have just gotten into the practice of repetitive sexual routines with little intimate connection. Others become frustrated with their spouse's inexperience, selfishness, or rough, inept hands and forego requesting or engaging in sensual touch rather than having expectations for enjoyment. For many, life is busy and full, and therefore this kind of intimacy is the first to go.

The challenge is that sex without sensual touch can quickly become an empty routine that is hard to change. *Yes, honey, that would be nice, but let's just keep things as they are. Don't rock the boat. If we do more of that sensual stuff, she/he will just want more. If I do all that he/she wants, sex takes forever.* The reality is that many men can reach orgasmic release without much sensual touch whereas for most women, reaching orgasm is difficult without a significant level of foreplay including loving, enjoyable touches. Women express that they become resentful toward sex because of how quickly things move to the genitals with little intimate connection or sensual caresses. What may be surprising to some, however, is that men often express that sensual touch is what they miss most from their sexual relationship. They feel that, yes, the orgasm was nice, but that a lack of intimate touch leaves them feeling empty and disconnected.

The Importance of Prioritizing Sensual Touch

Couples who do intentionally engage in sensual touch, without continuing on to sexual touch or orgasm, mention how the focus just on touch and sensual enjoyment is helpful when there are no expectations.[4] This can also greatly increase enjoyment when things do lead to sex at another time. For many men, and for some women, the idea of touching sensually and not finishing with intercourse or orgasm seems insane. However, in our experience, when couples purposefully pursue sensual touch for the sake of enjoying those erotic sensations, minus the orgasm, the level of satisfaction in the overall sexual relationship rises in a surprising and amazing way. This seems somewhat counter-intuitive. How can choosing not to engage in sex make sex better? The reality is, for many, the focus on orgasm can have a strong, detrimental effect on the ability to genuinely enjoy the prelude. Taking the focus off of orgasm often releases couples from pressures sometimes associated with sex, which can then lead them to relish a deeper, erotic pleasure and sheer enjoyment found only in each other. This is what God desires for every couple and what He describes in such vivid detail in the Song of Songs. For couples that have taken these steps to prioritize sensual touch, this kind of attention to sensuality takes their relationship to a higher level than they have ever experienced in their marriage.[5]

Kissing

"Let him kiss me with the kisses of his mouth." (Song of Songs 1:2)

Kissing is such a vulnerable way to be intimate. It is described in detail in every romance novel and shown in detail in movies and TV. It can be something that makes someone feel loved and cherished, whereas the lack of kissing can make someone feel unwanted and distant. Kissing can be highly arousing, especially when kisses are placed in tantalizing ways and in sensitive areas. As enjoyable as kissing can be, it can also be a source of frustration, guilt, sadness, hurt, and anger.

When sex becomes a problem in marriage, the different levels of intimacy often become a problem. Sensual touch, if it was even happening, disappears. Affectionate touch then, usually because it becomes connected with sex, begins to lessen or disappear. Kissing is also withdrawn. If couples are having sexual problems, the first area to check on is to see how these other areas are going. With kissing, ask yourselves, do you kiss hello and goodbye? Do you casually give one another kisses throughout the day when you are together? How do you feel about kissing in public? Do you engage in longer kisses for no reason other than showing love? Do you still make out like you did when you were dating? What do your hands do while you are kissing? Do you know what your spouse would like you to do while you are kissing them?

Some people like to be kissed while having their body caressed. Others prefer to explore their spouse's mouth with a hand on a breast or buttock. Some men like to kiss while thrusting during intercourse, mimicking with their tongue what their penis is doing. Others express the need for more gentle, tender kissing that doesn't lead to anything else. Couples often share that they are hurt, frustrated, or angry about how their spouse does or does not kiss them. Some wives share that their spouse kisses them only when they want to have sex, so they avoid kissing. Some men share that their wife will not engage in deeper kisses. Using the tongue during a kiss can become an issue of frustration when one spouse enjoys the use of the tongue while kissing and the other does not. Other couples differ over the length of time they enjoy a kiss, how much to open the mouth while kissing, and how hard or passionate to kiss. Some couples do not even kiss hello and goodbye. There are couples who did not kiss until they are married for the purpose of maintaining purity. Other couples, however, did not kiss due to cultural or societal constraints, and for some, when the wedding was over, kissing to show love, affection, and sexual desire never developed.

One couple we have worked with shared about an affair that had happened early in their marriage. The disclosure of the affair occurred when the wife found a note from her husband to the woman that described how he loved her kisses. Because this couple had a child, they decided to stay together to try to work on the marriage. They became Christians soon after, and working through the affair and coming to forgiveness was a part of that process. However, fifteen years later, when they sought counseling for their sexual relationship, it came out that the wife had not shared the specific pain she felt over the note about kissing and how kissing had been a source of hidden pain since then. Talking about this and working through this specific area was a significant moment of healing for this couple.

So how does a couple turn things around with their sensual touch and kissing? One of the first things to do is to talk to each other about this area of your lives. Read this chapter together and share your thoughts, concerns, and wishes. Then do the exercises below to begin communicating about and experiencing the joys of sensual touch. Take some time to discuss the passage about kissing as well and use the exercises below to begin talking about and experimenting with how to improve the level of intimacy in sensual kissing.

Talking About Sensual Touch

Exploring what type of sensual touch you enjoy is a part of the journey. You may not even know what you like. You may be more aware of what you do not like. Perhaps you know exactly what you like, but it is hard to tell your spouse. Or maybe you know and have told your spouse, but still are not experiencing that kind of touch. For some, you may love all types of sensual touch but your spouse does not. Or you may be the spouse that feels uncomfortable with sensual touch, especially if it happens where someone might possibly see it.

Sensual touch can be warm, romantic touches where a hand gently touches the thigh while whispering something loving or erotic to your spouse. Or it may be a light caress across a buttock accompanied by a kiss to the neck or shoulder in passing. Whole body sensual touch may be laying on a couch, watching a favorite show, while caressing the entire body or it may be laying naked in bed together with your back to your spouse's front, spooning and caressing. These touches can occur in the privacy of your home or in hidden touches in public. The classic foot under the restaurant table caressing your partner's thigh is one such hidden public touch that can be arousing.

However, for some, the reality is that all of those kinds of touches can also be accompanied by feelings of discomfort and embarrassment. It is vital to honor your spouse's inhibitions while both of you work on intentionally growing in this area of your intimacy. This is why we highly encourage couples to have open and honest discussions about preferences for sensual touch. Share with each other favorite memories you have of times you enjoyed sensual touch. Talk about the parts of your body where you enjoy sensual touch and the parts where you do not enjoy touch—such as the inner thighs, buttocks, neck, or small of the back. Tell your spouse how you feel about sensual touch when you are in public. Has there ever been a time when sensual touch happened in public and it became problematic? Have you talked about it? Tell each other if you like your neck kissed, if you like your butt massaged, how much tongue you prefer when you are kissing, or how you feel about being kissed on your stomach or your butt.

We would recommend that you begin first by reading and talking about this chapter. Talk through the different topics in the above paragraph and then do some of the exercises below.

Enjoying Sensual Touch

So now that you have talked about sensual touch, where do you go from there? How do you begin making changes, enhancing your sensual touch, and exploring what you enjoy? We could write more about it, but what you really need to do is go do it. So instead of reading more, do the exercises below. Talk. Touch. Talk some more. Step-by-step begin to make the changes that can shift your entire sexual relationship.

EXERCISES

SENSUAL COMMUNICATION EXERCISES

Sensual Communication Exercise 1: Prompt and Reflection

Below is a sensual communication exercise. Each of the sentence prompts are about *sensual touch*, which includes touch to the face, legs, stomach, butt, small of the back, inner thighs, behind knees, neck, bottom of feet, palms of hands, inside of the arms, lips, and eyelids. As explained before, sit in two chairs that can face each other. Husbands, sit with your knees spread. Wives, tuck your chair in so that your knees are touching your husband's chair. Get comfortable and then take each other's hands. When you share your sentence, look directly into your spouse's eyes.

Decide who will start first. Whoever goes first begins with the first prompt and finishes the sentence. The spouse then simply reflects the sentence. Then the spouse who is second begins with the first prompt and the spouse who went first reflects. Do this for each prompt. Also, as before, for some of these prompts, you may be sharing something from the history of your relationship. Begin.

Remember, each of these prompts are about sensual touch:
1) "One of my favorite memories was when we_____."
2) "I really enjoyed it when you _____."
3) "You are very good at _____."
4) "One way I like to sensually touch you is _____."
5) "One way I like to be sensually touched is_____."

148

6) "Something we used to do that I would like to do again would be
_____."

7) "One thing I feel insecure about is with sensual touch is
_____."

8) "One type of sensual touch I don't actually enjoy is_____."

After doing these prompts, ask each other:

9) "Is there anything I've said that you want to ask me about or have me explain?"

Sensual Communication Exercise 2: Intimate Marriage Cards

Purchase *The Intimate Marriage* cards, Deck 3 (see back page for ordering information). You may have used Deck 3 for the exercise in the *Touch and Affection* chapter. For this exercise, use either the entire deck or only those cards after the *Sensual Touch* card. Play this daily, and follow these directions:

1) Determine a time every day when you can spend five minutes playing this.

2) When you sit down to play, decide who is going to go first and then set the timer for five minutes.

3) The spouse to go first then takes a card from the pile, reads the card, and then answers the card.

4) The spouse listening simply reflects what their spouse has said. The card may say "Tell your spouse which of these areas you find touch arousing: inner thigh, neck, stomach, butt, feet, lower back." The spouse going first shares their answer and the other spouse reflects.

5) Now the spouse going second takes their turn. Take a card from the pile, read, and answer. The spouse reflects.

6) Continue until the timer goes off at five minutes, snap the lid on the box, and finish.

7) During the five minutes, only read, answer, and reflect. After the lid is on the box and you return to your day or evening plans, feel free to talk more about the questions and answers.

SENSUAL TOUCH EXERCISES

Directions for the Sensual Touch Exercises:

*Reminder: All of these exercises are to be done without being preceded by or followed by intercourse or orgasm. For some of you, you have decided to take a sexual vacation while you are working on these things (see *The Sexual Vacation* section of chapter eight, *Touch and Affection*). That could be a very good idea. However, whether you have decided to take a sexual vacation or whether you are still engaging in sex while working through these exercises, remember that it is vital that couples explore sensual touch without the expectation of orgasm. If you do one of these exercises in the evening, you can choose to have sex the next morning. If you do this exercise in the morning, you may decide to have sex later that night.

Several of the sensual touch exercises below include a Stop/Continue part of the exercise. Follow the directions in the following paragraph and apply them to those exercises where the direction is "Stop/Continue."

> Stop or Continue: Take turns practicing how to either choose to stop and do something different or to continue. The spouse giving the touch asks, "Do you want to stop or continue?" The receiving spouse can say "I'd like to continue," or they can say, "I would like to stop and what I'd rather do is_____." The choice to say, "What I'd rather do is_____" may be something like: "What I'd rather do is give each other foot rubs and then cuddle and watch a movie," or "What I'd rather do is hold hands while we go to sleep and try this again tomorrow night."

Before doing any of these exercises, make sure that it is a mutual decision to do so. These exercises are appropriate when conflict resolution, relational intimacy, and touch and affection are going well. Also, check in with each other on the level of anxiety you are experiencing during these exercises. If at any time it becomes problematic, stop, take a break, and come back later. If you need to, seek some help before beginning.

Sensual Touch Exercise 1: Foot and Calf Massage

Before beginning this exercise, read the directions below completely. Begin.

1) Before doing the foot and calf exercise, wash your feet and, if you prefer, choose a lotion or oil for the massage.
2) Decide who is going to give first. For the spouse that gives first, using the lotion, begin massaging your spouse's foot and calf.
3) For the receiving spouse, tell your spouse what you like about the touch they are giving. "I like it when you_____."

4) Tell your spouse verbally what you would like them to do differently, where you would like them to massage. Tell them the type of pressure you want. Use words like firmer, softer, faster, slower. "That is good there," and "Go ahead and do it firmer."

5) Take your spouse's hand and guide their hand to where you want them to massage. Using your hand, show them the type of pressure and movement you want.

6) Tell your spouse what you like about the way they are massaging your foot and calf and what it feels like. "That is very_____," and "I like how you_____."

7) Stop/Continue: For the giving spouse, ask, "Would you like to stop or continue?" For the receiving spouse, answer saying, "I would like to continue," or "I would like to stop, and *what I'd rather do is*_____."

8) Switch who is giving and receiving, then continue.

Sensual Touch Exercise 2: Head and Shoulder Massage

Follow the directions in the Foot and Calf Massage exercise above.

Sensual Touch Exercise 3: The Sensual Survey

Read the directions below completely before beginning.

1) Decide who is going to be the first "pleasure surveyor."

2) The receiving spouse, wearing light clothing (i.e., tank top and shorts), rests on the bed, first on their stomach and then on their back (approximately five minutes on each side).

3) The "surveyor" then gently touches various places all over the parts of their spouse's body that are not covered by clothing.

4) The receiving spouse then, in response to the touch, communicates, using numbers, the level to which the sensation is desirable or undesirable. The answer might be something like "plus one" or "minus two." The range is "plus three" to "minus three." Saying "zero" would indicate a neutral response. Saying "plus one" says that you enjoy that touch somewhat. Saying "plus two" communicates that you like it quite a bit. Saying "plus three" is like saying, "Oh my goodness, that is really great." The higher number for the "minus" answers indicates that the touch is even more undesirable.

5) For the surveyor, explore different types of touches such as light to firmer caresses. You can knead their body or lightly scratch with your fingernails. Make sure to pay close attention so that you can have a clear map in your head of your partner's body.

6) Now switch. The "surveyor" becomes the receiving spouse, and the receiving spouse becomes the "surveyor." Then repeat the directions above.

**Additional version (do this after the above version): wear very little clothing (i.e., underwear and bra)

Sensual Touch Exercise 4: Full Body Caress

Level Two Erogenous Zone (face, legs, stomach, butt, small of the back, inner thighs, behind knees, neck, bottom of feet, palms of hands, kissing, inside of the arms, lips, eyelids).

Enhancing the Touch: decide whether to use oils, scarves, lips, fingers

Read the directions below completely. Do this exercise fully unclothed. Begin.

1) The goal of this exercise is to explore the enjoyment of sensual caressing. Do not proceed to sexual touch or to orgasm.

2) Before doing the full body caress exercise, set the atmosphere (i.e., take a shower, light candles, put on music, etc.).

3) Decide who is going to give first. Start with the receiving spouse on their stomach. For the spouse that gives first, for ten minutes, using hands, fingers, lips, oil, or scarves, begin caressing the sensual parts of your spouse's body (face, legs, stomach, butt, small of the back, inner thighs, behind knees, neck, bottom of feet, palms of hands, kissing, inside of the arms, lips, eyelids).

4) Have the receiving spouse turn over onto their back to receive the caress for another ten minutes.

5) For the receiving spouse, throughout the exercise, tell your spouse what you like about the touch they are giving. "I like it when you____," or "Mmmm, that's nice."

6) Tell your spouse verbally what you would like them to do differently, where you would like them to caress. Tell them the type of touch you want.

7) Stop/Continue: For the giving spouse, ask, "Would you like to stop or continue?" For the receiving spouse, answer saying, "I would like to continue," or "I would like to stop and what I'd rather do is____."

8) Switch who is giving and receiving, and continue. The total time for this exercise is forty minutes (ten minutes on each side for each spouse).

Sensual Touch Exercise 5: Explore Kissing

In the Affectionate Touch Exercise 2 in chapter eight, *Touch and Affection*, you showed each other how you like to be kissed. In this exercise, you will explore the various ways to kiss your spouse.

1) Choose who will explore first. Begin exploring your spouse's mouth with your lips. Use your lips to nibble, kiss, suck, and peck your spouse's mouth and cheeks, both their upper and lower lip, sometimes taking the lip between yours. The spouse responds but is passive.

2) Switch roles. Take turns switching who is initiating the kiss, experimenting with light touches of the tongue and gentle licks both of the lips and within the mouth.

3) Remember this is an exploration. There is not right or wrong way to kiss. You are merely trying a range of possibly enjoyable choices to pick from, learning what you like and prefer when you kiss.

4) Settle together comfortably and talk about what you noticed, what you enjoyed, what you preferred and did not prefer.

Sensual Touch Exercise 6: Make Out!

1) Do the above exercise. This time, while fully clothed, add light hand touches throughout the body as you are exploring your spouse's mouth. Include touches outside the clothing to the back, the buttocks, the arms and shoulders, the hands, the face and the head. Add kisses to the neck and ears.

2) Now let your hands explore under your spouse's clothing. Unbutton the buttons, pull down the zipper, put your hands underneath their shirt against their skin and down the around their buttocks under their clothing. Feel the curves of soft flesh and follow the hidden nooks. Do this all the while exploring kissing your spouse's mouth and body with your lips.

3) After doing this, find a comfortable place to hold each other and talk about the exploration, what you enjoyed and what you would like more of. Talk about both what you experienced as the giver and as the receiver.

Follow Up Sensual Communication Exercise: Sensual Communication (do this exercise after **Sensual Touch Exercises 1, 2, 3, 4, 5,** and **6** above)

*The following communication exercises are *very important*. After you have fun exploring each other in the sensual touch exercises, make sure you take the time to do this exercise to cement your growing comfortability with being open with your spouse about your sensual time together.

Each of the sentence prompts below is about the sensual exercises above. As explained before, sit in two chairs that can face each other. Husbands, sit with your knees spread. Wives, tuck your chair in so that your knees are touching your husband's chair. Get comfortable and then take each other's hands. When you share your sentence, look directly into your spouse's eyes.

Decide who will start first. Whoever goes first begins with the first prompt and finishes the sentence. The spouse then simply reflects the sentence. Then the spouse who is second begins with the first prompt and the spouse who went first reflects. Do this for each prompt. Begin.

1) "What I was afraid of was _____."
2) "What I enjoyed was _____."
3) "What I wanted to say but didn't was _____"
4) "Something I was surprised to enjoy was _____."
5) "Something I didn't like was _____."
6) "Something that would make affectionate and sensual touch more enjoyable for me would be _____."

After doing these prompts, ask each other:

7) "Is there anything I've said that you want to ask me about or have me explain?"

14

Exploring Sexual Touch

"The King has brought me into his chambers."
(Song of Songs 1:4)

You walk through the grocery store line and are told by many different magazines how to make your sex life great. However, the reality is that it can be much more complicated than all those great sources of information make it sound. As we read His Word, God gives us clear direction on what the sexual relationship can and should be like. In the world of professional research on sexuality, there have been countless studies on what influences sexual satisfaction and on what makes sexual touch and the sexual relationship enjoyable and satisfying. Researchers have found, and common sense tells us, that the level to which a couple is happy about their marriage affects how satisfied they are in their sexual relationship.[1] When sex goes well, partners feel happy, passionate, and loved.[2] When sexual initiation goes well, when sex is frequent and regular, and when both partners achieve orgasm and sexual pleasure, couples are positive about their sexual relationship.[3] Researchers found that problems in sexual intimacy were often related to concerns with too little foreplay and unsatisfying amounts of time spent in tender interactions after orgasm or intercourse.[4] Kissing, cuddling, touching, and caressing play an important part in sexual satisfaction,[5] and the levels of empathy, relational intimacy, conflict, and sexual communication are all factors associated with sexual satisfaction.[6]

There are many different variables that influence how satisfied you may be feeling about your sex life; in order to make things enjoyable for both of you, it takes a lot of communication. Communicating in the midst of sexual touch is especially important. In earlier chapters, you have had the opportunity to practice expressing likes and dislikes around affectionate touch and sensual touch. You can now apply this to sexual touch. The next paragraph goes into explicit detail about types of sexual touch. If you find that you have a high level of discomfort as you read below, this may be reflected in how difficult it is for you to talk to your spouse about sex. Hopefully, the exercises included here will increase your comfort in speaking openly with your spouse about your sexual relationship and the type of sexual touch you prefer.

Sexual touch includes touching the penis, the vulva and vagina, the scrotum and testicles, the breasts and nipples, the anus or the perineum, which is the tissue between the anus and scrotum or vagina. These sexual parts of the body have some of the highest concentration of nerve endings and are the most sensitive to both pleasure and pain. It is important to let your spouse know what type of touch you prefer as they touch you sexually. When is a pinch enjoyable? How much pressure feels good when you touch her vagina? What type of movement on those very sensitive tissues brings pleasure? How firm should your grip be on his penis? When should you use your tongue or lips? How much pressure should you use when you touch your wife's breasts? Does she like it when you use your mouth or tongue on her nipples, and how much suction on her nipple feels good? Where on his penis does he experience the most enjoyment of your fingers, lips, or tongue? Does he like having you massage his testicles and, when you do, what type of touch is enjoyable? What type of lubricant feels good and where?

Talking About Sexual Preferences

It can be difficult to figure out what kind of touch we like and then to tell our spouse. Why is that? There can be a number of things that make it difficult. For some, even reading the sexual terms above raises your anxiety and discomfort level. For others, letting those words pass your mouth is highly uncomfortable. It can be especially hard for women to say what they like sexually or express something they want to try. When women are asked what words they associate with a woman who expresses an enjoyment and desire for sex, they say *slut* and *whore*. It is sadly common in most societies to associate women who like sex with these kinds of words. When men are asked what words they associate with being assertive with what they want sexually, they say words like *pervert* and *selfish pig*. During workshops, whenever we have asked those attending why they are uncomfortable with sharing their preferences, these associations are some of the reasons they give. Though it is true that within every culture it is more acceptable for a man to voice his sexual preferences than it is for a woman, both a husband and wife can have varying challenges with directly and specifically telling their spouse what they like, especially in the area of sexual touch.

It can also be hard to tell your spouse what you want them to do when they are touching you sexually because you honestly do not know what you prefer. You are enjoying what your spouse is doing, but you really have nothing to say other than "that's nice." You may not know what you like or do not like until they start doing it. It may also be hard to tell your spouse what you want them to do if you are concerned about their response, whether they might become irritated or upset. Men and women sometimes express that they feel frustrated when their spouse makes a request, tells them to stop doing something, or asks them to do it in a different way. When your spouse asks you to do something different, it may feel like you can't do anything to make them happy—that no matter what you do, they complain. It can be easy to get offended when you are trying your best to bring enjoyment to your spouse, and you feel like they get irritated or don't like what you are doing. Learning to hear corrections and requests for change takes humility, patience, and a genuine desire to bring pleasure. Check yourself and see if there is anything about how you communicate your desires to your spouse that makes it difficult for them to hear. Also, check yourself to see if you have an innate, negative response when your spouse asks for something different.

Arousal and Sexual Touch

When the atmosphere in your bedroom engages all of the senses, the pleasure of sexual touch can be greatly enhanced. To explore this more thoroughly, we highly recommend the book *The Five Senses of Romantic Love* by Sam Laing. Indulging all the senses might include background music, lowered lighting, or the use of candles, pleasant scents from lotions, oils, or incense, and having food like chocolates or strawberries or drinks such as wine or sparkling fruit juice. For some, having an intense focus on figuring out what is arousing can actually cause problems with becoming aroused. There is a strong difference between exploring what is pleasurable and worrying about arousal. Worrying about the level of arousal can create a significant loss of pleasure in sexual touch. Talking about the worry can be very helpful. You may also want to make sure your sexual time includes lots of play, such as sexual dice games, playing cards, or taking baths or showers together.

The challenge with sexual touch is that we have so many expectations, experiences, and underlying thoughts about those touches. It is important to communicate preferences and what is either arousing or may be a turnoff. If you have experienced any molestation or sexual violations, sexual touch can be problematic. If there are concerns about obtaining and maintaining erection, sexual touch can bring on many different levels of anxiety or frustration. You may have a medical condition that makes sexual touch uncomfortable or painful. If you grew up feeling like sex was a taboo subject, that can make talking so openly and specifically about sexual touch preferences rather challenging. Working through these kinds of areas, or adding attention to the other senses of the body, can aid in making sexual touch arousing.

The Timing of Sexual Touch

Some couples talk about how much they love giving each other sexual touches while in public that no one else can see: reaching under a skirt with a foot to touch the vagina, reaching across the seat of a car to fondle the penis, placing a hand over the breast for a light squeeze, or running the fingers along the ridge of the buttocks over clothing when no one else can see. This kind of *hidden* sexual playfulness, along with whispered sexual comments, can go a long way toward heightening sexual anticipation and feeling sexually desirable and wanted.

For some, however, this kind of sexual touch while in public, even though not seen, can be uncomfortable and embarrassing—and for some may even feel violating. A person's preference regarding sensual or sexual touch while in public is neither wrong nor right. It is helpful, however, to discuss your preferences regarding when sexual touch is fun, enjoyable, and honoring. Do not make fun of your spouse if they are someone who is uncomfortable with these types of hidden touches. This is a time to consider your spouse as better than yourself and put their needs above your own. In the same manner, you may need to examine whether including playful sexual touch between you, in a manner that does not feel unrighteous or worldly, might make your spouse feel more loved and wanted. You may need to overcome some embarrassment or some false beliefs that this is not appropriate for married couples. Talk with someone you trust in order to see if there are specific things in your background or in your thinking that you may want to work through in order to enjoy this kind of touch.

An area to be aware of in regards to sexual touch is that for those who have experienced sexual violations, unexpected sexual touches can bring up traumatic memories and feelings. The spouse may need to make sure that sexual touch never occurs from behind or without the spouse seeing them coming. Simple consideration, such as asking permission to touch, may go a long way toward creating safety. Find a way to talk openly about this as a couple or get someone to sit with you as you discuss this so that sexual touch can become something that enhances your relationship.

For some individuals, sexual touch is not enjoyable when they are feeling stress and anxiety. For others, when they feel stress, loving sexual touch actually helps relieve their tension. Talk about how this is for each of you. It is also important to understand that playful sexual touch may or may not lead to actual sexual activity later. One key to truly learning to enjoy random sexual caresses is having fun doing it even when you know things are not going to go any further. Sexually playful touch, when it is not vulgar or insensitive but loving and tender, can be another way a couple expresses the unique, erotic bond they have within a relationship that is pleasing to God. Learning how to have this kind of fun with sexual touch—both when connected with having sex and without sex as a goal— is a significant part of becoming a skilled artist in your intimate marriage.

Types of Sexual Touch

Sexual Touch for Your Husband. You can begin your caress at the base of his penis and run your fingers up along the shaft, circling the coronal ridge and caressing the head. The areas of the coronal ridge and the frenulum on the head of the penis are particularly sensitive for most men (see descriptions of these areas in chapter twelve, *Sexual Physiology 101*). You can use your tongue, lips, or fingers to caress, lick, or suck on the coronal ridge and frenulum to increase the pleasure of sexual touch. You can also orally stimulate his penis either by fully bringing his penis into your mouth, or by stroking his penis with your hand while having only the head of his penis within your mouth. You can use your tongue along the length of his penis. When touching him sexually, you can use your fingertips, caress him with all of your fingers or with the palm of your hand, use your entire hand to stroke his penis, or hold his scrotum with one hand while stroking with the other. To increase sexual pleasure, most men prefer a firm grip on their penis, with a harder, more rapid stroke than their wife might expect. Husbands, you may need to communicate with your wife, either verbally or through touch, to show her the kind of touch you prefer. You can place your hand upon your wife's hand or move her hand to indicate where you would like to be touched and the level of firmness of grip and the type of rhythm you find the most pleasurable. Wives, it may increase his enjoyment to use a lubricant as you stroke his penis. Also, for some men, firmly rubbing the perineum, the tissue between the base of the penis and the anus, is arousing, especially if you do this while stroking his penis. You can also gently hold and massage his scrotum as you simultaneously stroke his penis or suck upon his testicles for increased pleasure.

Male nipples are also sensitive to touching, caressing, and sucking and will become hard just as female nipples do. Run your fingers lightly around his nipple and then cup his chest within your hands using a light massage while sucking on his nipples. With your fingertips or with light kisses, follow the line of hair from his chest, over his stomach, leading to his penis. Stroking, sucking, and licking each of these areas, from his chest to his penis and scrotum, with your lips, tongue, and fingertips, can greatly increase his sexual pleasure.

Sexual Touch for Your Wife. Most women need to receive whole body touches and caresses before their husbands go to the breasts and vulva. You may want to take some time to lightly caress your wife or give her a massage before you begin caressing her genitals. When you do begin to touch your wife sexually, she may prefer a softer, circular touch to her labia (the lips of the vulva), clitoris, and mons pubis. As her arousal increases, she may want firmer, more direct touch, though this can vary significantly each time you engage sexually. At high stimulation, her clitoris may become very sensitive. Sometimes when this happens, she may want you to provide firmer stimulation or broader stimulation to lead her to orgasm or she may prefer a lighter, softer touch and a slower pace. Heightened clitoris sensitivity may also mean that you need to go back to stimulating her labia, mons pubis, or vagina, rather than directly stimulating her clitoris. Ultimately, the type of touch to your wife's vulva and clitoris needs to vary and fluctuate.

Wives, this is where you will need to let your spouse know what you need—either by verbally telling him or guiding his hand and mouth. Let your husband know when direct touch—and what type of direct touch— to the clitoris feels good or if it begins verging on pain or discomfort and you need something different. Husbands, you can also increase her level of pleasure by stroking, sucking, and licking her genitals with your lips and tongue with various levels of firmness. Your tongue, which can simultaneously be both firm and soft, can softly stroke her labia or it can firmly flick her clitoris. Experiment and communicate with your spouse to find out the types of soft or hard stimulation that will enhance her enjoyment of sexual touch and bring her to orgasm.

Place your fingers within your wife's vagina, sliding them in and out. Remember that it is the outer third of the vagina that is sensitive to touch, as the more internal part of the vagina contains very few nerve endings. It is important that there is enough lubrication, either her natural lubricant or a purchased lubricant, to make this kind of touch enjoyable. You can place your fingers within her vagina and stroke and press up, toward her belly button, to stimulate the erectile tissue that surrounds her urethra, the area called the G-spot. Some women can orgasm in this manner. The perineum, the tissue between the vagina and the anus, is full of erectile tissue and very sensitive to sexual touch as well. Use your erect penis to rub and stroke your wife's labia, mons pubis, clitoris, and perineum. Hold your penis and use it as a rod or wand. With plenty of lubricant, run the head of your penis up and down along her labia, firmly stimulate her clitoris, and then come back and slide in and out of her vagina. It is important that the wife communicate what is increasing or decreasing her enjoyment and arousal and if there is a need for increased lubrication to make the sexual touch pleasurable.

Stimulate your wife's breasts and nipples to increase her sexual pleasure. Most women prefer a gentle sucking or stroking directly to the nipple along with caresses and light massage to the breast. At times, your wife might find breast stimulation uncomfortable or even painful, usually because of hormonal changes due to menstruation, pregnancy, and breastfeeding. The type of touch she enjoys to her breast and nipples might fluctuate dramatically, so talk and ask openly about this. For increased arousal, stimulate her breasts and nipples with your mouth and one of your hands while simultaneously stimulating her vulva and clitoris with the fingers of your other hand; or stimulate her vulva and clitoris with your mouth and hand while caressing her breasts with your other hand. You can also have your mouth, lips, and tongue at her vulva while both your hands are at her breasts. This kind of concurrent sexual touch to the breasts and vulva usually increases sexual pleasure for women and will often be what leads to orgasm.

Positions for Enjoying Sexual Touch

There are a few different positions that can enhance bringing pleasure to one another through sexual touch. You can lie down beside one another on your backs, leisurely letting your hands explore one another's bodies as you both lay comfortably. You can then turn to your side, leaning on one arm and using your other hand to lightly caress and explore your spouse's entire body and allowing your hand to caress and stroke their genitals. Lean up against some pillows or a headboard while your spouse lays back against you within your arms and between your legs with their back against your chest. With your arms wrapped around your spouse, use your hands to explore their breasts/chest and penis/vagina. You can also either lie down or recline against the pillows while your spouse sits between your legs facing you on their knees or sitting cross-legged. This allows for mutual pleasuring as you look at one another, seeing the enjoyment on your spouse's face as you give and receive sexual, thoughtful touch. There are unlimited versions of these positions, each with the goal of enjoying and exploring the delights of non-demanding sexual touch.

EXERCISES

SEXUAL COMMUNICATION EXERCISES

Below are some fun exercises to explore sexual touch. Some of you may have jumped ahead to this chapter without reading the rest of the chapters and without doing the other exercises. We recommend that you go back and read and do those before diving into things found here.

*Before doing any of these exercises, make sure that it is a mutual decision to do so. These exercises are appropriate when conflict resolution, relational intimacy, touch and affection, and sensual touch are going well. Also, check in with each other on the level of anxiety you are experiencing during these exercises. If at any time it becomes problematic, stop, take a break, and come back later.

Sexual Communication Exercise 1: Prompt and Reflection

Below is a simple sexual communication exercise. Each of the sentence prompts are about *times you have had sex with your spouse or experienced sexual touch* both in the history of your sexual relationship and more recently. As explained before, sit in two chairs that can face each other. Husbands, sit with your knees spread. Wives, tuck your chair in so that your knees are touching your husband's chair. Get comfortable and then take each other's hands. When you share your sentence, look directly into your spouse's eyes.

Decide who will start first. Whoever goes first begins with the first prompt and finishes the sentence. The spouse then simply reflects the sentence. Then the spouse who is second begins with the first prompt and the spouse who went first reflects. Do this for each prompt. Begin.

1) "One of my favorite memories was when we _____."
2) "I really enjoyed it when you _____."
3) "You are very good at _____"
4) "Something I would like to try again would be _____."
5) "One thing I feel insecure about sexually is _____."
6) "Something sexually that I do not enjoy is _____."

After doing these prompts, ask each other:

7) "Is there anything I've said that you want to ask me about or have me explain?"

Sexual Communication Exercise 2: Sexual Preferences

Purchase "The Intimate Marriage" cards, Decks 4 & 5 (see back page for ordering information). Play this daily, and follow these directions:

1) Determine a time every day when you can spend five minutes playing this.
2) When you sit down to play, decide who is going to go first and then set the timer for five minutes.
3) The spouse to go first then takes a card from the pile, reads the card, and then answers the card.
4) The spouse listening then simply reflects what their spouse has said. The card may say, "What sexual position do you enjoy the most?" The spouse going first answers the prompt and the other spouse reflects.
5) Now the spouse going second takes their turn. Take a card from the pile, read, and answer. The spouse reflects.
6) Continue until the timer goes off at five minutes, snap the lid on the box, and finish.
7) During the five minutes, only read, answer, and reflect. After the lid is on the box and you return to your day or evening plans, feel free to talk more about the questions and answers.

Sexual Communication Exercise 3: Initiation and Refusal

*The following exercise is founded on all the work you have done in learning how to make a request (directly telling your spouse what you want) and how to refuse (including the *what I'd rather do* from the stop/continue portion from previous exercises). The request and refusal practice is also found in the Sexual Touch Exercise 2 below. Specifically, this exercise helps continue building how to make direct sexual requests and learning how to refuse a sexual request in a way that works, without slamming the door to any possibility or leaving someone feeling rejected.

1) Take turns role-playing how you would like your spouse to initiate sex. Be your spouse and show them how you would like them to ask about having sex.
2) Be thoughtful about how you role-play your spouse initiating sex. Do not do this in a mocking or sarcastic way. Consider their needs, personality, and preferences. A request might sound something like, "Hey, babe, I'd love to play around tonight. Wanna?"
3) After you each role-play each other, share with your spouse what

you felt about how they want you to communicate a desire to have sex.

4) Now take turns role-playing your spouse and how you would like them to refuse a sexual initiation. Again, be your spouse and show them how you would like them to respond to and refuse a sexual request. This might sound something like, "Honestly, honey, I am so exhausted. *What I'd rather do is* cuddle and watch something together tonight and then how about we play around on Friday," or "How about we have a quickie and then we take some more time to play on Saturday."

5) Share with each other what you felt about how your spouse wants you to respond to and refuse a sexual initiation.

SEXUAL TOUCH EXERCISES

*Reminder: Sexual Touch Exercises 1 and 2 are touch exercises that are not to proceed to either intercourse or orgasm. It is vital to initially explore sexual touch without the added focus or pressure to reach orgasm. See the sections *The Sexual Vacation* in chapter eight, *Touch and Affection* and *Prioritizing Sensual Touch* in chapter thirteen, *Exploring Sensual Touch* for more explanation.

Sexual Touch Exercise 1: Third Base

*Sometime after doing this exercise, do the follow-up communication exercise found at the end of this chapter.

1) Remain fully clothed for this exercise. Explore kissing your spouse and lightly touching and caressing their body. Touch and fondle each other over clothing on the back, the buttocks, the arms and shoulders, the hands, the face, and the head. Add kisses to the neck and ears.

2) Now let your hands explore under your spouse's clothing. Unbutton the buttons, pull down the zipper, put your hands underneath their shirt, against their skin, and down the around their buttocks under their clothing. With gentle caresses and massages, explore under your spouse's bra or underwear, caressing the breasts, vulva, clitoris, scrotum, and penis. Feel the curves of soft flesh and follow the hidden nooks. Do this all the while kissing your spouse's mouth, neck, and body with your lips.

3) Do not take any clothes off and do not go to orgasm.

4) After doing this, find a comfortable place to hold each other and talk about the exploration, what you enjoyed and what you would like to do more. Talk about what you experienced as the giver and what you experienced as the receiver.

5) At a later time, do the follow-up communication exercise below.

Sexual Touch Exercise 2: Erogenous Zone 1

*Sometime after doing this exercise, do the follow-up communication exercise found below.

Do this exercise at least twice in one week. Continue this for as many weeks as you need. As mentioned, this exercise is to explore sexual touch and is not to proceed to orgasm. If you do this exercise in the evening, you can have sex the next morning. If you do this exercise in the morning, you can have sex later that night. It is very important to experience this exploration without the expectation or pursuit of orgasm.

1) The goal of this exercise is to explore the enjoyment of sexual caressing.

2) Before beginning, set the atmosphere. Take a shower and soap each other up. In the bedroom, dim the lights and light some candles. Put on some music and, if you prefer, put on something sensual to wear.

3) While unclothed, take turns giving and receiving a full body caress, including caressing of the genitals (breasts, nipples, scrotum, anus, vagina, penis). Start with having your spouse lay on their stomach for ten minutes, then have them turn over on their back to receive the caress for another ten minutes.

4) After a time of whole body touch, make sure to include a focus primarily on the genitals in order to explore and enjoy different types of genital caresses. Feel free to alternate between using your hands, tongue, and lips, lotions and oils, lubricants, or pleasurable materials such as satin and silk. It is especially important that there is plenty of lubricant for the female labia/lips, vagina, and clitoris. If natural lubrication is not enough for comfortable genital play for the wife, consider the purchase of a good lubricant. We recommend Liquid Silk, a lubricant for both husband and wife.

5) When you are receiving, communicate to your spouse what you enjoy: what type of pressure you like, what type of touches you prefer, and if you would like them to go faster or slower, softer or

firmer. Tell them where you want them to go. Take their hand and show them where you want them to touch you and the amount of pressure you would like.

6) After twenty minutes (ten on each side), switch who is receiving and giving.

7) Stop or Continue: Take turns practicing how to either choose to stop and do something different or to continue. The spouse giving the touch asks, "Do you want to stop or continue?" The receiving spouse can say, "I'd like to continue," or they can say, "I would like to stop and *what I'd rather do is*_____." The choice to say, "What I'd rather do is_____," may be something like "What I'd rather do is give each other foot rubs and then cuddle and watch a movie," or "What I'd rather do is hold hands while we go to sleep and try this again tomorrow night."

8) Communicate throughout the exercise and end with a few moments of sharing what you enjoyed while you hold each other.

Sexual Touch Exercise 3: The Peak Experience

*Sometime after doing this exercise, do the follow-up communication exercise found below.

1) Do the exercise above twice in one week. This time, go ahead and pursue orgasm.

2) Be aware that this exercise can become problematic without gradually working on communication at other levels of physical touch (touch and affection, sensual touch). It is also important to realize that adding the possibility of orgasm can increase the level of anxiety. Communicate about this throughout the exercise. Discontinue this exercise if anxiety levels reach an uncomfortable point and talk later about what created anxiety and when you would like to try again.

Follow Up Sexual Communication Exercise: Sexual Communication (do this exercise after **Sexual Touch Exercises 1, 2,** and **3** above)

*The following communication exercises are very important. After you have fun exploring each other in the sexual touch exercises, make sure you take the time to do this exercise to cement your growing comfortability with being open with your spouse about your sexual time together.

Each of the sentence prompts below is about *the sexual exercises above.* As explained before, sit in two chairs that can face each other. Husbands, sit with your knees spread. Wives, tuck your chair in so that your knees are touching your husband's chair. Get comfortable and then take each other's hands. When you share your sentence, look directly into your spouse's eyes.

Decide who will start first. Whoever goes first begins with the first prompt and finishes the sentence. The spouse then simply reflects the sentence. Then the spouse who is second begins with the first prompt and the spouse who went first reflects. Do this for each prompt. Begin.

1) "What I was afraid of was _____."
2) "What I enjoyed was _____."
3) "What I wanted to say but didn't was _____"
4) "Something I was surprised to enjoy was _____."
5) "Something I didn't like was _____."
6) "I am wondering if you'd be willing to _____."

After doing these prompts, ask each other:

7) "Is there anything I've said that you want to ask me about or have me explain?"

15

Sexual Challenges for Men with Erectile and Orgasmic Functioning

Michael has been experiencing problems with erection for the last eight years. He and his wife have also not had sex in several years, their conflict is high, and he expresses that he rarely even thinks about sex.

Eduardo and his wife have been experiencing problems in their sexuality for a number of years. Eduardo has a long history of using pornography and masturbation. After much healing in their relationship, he continues to have issues with achieving and maintaining his erection.

Russ and his wife engaged in sex therapy and had some amazing results in their marriage and their intimacy, yet he still remains unable to reach orgasm, though he maintains his erection throughout sexual stimulation.

Davante shares that he always ejaculates within thirty seconds to one minute after entering his wife. He expresses that he thinks about this quite a lot before they have sex and is watching the clock while they are together sexually. Both he and his wife have a lot of frustration with this, though they feel that every other area of their relationship is going well.

Stewart has been unable to get an erection for over five years. He also has had severe back pain that resulted in several back surgeries. Though he initially tried a number of different prescribed medications, none helped his erectile difficulties. Over time, Stewart began to withdraw from all sexual contact with his wife, which has led to increased conflict in their relationship.

If you have experienced similar challenges as the men in the examples above, you are not alone. Many men experience a number of different challenges with erection, ejaculation, and orgasm. Men may feel they have a problem gaining or maintaining an erection. They may feel they ejaculate too soon. They may also have been unable to orgasm or ejaculate, even though they maintain their erection throughout sensual and sexual stimulation. There are countless books, research studies, and a number of different treatments available through the centuries for issues with erection and ejaculation. One thing that is important to note medically is that erectile difficulties in particular may be one of the early signs of heart trouble or other medical problems, hence the importance of making a medical appointment for an assessment. Having challenges with erection, ejaculation, or orgasm can sometimes point to other underlying physiological, psychological, and emotional issues. So let's examine some of these issues and how they affect the marital sexual relationship.

Erectile Difficulties

Some men, when their penis does not stay erect, have few concerns. They accept that their penis fluctuates between erect and flaccid and that things may go better sexually another time. However, for other men, regularly having a difficult time becoming erect, maintaining erection, or reaching orgasm is very challenging. The official diagnosis of *Erectile Dysfunction* is the experience and distress over difficulty obtaining or maintaining erection or a marked decrease in the rigidity of erection during sexual stimulation 75–100 percent of the time.[1] Especially during foreplay and sexual intercourse, men may become concerned about losing their erection or the strength of their erection, and this can cause a number of feelings including embarrassment, discouragement, frustration, anxiety, or loss. It can be particularly difficult if their wife responds in any manner that is negative—either by expressing disappointment outwardly or with silence; making negative, derogatory remarks; making comparisons with other partners; or wondering if their husband is not attracted to them or may be getting their needs met elsewhere. Some men disengage from sexuality altogether due to issues with and feelings about their loss of erection.

It is important to understand a few things about erection. It is common for the penis to regularly fluctuate between differing levels of erection during sexual stimulation. Men's penises also fluctuate between erection and flaccidity several times during sleep, thereby bringing in oxygen and maintaining health in the penile tissues. Testing this using a penile plethysmograph, or by merely using a roll of stamps at night (search *erection self-test* on the Internet), are some of the ways in which a doctor, or a concerned male, might begin to discern if the penis is showing signs of healthy functioning during sleep or if there are any complicating physiological factors that need to be addressed.

Erection can be elicited by direct touch to the genitals. This leads to an automatic, reflexive response controlled by the lower spine, much like the knee-jerk reaction you get when the doctor taps your knee with a reflex hammer during a physical examination. Erection can also be induced by nerve stimuli from the brain caused by thoughts, images, touch, sounds, and emotions. These various forms of nerve impulses (genital and brain) combine synergistically to increase blood flow into the penis and restrict blood flow out of the penis, causing erection.

Because men (and women as well) are not always aware of how normal it is to experience fluctuations in erection during sexual stimulation, any sign of the loss of erection may create high anxiety or frustration, which in turn can—in a complicated loop with the brain—cause a further loss of erection. The term generally used for this in the literature and in the field of sexual treatment is *performance anxiety*. There are, however, many different factors that affect levels of anxiety and levels of erectile functioning. As certain authors explain, "The causes of ED are frequently multifactorial, with psychological, neurological, endocrinological, vascular, traumatic, and iatrogenic components described."[2] What does that mean? That means that erection can be affected by what you think and feel, by blood flow, by trauma or accidents, by illness, by things going on in your brain (thoughts, hormones and chemicals, communication between neurons), and by how your brain—overseeing the control of nerves and hormones—interacts and communicates with the rest of your body. In particular, other physiological, psychological, and relational issues can affect erectile problems (see table below).

ISSUES THAT AFFECT ERECTILE PROBLEMS

Physiological Factors	Psychological Factors	Relationship Factors
Poor eating habits, lack of exercise, and poor sleeping patterns	Anxiety and Fear	Unresolved resentments
Biological issues: vascular issues, surgeries, high levels of fat in the blood	Depression	Relational injuries
Illness: diabetes, high blood pressure, cancer, surgery	Distractions	Sexual demands

(continued next page)

Smoking, alcohol, illegal drugs	Perfectionism	High conflict or avoidance
Prescribed medications (antidepressants and blood pressure medications)	Low self-esteem and negative body image	Lack of intimacy, trust, or safety

Treatment for these issues—either in pastoral counseling, professional therapy, or sexual medicine—can result in an improvement of erectile functioning. However, for some couples, the concern about erection is relieved when they come to a correct understanding of the normal fluctuations in penile erection.

Premature Ejaculation

Though premature ejaculation is a concern for many men, the actual diagnosis may not apply to many who describe themselves in those terms. Before you read on, ask yourself how many minutes of direct stimulation to the penis you think the typical male experiences before they ejaculate. No peeking ahead. What number are you saying in your head? Now read the following paragraph.

The typical male ejaculates after two to five minutes of direct stimulation. The actual diagnosis for *Premature Ejaculation* is given if someone ejaculates before one minute of beginning sexual intercourse (DSM-5). Though most men who believe they have premature ejaculation might not actually qualify for the diagnosis, they may still feel like they ejaculate sooner than they wish to, before they are able to thoroughly enjoy sexual intercourse or sexual stimulation as they would like.

Some men do not experience any worry over the length of time before they ejaculate. Others experience a moderate or high amount of anxiety and frustration when they feel like they cannot extend the amount of time before orgasm. For those men, working through these challenges may include learning to feel satisfied with a typical period of sexual stimulation. Others may decide to pursue treatment to prolong the time before ejaculation. For some couples, however, it is not the husband that is as concerned about the length of time that he lasts. Some wives express a significant amount of frustration as well. Wives may feel that their husband cannot last long enough, cannot remain hard long enough, in order to bring them to orgasm during vaginal intercourse.

Most women, in order to reach orgasm, need between twenty to thirty minutes of stimulation to their genitals. With most men taking between two to five minutes during vaginal intercourse to reach orgasm, this becomes a bit of a mathematical problem. If the goal is for her to reach orgasm during vaginal intercourse, and she needs twenty to thirty minutes, but he can only last two to five, then ... Hmmm .... As mentioned, the reality is that only 30 percent of women are able to orgasm from vaginal intercourse. This may be due to the distance between the vagina and the clitoris, and the lack of enough stimulation to the clitoris. It may also be that a male cannot sustain erection without going to orgasm for the twenty to thirty minutes of stimulation that *she* needs to reach orgasm. Most women experience orgasm through stimulation by their partner's hands, fingers, tongue, or lips or with the use of a vibrator. For men who feel they are experiencing premature ejaculation, and whose wives may feel frustrated, understanding and accepting these normal discrepancies can go a long way toward relieving the anxiety around ejaculating too soon.

Another factor that affects the frustration levels couples feel about premature ejaculation is that the media (in movies, books, magazines, and TV) predominately portrays couples as having their orgasms at the same time. While that might make for dramatic screen time, it is not most people's reality. Magazines and websites make simultaneous orgasms seem like the ultimate peak sexual experience. These kinds of expectations can put pressure on the poor penis that can cause all kinds of havoc. It can also lead someone to feel cheated and disappointed with their sex life. It may be necessary to reclaim reality and ditch the dream of simultaneous, dramatic, Hollywood-style, concurrent orgasms. It may help for a husband and wife to learn to recognize any automatic negative thoughts that cascade through their minds when they begin to engage sexually or when it feels like something is going wrong ... again. This may be the time to learn how to take those negative thoughts captive (2 Corinthians 10:5) and examine them, perhaps replacing them with more accepting and understanding thoughts. We would recommend the book *Enduring Desire*, and particularly the exercise entitled *The Sexual Self-Talk Quiz,* to learn how to manage these negative thoughts.

Delayed Ejaculation

Delayed ejaculation is considered an orgasmic disorder for men, and is one of the less common sexual difficulties men experience. A *Delayed Ejaculation* diagnosis includes the experience of a marked length of time maintaining erection during normal, exciting sexual stimulation that may or may not end with an ejaculation/orgasm (DSM-5).[3] The length of time that is considered problematic is not specified in diagnostic manuals. For some men and their partners, the amount of time and physical effort attempting to reach orgasm may become exhausting and frustrating, especially if the end result is not a sexual release. This can cause both a husband and his wife to begin avoiding sexual time together.

When ejaculation becomes a problem, men can feel insecure, anxious, and sexually incompetent. A husband may become self-conscious and wonder if his wife is getting frustrated or bored. Some men may keep a mental count of how long it is taking them to reach orgasm and think to themselves, "Why is this taking so long?" A wife may feel anxiety as well, interpreting the inability to reach orgasm to mean her husband is either not attracted to her or that she is not a good lover. This can, of course, be particularly anxiety ridden if a couple is trying to conceive, which may add an extra measure of stress to what should be a pleasurable time together.

There are other factors during sexual activity that could also affect delayed ejaculation. Some men with a history of frequent masturbation have expressed that—during sexual intercourse, oral sex, or hand stimulation given by their spouse—they are not able to achieve the level of firm stimulation their penis has become conditioned to receiving by their own hand. Other men share that they become over-focused and anxious about bringing pleasure to their wives, to the point that they have a difficult time releasing themselves to experience their own pleasure. Just as with erectile disorder and rapid ejaculation, anxiety levels about not reaching orgasm may play a significant part. There can also be a number of medical and psychological factors. Depression, traumatic experiences, spinal injuries, surgeries, age, lower testosterone, antidepressants and antipsychotic medications, alcohol, and heroin have all been connected to delayed ejaculation.[4] The section and exercises below give practical approaches to dealing with orgasm issues for men.

Treatment

Erectile Difficulties. A primary question men and their partners often have is how they can overcome erectile problems. Treatment can include pastoral counseling, bibliotherapy (reading a book), sexual medicine care, psychotherapy, sex therapy, holistic care, or lifestyle changes. As we mentioned earlier, for some couples, the level of anxiety connected to erectile difficulties lowers just by learning how normal it is for the penis to fluctuate in the level of erection during sexual interactions. Other couples will benefit from working on their overall intimacy, learning how to have conflict in a way that brings them closer, and exploring how to enjoy touch and sensuality more. This might include discovering the negative thoughts a couple may have about erectile problems and replacing them with more accepting thoughts. Some may also benefit from traditional sex therapy techniques to aid in reaching and maintaining erection, such as the stop/start method or the squeeze technique (explained below). Sexual medicine care may include the use of PDE5 inhibitors (such as Viagra, Cialis, or Levitra), suppositories placed into the urethra at the tip of the penis (i.e., MUSE), vacuum pumps, injections into the penis (intracavernosal injections), hormonal treatments, or vascular or surgical treatment. Some men begin eating healthier, start exercising and losing weight, or stop smoking or drinking. Others benefit from holistic remedies (i.e., herbs and supplements) or acupuncture. For the majority of couples, a combination of these different interventions has led to more satisfying erectile functioning. When men are willing to communicate openly about these issues with their wives, it can bring about greater understanding and enjoyable times exploring solutions.

Premature Ejaculation. For those who decide they want to pursue achieving a longer time of arousal before ejaculation, there are a number of treatments available, though they vary in effectiveness. There are penis-numbing creams available over-the-counter. For some men, numbing agents lower the penis' level of sensitivity to stimulation in order to lengthen the time before ejaculation occurs. Antidepressant medications, specifically SSRIs (i.e., Dapoxetine), have also been prescribed to treat rapid ejaculation since one of the side effects of antidepressant medication is delayed ejaculation. Sex therapists also coach men to use the two techniques explained below—the stop-start technique and the squeeze technique—to delay ejaculatory inevitability. Some men learn to modulate their level of sexual excitement by varying their muscle tension and breathing. Couples can do these various techniques together and make it a part of their sexual play. Having sex more frequently may also result in a longer time before ejaculation. For some men, using Viagra, Levitra, or Cialis takes the concern off the penis (knowing it will maintain erection) and thereby lengthens the amount of time before they orgasm. It is recommended that engaging in any of these techniques would benefit from professional direction.

Delayed Ejaculation. Many of the treatments described for erectile dysfunction and premature ejaculation are also used for delayed ejaculation. Learning to enjoy sexual intimacy and erotic touch, as mentioned in the chapters on sensual and sexual touch, may be beneficial. Finding ways to lower anxiety around sexual interactions might be important. See Sexual Exercise 3 below. It is also important to check with your medical doctor about the side effects of some of the medications you may be taking. Keep in mind that the timing of when medications are taken can also have some effect on sexual functioning. Taking a medication in the morning after having sexual intercourse the evening before (rather than taking it at night) may increase the ability to reach orgasm. These kinds of medical choices should only be done under medical care, but this does indicate the wide array of different factors that could be influencing your sexual functioning.

So What Happened?

What happened for Michael? He and his wife came to see Jennifer for sex therapy. They were experiencing high conflict and high disconnection. That was the primary focus of the first part of therapy. As they became more connected and learned to work through their disagreements in a way that brought them closer, the work on touch and affection and sensual and sexual touch progressed. Michael chose to pursue a prescription for Viagra. By the end of therapy, he and his wife felt closer than they ever had in their marriage, and he had been successful maintaining erection and achieving orgasm both with and without Viagra, though he did feel that the intensity of orgasm was higher when he used a medication. Both he and his wife began to experience exciting and mutual sexual fulfillment and pleasurable orgasms.

What happened with Eduardo and his wife? Like other Christian couples who have pursued sex therapy, some work and repair was done with the impact of pornography and masturbation on their sexual relationship. Eduardo got involved in support groups and Bible studies to strengthen his purity. Working through pain and broken trust were the focus of early treatment. As these foundations improved, both Eduardo and his wife learned to be less reactive around his erectile challenges, and they grew in how they talked about it openly, including how they wanted to involve medication. They were able to accept the reality of intermittent loss of erection and came to enjoy being together sexually, sometimes with the use of medications and other times without—even when sexual stimulation did not always end in an orgasm. The release of the tension around whether he was able to maintain an erection did allow both of them to enjoy their sexual life to a much greater degree.

And how are Russ and his wife? After participating in what they felt was successful sex therapy that had resulted in high sexual satisfaction, Russ was still not able to orgasm, though he remained erect during stimulation. He had earlier not been open to seeking help from a sexual medicine specialist. This was revisited in a follow-up appointment, and he made plans to go. Before attending his scheduled sexual medicine appointment, his primary doctor, in full support of that decision, did recommend that perhaps they first try changing his anti-depressant medication. Russ began to experience full orgasm from that point on. What a victory!

What about Davante, who'd been experiencing lifelong premature ejaculation? Actually, Davante wasn't worried or bothered by it and neither was his wife. Their main concern ended up being that his wife felt very pressured by him to have frequent sex while she herself was not receiving pleasure in their sexual relationship. Davante and his wife improved tremendously in genuinely expressing how they felt about their relationship, including sexuality, and in listening with a sincere desire to understand. As they focused on that, their overall sexual relationship improved tremendously, including his wife's sexual pleasure, and they were able to talk openly about frequency and sexual preferences. Davante did notice that as the level of tension in their relationship lowered—as his wife began to enjoy sex more, and as their frequency increased—the length of time before he ejaculated increased somewhat.

And how is Stewart doing? Stewart and his wife Margaret decided to engage in therapy to deal with the problems in their marriage and to address the sexual issues. Treatment initially consisted of dealing with conflict and increasing marital closeness. As their relationship improved, Stewart decided to see a sexual medicine specialist. Evaluation tests found venous leakage that would not be responsive to treatment using PDE5 inhibitors such as Viagra. Stewart was prescribed intracavernosal injections. The use of the injections was then incorporated into the process of therapy. Before beginning to use the injections, Stewart and Margaret had begun having increasingly enjoyable sexual time together, where each experienced sexual pleasure and Margaret reached orgasm. The work Stewart and Margaret had done on loving communication in their marriage aided tremendously in how they talked and worked together to incorporate the use of the injections into their lovemaking. With thoughtful use over several occasions, Stewart was able to maintain erection and reach orgasm without triggering his back pain. This was a wonderful addition to an already greatly improved marital sexual relationship.

EXERCISES

Sexual Exercises 1: For Premature Ejaculation (PE)

To prolong the length of time before ejaculation, try the techniques below. It is important that each of you read through the whole process and that both of you feel positive about engaging in this. One of the challenges in using these kinds of interventions is learning to talk about them and to get help about any feelings of frustration. Keep a spirit of curiosity, learning what your body finds enjoyable.

This should be a time of sexual fun and exploration that is intertwined with a lot of other play and pleasure. Research on these techniques has shown some success, though the most important goal would be the loving connection between you as you explore. Surround these exercises with a lot of fun sensual and sexual touch.

1) Squeeze: As your wife stimulates you to erection, before you reach the point-of-no-return (ejaculatory inevitability), ask your wife to place her thumb and forefinger around the head of your penis and squeeze until the urge to ejaculate recedes. Return to receiving stimulation and to other sexual play. Again, when you reach high stimulation, ask your wife to *squeeze*. Integrate all this within other sexual play.

2) Quiet Enjoyment: As your penis enters your wife's vagina, do not thrust. Gently enter and rest. Quietly enjoy the sensation of being enveloped within your wife. Gently thrust one time and then rest. Continue until you have done this several times. When you desire to, go ahead and thrust to orgasm.

Sexual Exercise 2: For Premature Ejaculation (Stop/Start)

1) In the midst of sensual and sexual play, ask your wife to begin manually stimulating your penis. When you are at a medium level of excitement and erection, ask her to stop. Engage in other sensual and sexual touch and allow your erection to recede. Begin manual stimulation again, having her stop whenever you reach the medium level and allow the erection to again recede. Through this process, you can learn to reach and enjoy erection and then allow erection to recede without any pressure to continue to ejaculation and orgasm.

2) Do the same process described above during intercourse. As you enter your wife, begin thrusting; when you reach a medium level of excitement, stop, withdraw, and allow the erection to recede while continuing to enjoy other sensual and sexual touch. Then start again, entering and repeating the same process.

3) Do steps 1 and 2 several times without proceeding to orgasm. After spending several times together learning to accept and enjoy the ebb and flow of erection as described above, without the pressure of orgasm, engage in the same process until you decide to continue to orgasm. Be aware that the pressure of wanting to last longer before orgasm may increase your anxiety. Talk about this together and find ways to breathe through and accept the anxiety, while still continuing to play.

4) Medication version: Under a doctor's recommendation, try out a medication such as Viagra, Cialis, or Levitra. Do the exercises as described above, exploring your bodily and penile response to sensual and sexual touch when it is influenced by the medication. Continue to orgasm.

5) After you have finished playing while doing one of these versions, lay with each other afterwards and have a conversation about your feelings regarding the different things you explored and experienced. Compliment one another on what you enjoyed receiving and giving. Tell your spouse in what ways they are a good lover.

Sexual Exercise 3: For Erectile Dysfunction - The Sensual to Sexual Survey

This exercise is very similar to the exercise in the *Sensual Touch* chapter. The survey provides an avenue to discovering both what is pleasurable and arousing in sexual touch. It also gives men an opportunity to learn to enjoy sexual touch without being inhibited by anxiety about erection. Read the directions below completely before beginning. This exercise is done unclothed. All three levels of this exercise are for exploring sexual touch *without leading to orgasm.*

1) First enjoy a time of pleasuring your wife. Because bringing a wife sexual pleasure is very arousing for most men, take plenty of time to explore what is arousing to her. While you touch and caress your wife, notice how your own body responds and pay attention to what is arousing to you as you continue to bring her pleasure. If your penis responds with an erection, relax and allow the arousal to ebb and flow.

2) **Level 3**: The "surveyor," the wife, now gently touches various places all over the parts of her husband's body that would be considered Erogenous Zone 3: the legs, arms, back, shoulders, hands, head, etc.

3) The husband then, in response to her touch, communicates, using numbers (from zero to ten), the level to which the sensation is arousing. For instance, saying "zero" would indicate a neutral response. Saying "three" would indicate that you enjoy that touch somewhat. Saying "seven" communicates that you like it quite a bit. Saying "ten" is like saying, "Oh yes! That is great!"

4) Husbands: As you receive touch from your wife, let yourself enjoy the sensations, allowing erection to build and subside. If you begin to feel anxiety about whether your penis is becoming erect or staying erect, notice your anxiety and go ahead and breathe through the anxiety. Then allow yourself to return to focusing on the pleasure of your wife's touch.

5) **Level 2**: The wife then, with the same light touch, begins to explore

various places of her husband's body that would be considered Erogenous Zone 2: the sensual parts of the body such as the inner thighs, the buttocks, the small of the back, the neck, the ears, the inner arms, the stomach, etc.

6) The husband again communicates, using numbers, the level to which the sensation is arousing.

7) Husbands: As mentioned above, let yourself enjoy the sensations. If you become tense or anxious about your erection, breathe through it. Do not try to force the anxiety away. Just breathe through it. Then return to paying attention to the pleasure of your wife's sensual touch.

8) **Level 1:** With her husband lying on his back, the wife then begins to lightly touch the genital areas of her husband's body that would be considered Erogenous Zone 1, including the nipples, testicles, anus, perineum, shaft and head of the penis.

9) The husband again communicates, using numbers, the level to which the sensation is arousing. Once again, notice the ebb and flow of your erection. Notice your penis become erect and notice the erection subside without trying to maintain the erection. Relax while taking note of what type of genital touch is particularly arousing.

10) Throughout the exercise, the wife can explore using different types of touch with varying levels of firmness. Make sure to pay close attention so that you can have a clear map in your head of your partner's body, and especially his responses to genital touch.

11) After some time of genital pleasuring, allow your erection to subside. Lie together after the survey, warmly holding each other, sharing about your experience, and expressing encouraging and loving words of appreciation.

Sexual Exercise 4: Prompt and Reflection

*This prompt and reflection exercise gives you a chance to share and reflect the concerns, worries, and fears that are attached to the challenges you are having with sexual functioning. Each of the sentence prompts below are about *challenges you have with sexual functioning*. As explained before, take the same sitting position in two chairs facing each other, holding each other's hands, looking at each other as you speak. Decide who will start first. Whoever goes first begins with the first prompt and finishes the sentence. The spouse reflects. Then the spouse who is second begins with the first prompt and their spouse reflects. Do this for each prompt.

1) "One thing I have been discouraged about is ..."
2) "Something that scares me is ..."
3) "I have been embarrassed that ..."
4) "I am hopeful that ..."
5) "Something I've wondered if you've thought is ..."
6) "In order to work on/deal with this, I've wondered if you'd be willing to ..."
7) "I have wondered if you have felt ____ about this problem"
8) "I worry that you might ..."
9) "I worry about ..."
10) "Something you do that can make this challenge more difficult is ..."
11) "Something you've done that has helped me is ..."

After doing all of the above prompts, ask each other:

12) "Is there anything I've said that you want to ask me about or have me explain?"

Sexual Exercise 5: Thoughts, Feelings, and Communication about Sexual Expectations

For both premature ejaculation and erectile dysfunction, purchase Metz and McCarthy's *Enduring Desire*. In the chapter *Your Expectations and Sexual Satisfaction*, find the page containing *Realistic, Constructive Cognitions* and do the *Self-talk Quiz*. Together, read through each pair of responses and discuss your thoughts about each sentence.

16

Sexual Challenges for Women with Sexual Pain and Orgasm

Simone and Mike had been married for seven years. They have two young children. They have sex periodically, though less and less in the last several years. Simone has never experienced an orgasm, though she has felt a tingling sensation at times. They have attempted many different sexual techniques, read many books, and spoken with a number professionals. Mike has felt discouraged about their sex life and has noticed that Simone has slowly become less and less enthusiastic about sex.

Gabrielle shares about feeling a burning, searing, ripping pain during sex for the last few decades. She has been happily married to a caring husband for twenty-eight years and they have three grown children. She has gone to her gynecologist many times over the years looking for answers. She has been on birth control since they were married and through the years she has been prescribed estrogen creams, kegel exercises, lubricants, and over-the-counter vaginal moisturizers. She and her husband have gone to a sex therapist who explored issues from her past and dynamics in her marriage that might be affecting the pain. Ultimately, nothing has helped with the sexual pain. Gabrielle has begun avoiding sex and anything possibly leading up to sex, and things between her and her husband have become tense.

Angela and Juan have been married for nine months. They had not engaged with each other sexually until their wedding night. Sex did not go well on their honeymoon, and they have yet to consummate their marriage. Juan is bothered by certain smells and textures and he has had a very difficult time with touching Angela vaginally, either with his fingers or his mouth. When Juan has tried to enter Angela to attempt intercourse, Angela says her vagina has felt too tight, and it has been very uncomfortable. Angela has yet to reach an orgasm, though she has brought Juan to orgasm manually. They would like to find out how to have intercourse and how to bring Angela to orgasm.

Cindy and Ted have been married for twelve years. In the first few months of marriage, sex was fun and they have great memories of that time. They had no physical problems with their sex life and both enjoyed orgasms. Since then, however, for the last eleven years, their intimate and emotional connection has slowly deteriorated, and Cindy has attained orgasm less and less frequently. Three years ago, Cindy was diagnosed with breast cancer and was treated with radiation and chemotherapy. She is in remission and recovering, but the rare times they have tried to have sex, things have not gone well at all, and she has had a high level of pain if Ted has tried to enter her.

Looking at the popular magazines at the grocery store checkout lane, you will find lots of suggestions on how to blow your spouse's mind sexually. However, some women have never had their minds blown by sex. Depending on the research study, 9–63 percent of women experience problems with orgasm.[1] A wide range of women experience issues with reaching orgasm, either never having had an orgasm or having regular problems reaching orgasm. Other women may have experienced orgasm, but problems with pain and discomfort during sex lowers their sexual drive and strongly affects their desire to have intercourse and their ability to reach orgasm. This chapter is devoted to exploring problems women have with orgasm or difficulties women experience with pain during sex.

Orgasm

Female Orgasmic Disorder is defined as having infrequent, delayed, or no orgasm, or having less intense orgasms (DSM-5).[2] There are many different things that can cause problems reaching orgasm.[3] Medical conditions, surgeries, and medications can have a significant influence. Antidepressant medications, such as SSRIs, can lower desire, lower arousal, and delay orgasm. Hormonal fluctuations due to age, birth control, and surgeries—such as a hysterectomy or surgery for breast, ovarian, and cervical cancers—can affect vaginal lubrication and elasticity, the enjoyment of sexual contact, and the ability to reach orgasm. Chronic pain can cause fatigue and challenges with nerve function. For older women, possibly because of hormonal changes during menopause, orgasms may either be shorter or feel less intense, or they may need a longer time of stimulation in order to achieve sexual arousal leading to orgasm.[4] Mental health also has an effect on orgasm. Problems with both depression and anxiety have been associated with lower sexual sensations, lower desire, and orgasmic dysfunction. Problems in the marital relationship, such as high conflict or low emotional connection, can also affect the ability to reach orgasm.

Stimulation. Outside of medical issues, one of the primary things that keeps women from experiencing orgasm is that they are not receiving enough sexual stimulation. As mentioned in the section about physiology, for most women, orgasm is primarily gained by stimulating the clitoris. There are women who experience orgasm through nipple stimulation or mental imagery. However, for many women, increased stimulation to the vulva and the clitoris is necessary. Also, some women share that their husbands go immediately to the clitoris and fail to caress the rest of their body or vulva. This kind of overstimulation or over-focus on the clitoris can actually be irritating and painful and make achieving orgasm difficult.

Having the right *amount* and *type* of stimulation to the entire vulva, and specifically to the clitoral tissues, can be vital for most women to be able to experience sexual arousal leading to orgasm. There may be several reasons why a woman is not receiving enough stimulation. It may be an issue of not taking enough time. Most women need between twenty and thirty minutes of sensual and sexual touch to achieve orgasm. There may also be a lack of understanding of sexual physiology. Remember, the head of the clitoris protrudes where the labia connect above the vagina (see chapter twelve, *Sexual Anatomy 101*). The legs, or crura, of the clitoris, and the surrounding erectile bulbs, curve around both sides of the vulva, underneath the tissues of the labia. If a husband is trying to stimulate his wife, but neither he nor his wife understand where her sensitive areas are, this can make reaching orgasm difficult. Understanding physiology can lead to victories in giving sexual pleasure.

Some women also feel deeply uncomfortable with their spouse touching their vulvar tissues with their hands, fingers, lips, or tongue. Some of the exercises included below help with talking about this. Reading the chapter on God's view of sex can also be helpful. Generally, women often have to learn what feels good and what they need in order to experience sexual release. They also need to learn how to communicate what they find pleasurable to their spouse since lack of good sexual communication has been connected to problems for women with attaining orgasm.[5]

The amount and type of lubrication used is important as well. This can include vaginal lubrication, which can be found by placing the fingers within the vagina and drawing out the natural lubrication. Moisture from the husband's tongue can be an effective lubricant. Couples can also use an over-the-counter water-based or silicone-based lubricant, such as Astroglide, Wet, Liquid Silk, or Utopia, as well as different natural oils, such as coconut or olive oil. Some lubricants contain cooling and heating ingredients that can enhance arousal, though these products can cause irritation or burning sensations for certain women. Replens, an over-the-counter vaginal moisturizing product, can also help with dryness or low lubrication. All of these products need to be used with thoughtful and careful experimentation, paying attention to any problems with skin irritation and effects on birth control products such as condoms, foams, and gels.

Giving enough stimulation to the vulva may take vigor on the husband's part. Some men talk about how their fingers, tongues, and hand become tired, but they are still not able to bring their wife to an orgasm, even though she is telling him the whole time that it feels good. This can be frustrating to both the husband and wife. It is important to remember that you are on a journey to discover what is enjoyable and to be patient with the process of learning. For some women, achieving higher sexual pleasure and arousal may include being more involved in increasing stimulation by thrusting against their husband's hand or mouth or engaging in self-stimulation to their clitoris while their husband brings pleasure to other areas. This can also include using sexual positions that place more friction on the clitoris, such as the woman on top where she can shift her pelvis to control the intensity and placement of stimulation to the clitoris.

The Vibrator. Couples may find the vibrator a helpful tool to bring the wife to orgasm. For some women, once they are able to reach orgasm with a vibrator, they are then able to tell their husband the kind of stimulation they need. Using a vibrator can help her learn what type of stimulation feels good and where she needs it. Some couples use the vibrator to bring the wife to orgasm before the husband orgasms during intercourse. Other couples use a vibrator while the husband is thrusting during intercourse. For some women, once their clitoral tissues have been stimulated to orgasm by using the vibrator, the tissues are sensitive enough to have another orgasm without the vibrator during intercourse or after intercourse.

Use of sexual aids and devices can be a great enhancement to the sexual repertoire. However, couples sometimes express a concern that they will come to depend on the vibrator and that it will cause their sexual time together to become mechanical, less intimate, or more impersonal. Before utilizing sexual aids, we encourage couples to examine their thoughts and feelings, looking at scriptures to help guide the process when needed. The *What's Allowed* exercise in chapter two can aid in that process.

Appreciating the vulva. Understanding your body, especially the sexual parts of your body, may be an important step for you and your spouse in achieving orgasm. We have been using a lot of terms, such as clitoris, vulva, mons pubis, and labia. As a woman, you may see these words or see the diagram of the vulva and realize you do not know where these different parts are or what they look like on your body. You may need to go take a look. In order to understand your own genitalia, go exploring!

We have included an exercise below to help you do this.

Some women experience a high amount of embarrassment and anxiety around being touched in the vaginal area. *It's so dirty down there, it smells,* and *how can he like doing that* are common things women express. Complete surrender to sexual sensations can also create some embarrassing sounds and may cause your body to flail. Embarrassment can keep a woman from allowing herself to become so uninhibited. If these things apply to you, this challenge with allowing yourself to be completely uninhibited may be connected to how you feel about your body. See chapter ten, *Body Image and Sexuality,* to address this issue.

If a woman has a background of being told or believing that touching the private areas of her body is *wrong* or seems *gross,* she may feel uncomfortable allowing her husband to touch, caress, and massage her labia and clitoris, especially with his mouth, tongue, or lips. Husbands can have a difficult time with vaginal stimulation if the experience of the smells and textures of the vagina are distasteful to them. Though many men are aroused by oral sex, some men have an aversion to certain textures or smells, which can cause them to be turned off by vaginal fluids and the scent of natural vaginal lubrication. For couples who deal with these kinds of responses, working openly through the embarrassment, aversion, and anxiety can be very helpful (see chapter seventeen, *Exercise 3*). This takes time, respect, and care. These automatic negative reactions are not in and of themselves wrong or bad. It may not even be possible to control such strong, almost instinctive responses, especially initially. However, openness and speaking with someone who is safe about these kinds of feelings may lead to lower anxiety and to some creative choices. Some couples decide to take showers prior to being sexual with each other. Others use edible or scented lubricants. Women can grow in their ability to accept and appreciate the sexual parts of their bodies that God created. This can lead to a shift in feeling and experiencing that sexual touch is good and enjoyable.

Staying in your body. Some women have to work on staying in their body and keeping their attention on the pleasurable sensations they experience during sensual and sexual touch. For some women, staying in their body may be difficult due to previous sexual violations and sexual abuse. Trauma therapy or sex therapy is frequently necessary to learn how to manage the fears and automatic responses that have caused a woman to disassociate from her body during sex. We also recommend reading Robin Weidner's book *Grace Calls* to work through some of the issues associated with these learned, and often distressing, responses.

It is also not uncommon for women (and their spouses) to express frustration with how much their mind may be on other things while they are engaging in sex with their husband. In general, women tend to be skilled at multi-tasking, which can be very helpful in everyday life but very distracting during sexual time together. If this describes you, learn to notice when your mind drifts to other tasks, to worries, to thoughts of your children or your work when you are engaging in foreplay and having sex. When you notice your mind drifting, accept the drifting without reacting negatively and then consciously bring your mind back to the feel of your husband's hands on your body. Intentionally pay attention to what touches are pleasurable and communicate that to your husband. If you find your mind drifting again, simply acknowledge the drifting and purposefully return your focus to what your body is experiencing. This simple practice can make a significant difference in a woman's ability to take in and savor the enjoyment of sexual touch and orgasm.

Sexual Pain

Like Gabrielle's story above, women may experience discomfort and pain during sex. Some of you may have experienced the same searing and ripping pain when your husband's penis enters your vagina. Other women talk about a dull or sharp pain during thrusting and stabbing pains during orgasm. Sometimes women describe their pain as minor and transitory, others as lifelong and constant. The diagnosis for female sexual pain in the diagnostic manual[6] is *Genito-pelvic Pain/Penetration Disorder* (GPPD). This can involve pain during vaginal penetration or fear of pain or penetration that causes the pelvic floor muscles to tense and tighten, which may in turn cause pain. In the sex therapy and sexual medicine fields, other terms commonly used have been vaginitis or dyspareunia (overall genital pain during intercourse, which may be in either the external vulvar tissues or the internal genital tissues of the vagina, cervix, uterus, etc.), vulvodynia (pain in the vulva), and vestibulodynia (pain in the vestibule, or entrance, of the vagina).

The challenge is, when something is painful, you do not usually seek that out on purpose. If you know that placing your hand on a burner causes excruciating pain, you are not going to keep putting your hand there. Our bodies and our brains work very hard to communicate to us about pain and work together to keep us away from it. It can then become very difficult for a woman who is experiencing pain during sex to feel much desire for sex. Many women who experience pain and discomfort during sex continue to engage in intercourse despite the warnings from their body. Women do this for a variety of reasons. A woman may reason that since she sometimes does not feel the pain, she should just keep trying. Or she may feel that she loves her husband and does not want to deprive him sexually or doesn't want him to struggle with sexual temptation if they do not engage despite the pain. A woman may be concerned about how her husband has reacted or may possibly react if she says she does not want to have intercourse due to the pain. She may feel that this is just what women have to endure. There can be so many different reasons.

Continuing to engage sexually in the face of pain can send very confusing messages to the brain. The pain is saying to the brain, "This is bad, this is bad," and the woman is trying to tell the brain, "This is good; really, this is good." But the brain will often win and the very idea of sex can become negative or begin to have little positive value attached to it. Often a woman will either knowingly or unconsciously avoid sex. It is not uncommon for women to say that they have no sexual desire, yet they fail to connect that to the sexual pain and discomfort they have experienced.

Sex should not be painful. It is not a good practice to continue to engage in sexual intercourse when pain is involved. Unfortunately, many women have attempted to talk to their healthcare providers about sexual pain, and many of the providers genuinely could not find any reason for the pain or failed to find a treatment that relieved the sexual pain. A gynecologist might do an exam and not find any physical signs that support the woman's experience of pain. Gynecologists often prescribe an estrogen cream, recommend using a different lubricant, or refer a woman to therapy for perceived stress that could be causing a tightening of the muscles of the pelvic floor leading to pain. There may be a recommendation to a sex therapist. The sex therapist might assume that since the woman's gynecologist found no medical reason for the pain, the issue is relational, or involves the woman's family background or negative sexual experiences, or is due to a personal challenge or stressor that needs to be resolved.

The reality is that many of these issues are often involved in the sexual pain. However, it is also possible that the actual medical problem has not been identified or resolved. There are many women who are mentally and spiritually healthy, who do not have inhibitions sexually or negative sexual experiences in their past, and who are involved in healthy, happy marriages with thoughtful partners—yet they are still experiencing vaginal pain and have not yet found answers in the medical community. Many of these women would benefit from seeing a sexual medicine specialist who does a more extensive evaluation that leads to a more definitive answer about the cause of sexual pain.

It is often assumed that since someone is a medical doctor with a specialization in a gynecological or urological field, they are trained thoroughly in sexual medicine. That is, however, not always the case. Jennifer has attended the same trainings that gynecologists and urologists take from sexual medicine specialists. Most of the doctors answer with a 'no' when asked if they had received training on some of the techniques they are now learning from the sexual medicine specialists. Medical practitioners and sex therapists should be asking a woman a lot of questions about exactly how she experiences the pain (when, where, how, and what intensity) and ascertain what kind of medical care she has sought. We recommend that a woman see a sexual medicine specialist or a gynecologist who has specialized sexual medicine training. This has made the world of difference for many of women who have been told through the years that they just need to learn to relax, or that they just need to figure out how to stop getting yeast or urinary tract infections. Though these things can be contributing factors, the picture may be more complicated or completely different from how it has been portrayed.

Discomfort and pain in these tissues can stem from many different biomedical conditions, such as: dermatological and skin disorders, hormonal changes, tissue and nerve damage, internal and external scarring, damage to the pelvic floor from traumatic accidents, tight muscles of the pelvic floor (hypertonic muscles), thinning and loss of elasticity of the vulvar and vaginal tissues (atrophy), endometriosis, genital infections, or bladder and gastrointestinal conditions and syndromes (i.e., interstitial cystitis or IC and irritable bowel syndrome or IBS). Hormonal challenges may be the result of aging and menopause, hormonal contraceptives, cancer and fertility treatments, and uterine and ovarian surgeries. Women who have experienced breast cancer may receive chemotherapy treatments that can lead to sudden ovarian failure, which induces hormonal changes leading to vaginal and clitoral atrophy, vaginal drying, and a loss of elasticity in the vulvar tissues. For a very readable and extremely helpful text addressing these issues in more detail, read *When Sex Hurts* by Goldstein, Pukall, and Goldstein.

If you are experiencing any of these challenges, it is worth your time and money to pursue good care for sexual pain. This could include sexual medicine treatment in collaboration with couples sex therapy for you and your husband.

The Sexual Vacation

For many women who experience sexual pain, it may be necessary to take a break from intercourse and orgasm (the sexual vacation) while they are in sex therapy with their spouse or while they are being treated for sexual pain. Women often become so sensitized to pain and the fear of pain that they withdraw from all intimate interactions, especially intimate touch. For many couples, it is important to relearn safe touch and the right of refusal before reengaging in sexual touch and intercourse.

Some couples are able to continue to engage sexually with oral and manual stimulation while working through issues with pain. However, for many couples practicing the sensual and sexual touch exercises below, it is important to forego sexual intercourse and orgasm until the pain is resolved and the automatic reactivity to any kind of sensual and sexual touch due to the pain has been worked through.

This is often quite an emotional decision for men who already feel rejected by their spouse or for whom sexuality is very intertwined with how they view themselves as a man, especially if sex also helps with how they manage the stresses and challenges of life. Wives sometimes feel guilty about making the decision to take a sexual vacation, although some express relief. The idea of making a decision not to engage in sex can feel very scary and like a decision to give up. You may wonder if you will ever return to having sex or engaging in intercourse. The reality for many couples is that the quality of their sex life has already decreased dramatically or is non-existent. Putting a name to this process and making a strategic and mutually understood and agreed-upon decision to not engage in intercourse and orgasm during a period of treatment—while initially accompanied by frustration and tears—usually results in brand-new experiences of sexuality full of genuine joy, connection, and sexually fulfilling interactions.

Treatment

Sexual medicine and sex therapy treatment have led to important changes for women experiencing problems with orgasm and sexual pain. For the women in Jennifer's research study, those who had never had an orgasm were able to experience orgasmic release for the first time, and those with sexual pain were able to experience pain-free intercourse and orgasm.

Sexual medicine treatment may include hormonal treatments (such as testosterone, estrogen, or progesterone), pelvic floor therapy, dermatological treatments, and surgeries for nerve proliferation and nerve damage. Medical care may include dermatological treatments or hormonal treatments such as testosterone, estrogen, or progesterone. Pelvic floor therapy may include treatment for irritation to the pudendal nerve, rehabilitation of constricted or weak muscles of the pelvic floor, mobilization of the joints, nerves and tissues of the pelvic floor, physical therapy to break down scar tissue, and therapeutic exercises to improve blood flow. Other medical treatments may include surgeries and treatments for issues involving endometriosis or internal scarring. Nerve damage and nerve proliferation (excessive number of nerves in the pelvic region) have been treated medically with pelvic floor therapy, surgery to the pudendal nerve, TENS therapy (transcutaneous electrical nerve stimulation), and nerve blocks through anesthetic injections or prescribed anesthetic agents (such as lidocaine).

Sex therapy treatment usually includes increasing intimate communication, resolving conflict around sexuality, working on overall intimacy, addressing both affectionate and sensual touch, sexual touch exercises, treatment for anxiety, the use of vaginal dilators, techniques to enhance pleasure and orgasm, and interventions that address how to enjoy sexuality during the process of treatment for pain. Lifestyle changes can also make a difference in sexual pain, such as using only cotton liners and pads with no perfumes, using hypoallergenic soaps with no fragrance, and engaging in a more thorough cleansing with warm water after urinating or defecating.

So What Happened?

What happened with Simone and Mike? In the process of therapy, Simone took time to explore her body and come to a better understanding of her vulva. During sensual touch exercises, Mike learned to caress the many sensitive areas of Simone's body, and Simone learned to enjoy sensual and sexual touch. Through sexual touch exercises, Mike began to explore Simone's vulva more with his fingers, lips, and tongue and to spend more time stimulating her clitoris and labia. Simone learned to be more vocal about what type of touch she enjoyed and found arousing. Simone and Mike also spent time learning how to communicate openly without embarrassment about sexual topics. Over a period of time spent exploring and communicating, Simone began to enjoy their time together sexually. While using a vibrator during love making, Simone experienced her first orgasm. She was then able to share with Mike more specifically the type of touch and stimulation that created sensations that were highly arousing to her; and after a lot of fun experimentation, had an orgasm during oral sex. Sex then became more frequent and mutually fun and satisfying.

What about Gabrielle and her husband? They came in for therapy and were asked a number of medical questions during assessment. As she described her pain, it was suggested that she see a sexual medicine specialist, as it was possible that she had hormonally induced vestibulodynia (pain in the vestibule of the vulva, the tissues immediately surrounding the vaginal opening). While she and her husband sought medical care, they continued to participate in sex therapy on the issues in their sexual relationship that had become problematic. She did receive the suspected diagnosis, as the sexual medicine specialists found severe inflammation in the four glands surrounding the vestibule and a severe pain response. Her blood tests also revealed problematic hormone levels, and she was prescribed hormonal treatments, including testosterone. Her process of medical care, which also included pelvic floor therapy, was incorporated into the process of couples sex therapy. By the end of therapy, Gabrielle was experiencing pain-free sex, she and her husband had worked through conflicts in their sexual relationship, and they had achieved a renewed relational and sexual passion in their marriage.

How are Angela and Juan doing? Juan and Angela were able to talk about his discomforts with the idea of touching Angela's vulva and together they came up with several options. They began to shower together and have sensual fun while playing in the shower. They purchased a number of flavored lubricants and a can of whipped cream. They enjoyed using these for exploration of the vulva, though things sometimes got a bit sticky. Over time and much experimentation, Juan also learned to combine orally stimulating Angela's breasts while using a slick lubricant on his fingers to stimulate her clitoris and labia. This led to Angela's first orgasm. She also had to deal with her fears about penetration and learned progressive relaxation exercises to use when she became tense during attempts to have intercourse. With patience and lots of fun exploration, they were able to achieve intercourse and mutual orgasms.

And what about Cindy and Ted? Cindy went to see a sexual medicine specialist and found that her free testosterone levels were very low and that the tissues of her labia were extremely red and inflamed. In consultation between her oncologist and her sexual medicine specialist, it was determined that certain hormone therapies were safe. Cindy and Mike received therapy to help with communicating openly and lovingly about the frustrations they had been feeling about their sex life. They also learned to find ways to enjoy loving, warm, affectionate touch again, as almost all touch had become painful to Cindy during treatment and recovery. After a vacation from sex during the beginning of therapy, they were able to engage in mutual oral and manual stimulation leading to orgasm. After a time of medical treatment, along with the use of coconut oil, they were then able to have pain-free intercourse.

EXERCISES

Below are several exercises to understand your body, to identify any area where touch is uncomfortable or painful, and to explore enjoyable sexual touch that can lead to orgasm for women.

Sexual Exercise 1: Learning About Your Sexual Body

*The exercise below is for the wife alone. The purpose of this exercise is to understand how God has formed the external sexual parts of your body. The goal of the exercise is not self-stimulation or orgasm, but to be able to see and explore each part of the vulvar tissues and discover how each part responds to touch.

1) Make a copy of the diagram of the vulva from chapter twelve,

Sexual Physiology 101.

2) Set aside some time when you can be alone in your room, without any distractions from children or a husband.

3) Find a comfortable place in your room. Have a large handheld mirror, the copy of the vulva diagram, and a container of lubricant with you.

4) As you begin genital exploration, first practice by using the fingers of your hand to gently touch your other hand and forearm. Notice how the nerves beneath your skin respond as you run the tips of your fingers over the skin of your hand and forearm. Use this same gentle exploration for the steps below.

5) Remove your clothing entirely or from the waist down. Using the handheld mirror, angle the mirror so that you can see your vulva clearly. As you look in the mirror at the reflection of your vulva, compare what you are seeing with the diagram, noting how your own vulva may be the same or different from what you see in the picture. Using your fingers, identify each part of your vulva: the clitoris, the mons pubis, the labia minora, the labia majora, the urethra, the vestibule of the vagina, the vagina, and the perineum.

6) Using lubricant on your fingers, explore the tissues of your vulva. Notice the sensations you feel when touching each part. Take note of where you are especially sensitive. Gently explore the opening to your vagina, your outer and inner labia, and your clitoris. Glide your fingers inside your vagina to explore internal sensations. Explore the clitoris using different levels of touch, both directly on the clitoris and around it, to identify the various points that are sensitive. You may need to carefully nudge back the hood over the clitoris to see your clitoris. Explore your mons pubis. Run your finger down your inner labia and around the tissue between your vagina and anus, the perineum. Notice where touch is pleasurable. Also pay attention to any area where touch is uncomfortable.

7) As you do this exercise, remind yourself that you are fearfully and wonderfully made (Psalm 139; see *Body Image Exercise 2* in chapter ten, *Body Image and Sexuality*). Take some time after the exercise to breathe and relax.

Sexual Exercise 2: The Sensual to Sexual Survey

This exercise is very similar to the exercise in the *Sensual Touch* chapter, though in this exercise the only one receiving touch is the wife. The survey is usually quite important for women who have experienced sexual pain, in order to discover both what is pleasurable in sexual touch and what is uncomfortable or painful. This exercise can be used both during the sexual vacation as described above when a woman is being treated for sexual pain or after the pain has been resolved.

Read the directions below completely before beginning. This exercise is done either unclothed or very lightly clothed with a discussion of whether articles of clothing will be moved or removed. All three levels of this exercise are for exploring sexual touch *without leading to orgasm.*

1) The wife rests on the bed, alternating between being on her stomach and then on her back as desired.

2) **Level 3**: The "surveyor," the husband, gently touches various places all over the parts of his wife's body that would be considered Erogenous Zone 3: the legs, arms, back, shoulders, hands, head, etc.

3) The wife then, in response to his touch, communicates, using numbers, the level to which the sensation is desirable or undesirable. The answer might be something like "plus one" or "minus two." The range is "plus three" to "minus three." Saying "zero" would indicate a neutral response. Saying "plus one" says that you enjoy that touch somewhat. Saying "plus two" communicates that you like it quite a bit. Saying "plus three" is like saying, "Oh my goodness, that is really great." The higher number for the "minus" answers indicates that the touch is even more uncomfortable or undesirable.

4) **Level 2**: The husband then, with the same gentle touch, begins to explore various places of his wife's body that would be considered Erogenous Zone 2: the sensual parts of the body such as the inner thighs, the buttocks, the small of the back, the neck, the ears, the inner arms, the stomach, etc.

5) The wife again communicates, using numbers, the level to which the sensation is desirable or undesirable.

6) **Level 1**: With his wife laying on her back, the husband then, with his wife's permission, begins to gently touch the genital areas of his wife's body that would be considered Erogenous Zone 1, including the breasts and the vulva: the nipples, the entire breast, the clitoris, the labia (the lips, both major and minor), the perineum, the vestibule (the entrance to the vagina), and within the vagina.

**Touch to the vaginal tissues needs to include the use of lubricant, either natural or artificial. Touch could begin with unlubricated fingers to explore the sensations of touch with light, dry fingers to the breast and to the mons pubis, followed by touch with lubricated fingers to the rest of the vulva.

7) The wife again communicates, using numbers, the level to which the sensation is desirable or undesirable. If any of this touch causes

195

pain, stop or moderate the touch. Note the areas that feel painful and share this with your doctor.

8) Throughout the exercise, the husband can explore using different types of touches such as light to firmer caresses, circular, and back and forth. Make sure to pay close attention so that you can have a clear map in your head of your partner's body, and especially her responses to genital touch. Remember that what is pleasurable for a woman at one time can differ dramatically the next time.

9) Lie together after the survey, warmly holding each other, sharing about your experience, and expressing encouraging and loving words of appreciation.

Sexual Exercise 3: Getting the Engines Revved

Do the exercise below to explore the type of sexual touch that can lead to orgasm for the wife. Read all of the directions before you begin. Set up a sensual atmosphere with candles and music. Take a shower, soap each other up, dry each other off.

1) **For the husband**: With both of you remaining unclothed, give your wife a full body caress. Start with having her lay on her stomach and use your hands, lips, and tongue, as well as lotions and oils.

2) Have your wife turn over onto her back. Continue giving her a full body caress, paying special attention to all the areas you have learned where she enjoys sensual touch (see chapter thirteen, *Sensual Touch*).

3) After a time of whole body touch, when she says she is ready, begin to include caressing and stimulating her breasts, nipples, and vulva. Alternate between using your hands, fingers, tongue, and lips. Follow her direction for how firm to touch and the type of touch she prefers. When you touch her vulva, if natural lubrication is not enough for comfortable genital play, use plenty of lubricant for her labia/lips, vagina, and clitoris.

4) **For the wife**: It is important to communicate to your husband the level of pressure you like, what type of touch you prefer, and if you would want him to go faster or slower, softer or firmer. Tell him verbally where you want him to go. Move his hand to the areas you would like him to concentrate on. Show him with your hand the type of pressure you would like and the type of movement you prefer. Use the communication skills you learned during the "hand and forearm" and "foot and calf massages" in earlier exercises.

5) For this exercise, go ahead and pursue orgasm. However, remember

this is a time of exploration, and it can be sexually enjoyable even if you do not reach orgasm. Realize that adding the possibility of orgasm can add a level of anxiety. Recall that women take longer to achieve orgasm. It is important just to explore and not be concerned about the amount of time or the level of your husband's possible fatigue. Communicate about this throughout the exercise. If your anxiety level does reach an uncomfortable level, you can discontinue and return to do the exercise at a later time or make a request to be intimate in another way (a foot massage, talking, watching a show together while cuddling, etc.).

6) If the use of a vibrator is an option and something you are wanting to explore, include experimenting with different levels of vibration and stimulation throughout the vulva, and specifically to the clitoris.

7) **For the husband**: Combine stimulation to both the breasts and the vulva simultaneously, with your hands at her breasts and your mouth at her vulva, or your mouth at her breasts and your hands and fingers at her vulva. Follow your wife's verbal direction or her hands as to where she would like your lips, mouth, tongue, and fingers. If you use the vibrator, let her tell you if she wants you to hold the vibrator or whether she wants to hold it. Follow her direction on where to place it and what level of vibration to use.

8) After a period of enjoying sexual stimulation, or after orgasm, end with a few moments of holding each other and sharing what you both enjoyed.

Sexual Exercise 4: Prompt and Reflection

*This prompt and reflection exercise gives you a chance to share and reflect the concerns, worries, and fears that are attached to the challenges you are having with sexual functioning.

Each of the sentence prompts below are about *challenges you have with sexual functioning*. As explained before, take the same sitting position in two chairs facing each other, holding each other's hands, looking at each other as you speak. Decide who will start first. Whoever goes first begins with the first prompt and finishes the sentence. The spouse reflects. Then the spouse who is second begins with the first prompt and their spouse reflects. Do this for each prompt.

1) "One thing I have been discouraged about is ..."
2) "Something that scares me is ..."

3) "I have been embarrassed that ..."

4) "I am hopeful that ..."

5) "Something I've wondered if you've thought is ..."

6) "In order to work on/deal with this, I've wondered if you'd be willing to ..."

7) "I have wondered if you have felt ____ about this problem"

8) "I worry that you might ..."

9) "I worry about ..."

10) "Something you do that can make this challenge more difficult is ..."

11) "Something you've done that has helped me is ..."

After doing all of the above prompts, ask each other:

12) "Is there anything I've said that you want to ask me about or have me explain?"

17

Overcoming Challenges with Low Sexual Arousal and Desire

Greg and Sharon have been married for five years. Sharon came into their marriage as a virgin and had been eagerly looking forward to enjoying a sexual relationship with Greg. Although their honeymoon was fun, and sex in their early marriage was good, Greg has since rarely initiated sex after those first few months, and Sharon has become sad and sometimes angry about their lack of intimacy. Greg says he has never thought that much about sex and, when he is tired, has little interest in engaging sexually.

Cesar and Isa have been married over twenty years. They rarely have sex. Cesar expresses that he loves his wife, but he is often hurt by how frequently she turns him down sexually. Isa shares that early in their marriage, sex was OK, but that even then she had no actual desire for sex herself. Since then, she has had little self-motivation to engage with Cesar sexually. For most of their marriage, Cesar has initiated sex, and Isa has often responded out of duty and with a deep sigh.

Amar and Nyala have a busy family with three young children and have been married for eight years. They are best friends and truly enjoy being married. Their sex life was always very enjoyable, but over the last several years, Nyala only experiences desire for sex every few months. They have continued to have sex regularly, but Nyala has little enthusiasm for it, experiences some discomfort, and even when Amar tries to bring her to orgasm, she does not feel any physical arousal. She expresses that she is often tired, and since they had their second child, she has found it hard to relax and enjoy herself with her husband sexually.

Sexual desire is a rather elusive idea. Is it the feeling of wanting to have sex? Is it the physiological sensation of arousal? Is it thinking and fantasizing about having sex? Is it a pull toward sexual release? Is it just a need for closeness and intimacy? Is it the desire to have an orgasm? The answer depends on who you ask. Sexual desire goes by different names: libido, attraction, drive, appetite, lust, urge, etc. Sexual arousal is a little bit easier to label, as it is usually described in terms associated with certain physical sensations, especially in the genitals: throbbing, pulsing, erection, tingling, buzzing, heat, etc. Sexual arousal is often connected with positive feelings about those sensations and the sexual thoughts that accompany them. On the other hand, the lack of sexual desire definitely causes a significant level of confusion, hurt, and frustration for many individuals and couples. We will define desire and arousal, describe the problems that arise for some couples sexually when desire and arousal are low, and share some of the different ways a couple can learn to respond to these challenges.

Desire

When doctors ask patients about their sexual lives, low sexual desire is one of the primary complaints shared. Low desire is one of the top sexual disorders reported in research. It is also one of the more difficult challenges to treat in sex therapy. The FDA has recently approved the first sexual medication for women, Flibanserin, a pharmacological treatment for low desire in premenopausal women. Its release may increase the number of patient/doctor conversations about the quality of sexual relationships and will most likely create some very interesting conversations at parties. Male low sexual desire has been treated in many different ways, as we will review below.

Some question whether low sexual desire should actually be considered a disorder. According to the diagnostic manual used by mental health practitioners,[1] low sexual desire disorder (*Male Hypoactive Sexual Desire* for men and *Female Sexual Interest/Arousal Disorder* for women) includes low or absent sexual thoughts, fantasies, or desire for sexual activity. For women, the diagnosis also includes a lack of initiation or receptivity, low excitement or pleasure during sex, and a lack of interest, arousal, or physical response to internal (thoughts and feelings) or external (written, visual, or verbal) sexual cues. The ongoing debate in the sexual health community is whether the cause for low desire is biological, relational, or psychological. The reality is often a combination of a number of things, such as anger and disconnection in marriage, negative body image, sexual abuse, biological and medical issues, spiritual beliefs, psychological challenges, and lifestyle.

When there are challenges in the overall relationship, such as bitterness and conflict, it can be difficult for someone to desire sex. Not surprisingly, feelings of anger—or being spoken to or yelled at in anger—can lower sexual desire. Overall disconnection in marriage can also kill sexual interest. Unresolved conflict lowers sexual desire and arousal, undermining a couple's experience of intimacy and sexual satisfaction.[2] Challenges with body image, especially for women, though in some degree for men as well, can also affect sexual desire, sexual initiation, frequency of sex, and how sexually attractive someone feels.[3] Men and women who have experienced changes to their bodies due to surgery and illness have also had problems with desire and arousal connected to how they felt about their physical appearance.

Low desire can also be influenced by the world in which we were raised and someone's history of sexual experiences. Religious upbringing has been associated with sexual avoidance and lower sexual desire.[4] Fear of intimacy has been reported to lower sexual desire.[5] Desire can also be affected by sexual trauma, such as sexual molestation, rape, and other sexual violations.[6]

It may be important to rule out biological causes for low sexual desire such as illnesses, diseases, or hormone deficiencies. These are covered in more detail below. The same process may be necessary to rule out or identify psychological factors influencing desire. Getting help with depression and anxiety, for instance, can have a positive impact on levels of desire. However, certain medications for depression can actually lower sexual desire and arousal. If you suspect your medications may be causing low desire, it may be beneficial to speak with a medical doctor about changing the level of medication or switching medications.

Expectations that your spouse will feel sexual desire in the midst of daily life may have caused conflict for you in your marriage. However, there are

Sexual Response Cycle

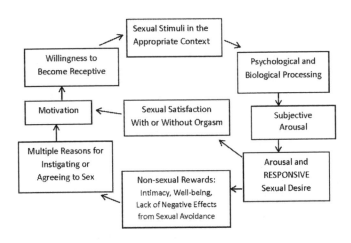

different beliefs about where desire should occur in the sexual response cycle (the components of the sexual response cycle are covered in chapter twelve, *Sexual Physiology 101*). Some specialists believe that if things are going well in a couple's relationship, it is relatively automatic for people to feel sexual desire before engaging sexually. Others think that many people may not experience sexual desire before engaging sexually for any number of understandable reasons.

If this is you and your mate's experience, you'll be relieved to hear that desire may not always come before engaging in sex, and that low desire is not that uncommon. Rosemary Basson, a sexual medicine specialist,[7] has shown how many women and some men experience desire *responsively* (see chart). When there is a willingness to engage sexually and sexual stimuli begins in an appropriate context, desire then kicks into gear—a responsive desire. This means that desire may not necessarily happen before sensual and sexual stimulation has started and that desire can be greatly affected by the atmosphere of the overall relationship and the immediate circumstances.

Women will often say that they do not feel sexual desire during the routine of their day. But when things are going well in the relationship and they begin to engage in foreplay, they desire to continue and to have an orgasm. In a healthy marital relationship, you do not necessarily need to wait for desire to occur in order to engage sexually. You can instead pursue the different things that cause desire to build as you spend time together sexually. Basson insisted that healthy sexual functioning and desire needs to include feelings of trust, intimacy, respect, and pleasure, as well as affectionate touch, satisfying communication, and safety in the relationship in order to be vulnerable.[8]

In our experience as well, many women and some men describe their desire as a responsive desire. Women and their husbands have expressed outright relief when this is explained to them. In general, women with low desire tend to wonder, "What is wrong with me?" when they feel they do not have a sexual libido or do not experience sexual desire throughout the week. Their husbands often express that they feel unwanted because their wives do not express sexual desire or interest. Exploring the ideas above helps them release misplaced shame, as they learn that women (or men) may not experience sexual desire before engaging in sex, especially those in the childbearing years, those with physical illnesses, and those experiencing high levels of stress. It also helps men to understand that their wives might still feel attracted to them and love them but not necessarily think much about having sex.

When a man does not experience much (or any) desire prior to having sex, this can have multiple levels of challenge, especially because society says, "All men want sex." The wife of a man with low desire often feels that if he does not want sex as often as the typical male, he must not be attracted to her. She wonders if there is something wrong with him or whether he is fulfilling his sexual needs somewhere else. A man may wonder whether his low desire means there is something wrong with him. The reality is he may just have an innate lower desire. It is also possible that there may be biological factors affecting his desire levels. For instance, male hypogonadism (determined by low hormone secretion or sperm production from the testes) is identified with low sexual desire, as are a number of other health challenges as explained below. Repetitive masturbation and/or pornography use may also have a negative effect on libido, which is discussed in chapter eleven.

Lowering the anxiety and frustration of the husband having a lower sexual drive can release a couple to make healing changes. This cycle of blame, defensiveness, and accusation begins to dissipate as his wife realizes that her spouse's lower desire could be biological or innate. As he begins to initiate more sexually, rather than wait until desire kicks in, his wife may find reassurance.

Arousal

Arousal is generally considered the physiological state of heightened awareness to sexual sensations and responses. As explained in chapter twelve, the stages of the sexual response cycle include desire, arousal/excitement, orgasm, and resolution. The illustration included below is a play on the differences in male and female arousal, with male arousal depicted as one button and female arousal depicted as multiple different buttons and dials. This humorous illustration shows the common view that it takes a relatively simple level of stimulation to arouse a man and a rather complicated number of steps to arouse a woman. A husband feels a great sense of accomplishment when he figures out just what brings his wife pleasure and what brings her to orgasm. On the other hand, he may experience a great sense of frustration

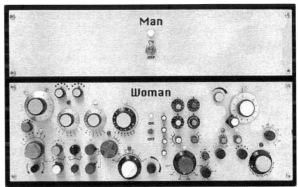

Differences in Arousal between Men and Women

when he uses the exact same techniques the next night, and the bells and whistles fail to go off.

If a woman rarely experience sexual arousal, it is possible she isn't receiving a high enough level of stimulation. She might benefit from some direction on how to build arousal and how to improve stimulation to the genitals (see chapter sixteen, *Sexual Challenges for Women*). During arousal, the brain sends signals of "I like this" to various parts of the body. Physical sensations may include tingling, throbbing, wetness, and swelling in the vagina and labia, and erectile responses in the penis. The ability to become physically aroused can be influenced by some of the same issues affecting desire, such as physical illness, medications, problems in the marital relationship, job issues, problems with the kids, worry, and stress.

Some people get aroused by thoughts or images. Others need a lot of sensual, intimate touch to begin feeling aroused (caresses, kisses, touches to more intimate areas of the body). Some, however, though enjoying those sensations, do not necessarily start to feel any of the tingling and throbbing of arousal until the genitals are touched. As mentioned in the chapter on sexual physiology, the female clitoris is more than just the pea-sized head that protrudes from the vulva just above the vagina and urethra. The clitoris has legs that extend down around the vagina. In order for most women to experience an increase in arousal, there usually needs to be an increase in the kind and amount of stimulation to the clitoris, both at the head and around the legs, or crura. Arousal is also often heightened for women when the breasts and clitoris are stimulated at the same time. See chapter fourteen, *Exploring Sexual Touch*, to learn more about this level of touch.

For many men, arousal is reached quickly and easily. However, other men who have challenges with arousal or erection may not become aroused by simple thoughts or touch. Some men may need an extended time of sensual and sexual touch to allow arousal in the penile tissues to build. As men age, experiencing arousal spontaneously, without direct touch, may happen less and less. He may need more time, caressing, oral stimulation, and/or vigorous stroking to become aroused in connection with erection. When a woman gives to her husband in this way, it is an expression of her love.

Medical challenges with Low Arousal and Desire

Reduced sexual desire has been associated with a number of medical issues including illnesses, surgeries, medications, and chronic syndromes. Individuals with chronic renal failure, chronic pain, diabetes, and hypogonadism experience low desire. Reduced sexual arousal is associated with blood sugar fluctuations in connection with diabetes and hypothalamic and pituitary diseases. Chronic illnesses were found to lead to depression and fatigue that affected sexual activity, as well as a reduced energy and mobility that affected the ability to hug, caress, and give pleasure to a partner.[9]

Frequency of sex and sexual desire also decrease as age increases for men and women.[10] Older women who experience lower sexual desire may also have greater difficulty reaching orgasm. This may be due to the level of discomfort they experience during sex caused by the physical changes of menopause.[11] Within these difficult circumstances, a man and wife have the opportunity to connect even more closely through showing self-restraint, patience, and a willingness to serve in the ways that best benefit the other.

Treatments for mental health and medical issues can influence levels of desire and arousal, including androgen deprivation therapy for prostate cancer, chemotherapy for breast cancer leading to ovarian failure, chemotherapy leading to testicular failure, the use of narcotic medications, and depression medications such as selective serotonin reuptake inhibitors (SSRIs).[12]

Treatment

There are a variety of pharmaceutical treatments that have been used for low arousal and desire in women, such as bremelanotide (or Flibanserin) and Intrinsa, which is a transdermal androgen for women. Low desire and arousal in men is sometimes treated with a PDE5 inhibitor, such as Viagra, Cialis, and Levitra. These medications are labeled as not activating unless a male is already experiencing desire. However, for some men, achieving some level of erection, and sensing their bodily arousal, leads to feelings of a greater desire for sex and orgasm and a more pleasurable orgasm. This in turn leads to a greater desire for future sexual activities. Women have also been treated with PDE5 inhibitors with limited success. Testosterone treatments have been shown to increase motivation for sex and sensations of arousal for men and women, though research results vary significantly as to the effectiveness of testosterone on increasing desire. The same can be said for herbal remedies such as Arginmax or Zestra. A small amount of data suggests that women who took these experienced greater sexual desire. Remember, if you need to use a medication or supplement, please know that this doesn't make you less than others. Using available tools to solve problems shows humility and commitment to your partner. As you do so, you honor the marvelous sexual and hormonal wiring that God instituted.

Since certain depression medications have sexual side effects, such as SSRIs like Paxil or Prozac, switching to Wellbutrin or lowering the level of an SSRI can have an effect on desire levels. Going off of these medications may raise feelings of desire and arousal, but this should only be done under medical supervision. Lifestyle changes can also have an effect on desire and arousal levels, such as increasing exercise, lowering stress levels, and better communication. Certain lifestyle choices have a negative effect on sexual drive, such as smoking and drinking. Making changes in these areas can have a marked impact on sexual functioning.

Some married individuals and couples seek sex therapy to treat low desire and arousal. In Jennifer's research study, the couples who completed therapy experienced an increased desire for emotional intimacy. They found the very process of therapy healing. Partners also experienced more non-sexual intimacy (i.e., affectionate touch, intimate verbal communication) and began to initiate more sexually. Women in the study, including those diagnosed with low sexual desire or arousal, experienced a significant improvement in their sexual satisfaction and sexual functioning and reported an increase in desire and arousal levels. Men in the study who experienced erectile dysfunction that had affected their level of sexual desire showed a change in their desire levels and their sexual functioning. These kinds of changes point to the rich benefits you may receive by seeking professional help.

"Blow on My Garden" (Song of Songs 4:16)

Aside from checking up on medical or psychological issues or seeking other professional help, couples can work on the areas of their relationship that may be influencing desire and arousal. Couples can talk about and explore ways to add romance to their relationship and to their sexual times together. Simply changing the atmosphere and circumstances of when sex occurs can make a difference, which is why "vacation sex" can be so enjoyable. No schedule and plenty of rest can have a significant influence on desire levels and the ability to relax enough to become aroused. Working on all of the areas already suggested in previous chapters can also make a significant impact on desire and arousal: working through conflict, spending time together having fun, talking more and having more intimate conversations, greater touch and affection, and engaging in a higher level of sensual play.

For some Christians, there are a number of things that can make a difference in how much sex is on their minds and the level of desire they feel to engage in sex. One of the markers of low desire is not spending time thinking about sex. For some people, giving themselves permission to think about sex can be a big part of building desire. As followers of Jesus, it may feel wrong to think about sex or to fantasize. Isn't fantasizing about sex lusting? And isn't lust a sin? Biblically, we know that lusting after someone else's husband or wife or about a man or woman who is not your spouse is sin (Matthew 5:28; Exodus 20:17). The scriptures here, however, are talking about committing adultery, having sex with someone other than your spouse. The word used in Matthew is lust, or *epithumeo* in the Greek, which means *desire, longing, and having a passionate yearning*. In the scripture from Exodus, the word for covet, *chamad* in Hebrew, means *to desire and take pleasure in*. In Matthew, Jesus is saying that if you even have those *feelings* for someone that is not your spouse, then you are committing adultery in your heart. In fact, you are having adulterous sexual intercourse in your heart even if you are not having it physically. In Exodus, Moses is saying that we break God's commands when we covet by having a desire for someone else's spouse.

We know from the other scriptures about marital sex that we are *supposed* to experience those feelings for our spouse: desire, longing, passionate yearning, sexual pleasure. God wants us to be captivated by one another. He wants us to be intoxicated with love and sexual desire (Proverbs 5:19).

In a similar way, in 1 Corinthians 7:9, Paul says that single men should get married rather than burn with passion, meaning that burning with passion belongs only in marriage. We should act that passion out in marriage. In other words, God wants us to take that flaming passion and focus it on our spouse rather than let it lead us to commit immorality or to have sex outside of the marital relationship. So what does all this mean? God wants sexual desire and longing to occur in our marriage. Indeed, it is good and godly to think about your spouse sexually. Just reread Song of Songs and you will find a clear picture of the beauty of desire.

So what would this look like in the life of a disciple of Jesus? Do sexually enjoyable encounters with your spouse ever replay through your mind? They should. There is so much junk that Satan has put out there on the screen of the world to fill our minds with images of sex that are not godly. Just watch any network show, pass many a billboard on the freeway, look at the ads next to your email site, or watch the previews at the movie theater. You do not even have to engage in cybersex or watch pornographic movies. Just turn on a screen or look at an advertisement.

Satan inundates us with the wrong kind of sexual pictures so that we don't think about the right ones. *And there are right ones.* Thinking about your spouse sexually, getting aroused thinking about having sex with them, not only replaces the pictures Satan throws at us, but it can also potentially fan into flame needed anticipation and physical arousal.

Within your religious background or upbringing, you may have only heard sexual thoughts and feelings talked about in negative terms. Because Christians focus on sexual abstinence before marriage, sexuality in church is often shared in terms of what *not* to do or how to abstain from lust or masturbation.

It can be a challenge for some to believe that having sexual thoughts when thinking about your spouse—feeling your vagina throb or your penis become erect—could be a good and right thing. However, God did a fantastic job of creating your physiology, including the sexual parts of your body. What a blessing when merely thinking about your spouse can result in a sexual, God-given response.

Building Desire and Arousal

Intentionally fantasizing about your spouse can be one way to increase your level of desire and arousal. Reviewing videos in your mind of the last time that your spouse brought you to orgasm can get the body tingling in a good and righteous way. Doing small gestures to tease your spouse can be arousing for both of you. Flash your spouse with a view of your intimate parts. Lightly caress theirs. Send each other emails or texts, and then erase them. Tell your spouse how you are attracted to them and talk about their sandaled feet (Song of Songs 7:1) and arms of gold (5:14). It is important to note here that one of the greatest aphrodisiacs for women is hearing what their husband admires about them (not just their looks or how sexy they are). They love receiving encouraging notes or expressions of affection. It makes a wife feel cherished when her husband takes the children away to give her non-children time, or vacuums, folds laundry, and does the dishes. Those little touches of domestic help, encouraging words, and gentle, warm touch can make quite a difference in how she feels when you do decide to touch her intimately.

Feeling confident in how you look can go a long way toward opening the doors to increased feelings of desire. Yes, getting thinner or more muscular could aid your self-confidence. Working out to get in better shape does make some people feel more desirable, thereby increasing their desire. However, for some, pursuing that body ideal may not be the wisest course. Consider instead how to feel confident about your body just as you are (see chapter ten, *Body Image and Sexuality*). Also consider changing the atmosphere to help pave the way to higher arousal—how the room feels (atmosphere); the materials clothing your body; a cleansing and aromatic bath or shower; or sensual lotions. Some women wear feminine negligees made of satin, silk, or lace that help them feel more confident. They find that adorning the parts of their body they are self-conscious about with something beautiful, soft, and sexy helps them feel sensuous and aroused. Other women feel more comfortable and sexy in a cotton tank top.

Husbands ask your wife what she prefers you to wear, or not wear, especially during sensual and sexual time together. Taking a shower and smelling clean can go a long way toward influencing desire. Talking openly about this as a couple can, in and of itself, be arousing.

Reading the erotic passages found in Song of Songs, and purposefully dwelling on the imagery God has placed in His Word, can also help overcome barriers and increase desire. Consider passages such as Song of Songs 1:2, 4, 13, 16; 2:6, 9, 16; 3:4; 4:3, 5-6, 11, 12, 16; 5:2-4, 13-14, 16; 6:5-9; 7:7-9. Notice the erotic imagery such as taking off a robe, wine gently flowing over lips and teeth, browsing among the flowers, kissing on the mouth, resting between the breasts, flowing springs, choice fruits, and a hand thrusting through the door. The beloved says that she roused her lover while they were under the apple tree (8:5). Roused here means stirred up, awakened, aroused and excited to love. So, get yourself all stirred up! Stir each other up! Fantasize, dream, imagine. And then plan and execute, knowing that God is glorified.

The Continually Flowing Stream

For your sexual relationship to be arousing, the streams need to continually flow. The terms used in both Proverbs and Song of Songs allude to water that is constantly refreshed. Proverbs 5:15-18 uses words such as running water, a river, a stream, and a flowing channel. This passage also talks about a cistern, where water should be kept fresh and cool. Cisterns were also used as hiding places in certain biblical accounts. Your marriage bed will benefit from being kept fresh and cool and can definitely become a place where you can hide together from the cares of this world. The writers of both Proverbs and Song of Songs also illustrate their thoughts using the idea of a fountain (Proverbs 5:18; Song of Songs 4:15). Picture a flowing fountain in a beautiful garden, resplendent with sparkling water, surrounded by lush, fragrant greenery and flowers. These flowing, refreshing pictures of water are what God uses to describe erotic, spiritual sexuality.

As in Proverbs, in Song of Songs 4:15, the lover says of his bride that she is a well of flowing water. The Hebrew translation here denotes a well created by digging. You may need to dig deep to bring up from within yourself new delights, desires, thoughts, ideas, gestures, and actions that help build and increase sexual desire, keeping your sex life fresh and arousing. Making your sex life a flowing stream, a fountain, a cistern, or a refreshing well may take a significant shift in the priorities of your life. If you are not naturally creative, ask others and consider some of the exercises at the end of this chapter.

So What Happened?

Let's look back at the couples mentioned at the beginning of this chapter. How did things go with Greg and Sharon? Greg had a highly stressful job and a lot of guilt about his background in pornographic addiction. Sharon had a lot of embarrassment about her stronger sex drive and believed Greg's lower sexual desire meant he was not attracted to her. Helping them understand and accept their differences in desire was a very important first step. They also had to spend some time working through the feelings of shame and guilt associated with sex. After both of them learned to be more assertive and express their sexual preferences, fears, and expectations openly, they were able to experience lower anxiety when they did engage sexually. Greg also made some decisions about initiating time together both sensually and sexually, even when work stressors were high. By the end of treatment, they had a much greater confidence in their relationship, lower anxiety about their varying levels of sexual desire, and a significantly increased enjoyment in their sexual relationship.

And how were things with Cesar and Isa? Isa did quite a bit of work on body image and her feelings about sex overall. When she became more assertive about what she liked for Cesar to do for her sexually, including emotional and relational intimacy and sensual touch, her level of enjoyment in sex increased significantly. Once she learned how to refuse a sexual initiation in a way that did not slam the door to other intimacy, she became much more responsive to Cesar's requests. She shared how much more she was enjoying their sex life to the point that sometimes she even thought about it during the day. Cesar learned to be more direct and less demanding in his requests, open with his disappointment, and more attentive to the different things Isa needed in order for sex to be more enjoyable.

And how about Amar and Nyala? Nyala pursued receiving care from a sexual medicine specialist that made an important difference to the level of physical discomfort she was feeling during sex. She also learned to take time for herself to do enjoyable things and to get more rest. Amar learned to spend a greater amount of time caressing and massaging Nyala and enjoying her entire body. This made a significant difference in the level of physical enjoyment Nyala experienced when they engaged sexually. Nyala grew more comfortable telling Amar specifically what types of touch were arousing to her, and Amar learned how to take the time to stimulate her vulva and her breasts. During treatment, Nyala also decided to make their sexual time together a greater priority, which was a great encouragement to Amar.

You may have decided to let go of the expectation that desire has to be there before engaging in sex. You may also now see a need to pursue how to make your initiation and participation in sex more arousing. Or you may have decided you just need to do some things to help build up a greater desire for having sex or to find greater ways to increase your feelings of arousal during foreplay. The exercises on the next page provide direction to help you put these into practice.

EXERCISES

Sexual Desire and Arousal Communication Exercise 1: Mutual Review

1) Make sure that both of you have read this chapter. Mark the passages that stand out to you.
2) Spiritually prepare yourself for a conversation about this with your spouse. Be ready to share honestly but lovingly, and make sure you are in a state of humility to listen openly.
3) Spend some time together sharing your thoughts about this chapter with one another and what passages you marked.

Sexual Desire and Arousal Communication Exercise 2: Prompt and Reflection

*This prompt and reflection exercise can be done about your overall sexual relationship and can also be used after you have engaged in the sexual touch exercises in the various chapters.

1) Using the prompts below, communicate about *desire and arousal.* As explained before, sit in two chairs that face each other. Husbands, sit with your knees spread. Wives, tuck your chair in so that your knees are touching your husband's chair. Get comfortable and then take each other's hands. When you share your sentence, look directly into your spouse's eyes.
2) Decide who will start first. Whoever goes first begins with the first prompt and finishes the sentence. The spouse then simply reflects the sentence. Then the spouse who is second begins with the first prompt, and the spouse who went first reflects. Do this for each prompt.

   a) "It is very arousing to me when you _____."
   b) "The idea of doing _____ is a turn on for me."
   c) "It is very arousing to me when you touch _____."
   d) "I have felt sexual desire when _____."
   e) "When _____ happens, I think it dampens my sexual desire."
   f) "When you _____, it helps me feel aroused."
   g) "Something that is not arousing to me is _____."
   h) Ask: "Does it affect your desire for sex or your arousal if I _____?"

211

After doing these prompts, ask each other:

> i) "Is there anything I've said that you want to ask me about or have me explain?"

Sexual Desire and Arousal Communication Exercise 3: Turn Ons and Turn Offs

*The following exercise is somewhat similar to the exercise above. However, this exercise is specifically focused on the turn ons and turn offs associated with the five senses of sight, smell, taste, hearing, and touch.

**Remember to share your preferences from this list without sarcasm or mocking. It can be very difficult to share these things, so be thoughtful in your attitude and tone.

1) Read the following examples of turn ons and turn offs.

Sight
Turn ons: showing up naked, strategically placed mirrors, satin boxers, teddies, beautiful sheets
Turn offs: bright lights, dirty room, same bedclothes over and over

Smell
Turn ons: perfumes, candles, incense, scented lotions, bubble bath, semen
Turn offs: body odor, dirty sheets, dragon breath, semen, alcohol or tobacco breath

Taste
Turn ons: chocolate and strawberries, minty kisses, wine
Turn offs: garlic, certain lubricants, wine

Hearing
Turn ons: favorite music, sexy talk, uninhibited groans and squeals
Turn offs: silence, squeals in ear, television, slang

Touch
Turn ons: soaping each other, ice cubes, fur rug, satin gloves, feathers, lotions, sweaty bodies, pinching nipples, tongue kissing
Turn offs: unshaven, rough hands, sweaty bodies, types of tickling, touch too rough/fast, pinching nipples, tongue kissing

2) Using the prompts below and the list above, communicate about your *preferences, likes, dislikes, turn ons and turn offs*. As explained

before, sit in two chairs that can face each other. Husbands, sit with your knees spread. Wives, tuck your chair in so that your knees are touching your husband's chair. Get comfortable and then take each other's hands. When you share your sentence, look directly into your spouse's eyes.

3) Decide who will start first. Whoever goes first begins with the first prompt and finishes the sentence. The spouse then simply reflects the sentence. Then the spouse who is second begins with the first prompt, and the spouse who went first reflects. Do this for each prompt.

    a) "One thing that is hard for me is _____."

    b) "What really turns me on is _____."

    c) "I am turned off when _____."

    d) "Something in the list above that is a turn on for me is _____."

    e) "Something that happens between us that makes it hard for me to feel turned on is _____."

    f) "Something that embarrasses me is _____."

    g) Ask: "Does it bother you when I _____?"

    h) Ask: "Do you like it when I _____?"

After doing these prompts, ask each other:

    i) "Is there anything I've said that you want to ask me about or have me explain?"

Sexual Desire and Arousal Touch Exercise 1: The Desire and Arousal Survey

*This exercise is very much like the Pleasure Survey exercise in the *Sensual Touch* chapter, though this exercise is for both the husband and wife.

Read the directions below completely before beginning.

1) Decide who is going to be the first "Arousal Surveyor."

2) The receiving spouse, wearing no clothing, rests on the bed, first on their stomach and then on their back (approximately five minutes on each side).

3) The surveyor then gently touches various places all over the parts of their spouse's body, paying special attention to the sensual and

sexual parts of the body.

4) The receiving spouse then, in response to the touch, communicates, using numbers, the level to which the sensation is enjoyable, stimulating, or arousing. The answer might be something like "plus one" or "minus two." The range is "plus three" to "minus three." Saying "zero" would indicate a neutral response. Saying "plus one" says that type of touch is enjoyable. Saying "plus two" communicates how that type of touch is somewhat arousing and stimulating. Saying "plus three" is like saying, "Oh my goodness, that gets my juices flowing." The higher number for the "minus" answers indicates that the touch is either undesirable, does not create enjoyable sensations, or is not arousing.

5) For the surveyor, explore different types of touches, such as light to firmer caresses. Make sure to pay close attention so that you can have a clear map in your head of what is arousing to your partner. Remember that these are answers to what is arousing at this time and that this can vary each time you are together.

6) Now switch. The surveyor becomes the receiving spouse, and the receiving spouse becomes the surveyor. Repeat the directions above.

7) After doing this, find a comfortable place to hold each other and talk about the exploration, what you enjoyed and what you would like more of. Talk about both what you experienced as the surveyor and as the receiver.

18

The Fun and the Romance

Take me away with you—let us hurry!

Leaping, climbing, and seeking
Jewels, earrings, and ribbons
Battles, chariots, and buffets
Crowns, swords, and shields
Trees, wind, and rivers

When you read over these words, what do you picture? What do they remind you of? Fantastic novels of exploration and adventure with kings and queens? Children playing make believe, running all around with their play swords and shields, climbing trees and fording rivers? Beautiful scenes of gorgeously dressed lords and ladies, feasting and loving? Adventure and Fun?! These are actually the literal words found in God's Word in Song of Songs. These are playful, adventurous words. These are the words God chose to include in His Holy Scriptures to describe the sensual, sexual relationship between a man and woman who both love God and love each other.

Sex is intended by God to be fun, playful, and intoxicating. Many couples, however, end up with routine and duty. If the words above do not have any association with what happens in your bedroom, in your intimate relationship, it is our hope that this chapter can help revolutionize the party in your garden.

You may have jumped ahead to read this chapter. You saw the title and thought, "Now this is what I'm looking for!" Or there are problems in your sexual relationship and you are looking for some quick answers on how to spice things up. Please go back and read the rest of this book before you return to this chapter. If your friendship is not all it should be, work on that first. If you feel like your spouse does not really know you or if they say you do not understand them, check out those chapters and exercises first. If you struggle with body image, sexual dysfunction, or sexual sins, read about that before diving into the material here. If the time you spend together sexually is still challenging, go to the sections on sensual and sexual touch. Heal the areas of your marriage that need attention before trying out the enhancing things found in this chapter. The truth is that a great, fun, playful sex life is only truly possible when your relationship is one of genuine connection, satisfying adventure, and respectful, loving communication saturated in God's Word.

There are so many books on how to create romance in your marriage. We're not going to include that information here. Just kidding. Some of you might shoot us. The reality is, there are a lot of books on romance, and one of our favorites is Sam Laing's *The Five Senses of Romantic Love*. We also recommend reading the Louis' *I Choose Us*, and do the *Being a Romantic Lover* and *Participation* exercises in their book. So, when it comes to romance and fun, ask yourself, "What does my spouse need?"

Husbands: What Your Wife Needs

Learn her. "Be considerate as you live with your wife" (1 Peter 3:7). The meaning of the word *considerate* here, *gnosin* in the Greek, is to investigate, to seek to know, to live according to knowledge. Husbands, be a lifelong student of your wife's body. Investigate her body but always remember that before you touch her body, touch her soul. Make the choices for your sexual relationship that reflect your knowledge of her. Learn her preferences for sensual and sexual touch. Also, learn what makes her feel loved, special, important, cherished. What does she like to do for fun? What makes her feel heard? What does she need that will help her enjoy your relationship more? Does she need a nap before you take off on that date? Remember that she may not yet know what her preferences and needs are sexually or otherwise, so be patient as she herself learns. Ask her questions about her sexual likes and dislikes. Find out what she thinks about sex and what the draws and drawbacks are for her.

Talk to her. Ask her questions. How was her day? What is she worried about? How is she doing? What does she need? What is she excited about? *Share your feelings. Share your feelings. Share your feelings.* Be vulnerable and real about your dreams, your hopes, your worries, and your mistakes. It might surprise you how much your sharing could be an aphrodisiac for her. Compliment her. Tell her what you admire. Tell her what you noticed about her during the day, last night, or last week. Imitate the Lover in Song of Songs and tell her how she is attractive to you—physically, spiritually, intellectually, and socially. Compliment her sandaled feet. Talk to her every day. If you are the greater talker, learn to be the greater listener. If you are more the silent type, learn to ask questions and share openly. Take the time to discuss how she feels about your sexual relationship. Together, read the different chapters and then get some time somewhere quiet and uninterrupted to talk about what you both thought.

Romance her. Romance can be defined in a variety of ways: feelings of excitement and mystery associated with love; doing something special and unexpected; or feelings of emotional attraction and belonging. A sense of lovability is at the core of healthy development. Romantic gestures communicate to a woman, "I am lovable," "I am important to him," "I am wanted." When a husband chooses to do something for his wife, takes the time to plan something special, or does thoughtful gestures at random moments, a wife will often feel desired, chosen, and special. There is no one-size-fits-all formula for romance. What feels romantic can be completely unique to each woman. Some women love flowers. Others prefer a great steak. So go ahead and get the flowers, buy the steak, light the candles, take her somewhere unique and special. Make her a special meal, plan an evening of sensual fun, cuddle watching something together, give her a massage, and make your sexual time together romantic with music, candles, warm touches, and special fun.

Resolve conflict. Be the one to initiate doing the Validation exercise in earlier chapters. Be the one to ask, "Can we talk about that?" If you are the one who usually initiates conflict resolution, make sure to give her the space and time to get to a better place when she is able to talk. As you talk about the conflict, ask her if she feels like you really understood and if she feels truly resolved. If things don't get resolved, be the one to seek help from the other couples in your life. When you get the help, find out first what you need for yourself rather than vent about your frustration with her. When you've had a conflict, go and pray and then come back when your heart is in a better place to resolve the issue. Remember, reaching out for sex when conflict is unresolved can leave a woman feeling used and unloved.

Make sex work for her. Make sure your time together is private. Do you need to teach your children not to come into your room without knocking? Do you need a lock on your door? Find out if she likes to know ahead of time that you'd like to have sex and when and how she'd like you to tell her. This may allow her anticipation to build up and allow her to prepare herself mentally to participate and enjoy your sexual time together. What kind of atmosphere makes sex more enjoyable for her?

Consider flickering candlelight, room temperature, music, lotions, oils, incense, and satin sheets (go spend the money and buy them if you think she'd like that). Atmosphere could be quite important for your wife.

Make sex fun for her. Talk first. Talk some more. Then play. Buy a sexual board game like those found on the *Covenant Spice* website. You can also play any regular board game (like Pictionary or Monopoly) and make up sexual rules. Or just play a card game naked, doing sexual favors for whoever wins the hand (well, as long as no one is winning *all* the hands). Play the card games and dice games in bed with yummy food and drinks on the side. Have pillow fights and play with water pistols (Really? How?). Fingerpaint each other's bodies with glow-in-the-dark body paint. Use whip cream, letting her squirt it where she'd like you to kiss, lick, or suck and then you do the same. Dance together. Ask her the kind of music she likes. Put the music on, both of you wear lingerie, light some good smelling candles, and dance.

Caress and then caress some more. Ask yourself, how is your affectionate touch? Make sure that, throughout the day, you give your wife warm affection and touch that is not connected to sex. Cuddle and hold your wife, spooning and caressing, even when you are not going to have sex. Watch a show together, holding her and caressing her as you watch. We dare you to spend an evening touching her sensually and intimately, giving her a great massage and then pulling the blanket up and sending her off to sleep with a kiss. And then, when you do have sex, take plenty of time to touch your wife when you engage sexually. Use the exercises in the previous chapters to learn the type of sensual and sexual touch she likes. Do not go immediately for her vagina and her breasts. Caress her entire body and give her massages. When you do go to genital touch, go light and slow at first. Follow her direction.

Initiate and plan. If your wife has the greater sex drive, initiate. Plan sexual times and make them special. Show her by your initiation that you want her and find her sexually attractive. "Arise, come with me" (Song of Songs 2:10). Think ahead. Planning makes your wife feel special. Take the opportunity to include thoughtful additions to your times together, both on dates and during sex.

Dates, Dates, Dates. She needs lots of them. Enough said!

Wives: What Your Husband Needs

Sex!

Well, OK. We'll add a few more things. The reality is that for many men, they desire all the things below almost more than they desire intercourse and orgasm.

Admire him. Your encouraging words hold so much power. Put them in cards, texts, and phone calls. Put notes in his lunch. Compliment him in front of others. Look at Proverbs 31:23. "Her husband is respected at the city gate." Why would this passage be included in a chapter on the wife of noble character? The respect this husband experienced among the elders of his land was connected to his wife in some way. Our guess is that her respect for him, her open admiration of him in front of others, was a part of the view that others had of him, the respect they held for him. Let him hear your respect for him, your admiration for him, from the city gates, when you sit in your home, as you walk along the street, as you spend time with friends. Admire him sexually as well. Tell him how he is a good lover. Send him a text and tell him, whisper it to him in the middle of a gathering, or tell him over coffee. What are the things he does with his hands, fingers, tongue, and lips that bring you pleasure? Tell him specifically.

Watch him. When your husband walks around naked, when he is getting dressed, when he puts on an outfit you like, when he wears something that looks good on him, watch him. Tell him. Admire his body and put Song of Songs into practice.

Touch him. Many men hear their wives say, "He only touches me when he wants sex," or "He's not very affectionate." The reality is that many men long for more touch from their wives as well. There is a whole chapter dedicated to affectionate touch in this book. This is just an important reminder that men often love being touched all over, all the time. If that is your husband, appreciate your man's body—and not only when you're in bed. Give him random kisses. Touch his back and butt as you walk by. Reach over and touch his arm, his thigh, his chest.

Prioritize him above all others. "Place me like a seal over your heart" (Song of Songs 8:6). The Hebrew word here for seal, *chotham*, means the seal made from a signet ring that a king would use to make a royal decree or send a royal missive. The Beloved here is letting him know the level of importance she wanted their relationship to have in their lives. Make your spouse your most important relationship: above your kids, your job, your parents and siblings, the other Christians in your life. Prioritize your sexual time together. Don't allow all of your energy to go to everyone and everything else, leaving him only the dregs. Prioritize your dates with him, sex with him, going to bed with him, talking with him.

Indulge your own sensuality. Don't wear underwear and go about your evening, noticing what it feels like. Tell him you have nothing on underneath what you are wearing. Take bubble baths or put scented oil into your bath. Use bath gels and scented lotions that make you feel good.

Wear clothing and materials that are sensual on your skin: lace, satin, or silk. Why is this in a section about what to do for him? Because for most women, when they purposefully and intentionally indulge their own God-given sensuality, become more sensually and sexually attentive to their husbands.

Tell him what you need. When it comes to sex, he needs to know what you would like. Tell him what kind of touch you like and what is arousing to you. Use the exercises on sexual communication in earlier chapters to learn how to talk while you are having sex and how to talk after and before sex, so that he knows what you like and what you prefer. Your husband needs direct requests and assertive communication about your needs.

Spend some money. Spend money on lingerie and on making your bedroom look good. Rejuvenating your sex life may mean buying new sheets and a new comforter. Make your room the most important room in your house and show this by spending a little money to make it look that way. For sexual fun, if you both like the idea, buy some sexual toys and some sexual dice or board games.

Romance him. Who said the only one who likes romance is the wife? Though most men would not be caught dead saying the words, "I wish she were more romantic," many men express that they wish their wife longed for them, wanted them, and thought of them. When he's working at the computer or reading something, kiss his neck and tell him what you love about him. Put notes in his briefcase, his tool belt, his lunch. Text him. Buy his favorite candy bar out of the blue and throw it in his lap. Plan a date somewhere unique and beautiful. Surprise him with an expected fun time or night away.

Understand. Be understanding rather than derogatory about the fact that—for your husband, as for many men—sex may be a major way in which he feels connected to you and experiences comfort (Genesis 24:67). He may want to have sex with you when he gets a raise or loses his job; when he is frustrated or when he is excited; when he is sad or when he is happy; when his team loses or when his team wins. This doesn't mean that it is OK for a husband to demand sex or to become angry if he wants to have sex and it doesn't happen. However, it is easy for women, and the world, to mock men for their desire for sexual frequency. You may need to have an honest and thorough conversation on your differing preferences for how often you have sex, but if he has a greater drive than you, making sarcastic comments can be harmful to your relationship. If, on the other hand, you have the greater sexual drive, read the chapter on desire and arousal and make sure that you come to understand that his lower desire may have nothing to do with his level of attraction to you.

Indulge his senses. He may like your excited sounds as you enjoy his touch and your orgasm. He needs the sight of your naked body. He probably likes to feel you touch his body and the feel of your hands on his testicles and penis. He may be a man who likes the smell of certain perfumes or bath gels on your skin. And remember, Satan has inundated the world with sexual pictures. You can find creative ways to indulge his visual need for pictures of you sexually. One way both of you can get those pictures is by keeping your eyes open while you are having sex together and coming to orgasm. Replaying those images can be very arousing for both of you.

Blow his mind. Share your sexual fantasies with your husband. Purposefully think about sex more and tell him what you thought about. Blindside him with a sexual surprise (a sexual dance, serving dinner naked, putting a pair of crotchless panties in his lunch bag, playing strip poker). Be fully engaged in your sexual time together: be there, talk, tell him what you want, and ask him what he wants. After you've shared what kinds of things you both feel good about in your sexual repertoire, be the one to initiate making things happen. Buy some toys or fun products and use them.

Be creative. See the suggestions above for the husband for games and fun. Initiate this kind of play and put your twist on it. Show your husband you thought of him by setting the whole thing up. When he gets home or is done with work, have a trail of rose petals laid out that lead him up to the bedroom. Let him know you've got some sex planned by hanging a piece of lingerie where he can find it on the bathroom mirror or the door handle as he walks into the house.

Initiate. Many husbands feel loved and wanted when their wife is the one to initiate sex. Be the one to reach over. Be the one to set the atmosphere. Reach for his genitals first. Grope him in the car and in the kitchen. Tantalize him by how you sit (especially if you've told him or shown him ahead of time that you are wearing no underwear or crotchless underwear), give him hidden touches, and whisper to him about what you're going to do to him later.

Okay, you may be having all kinds of bodily sensations after reading this chapter. Now go do something about it.

EXERCISES

Fun and Romance Exercise 1: Creating a Sexual Script - A Couples Exercise

*This exercise is about reclaiming the beauty and possibilities within your sexual relationship. Many of us have negative sexual scripts that play in our minds when we engage sexually. These scripts are developed over time by our experiences both before and during marriage. The lines in the script can be full of assumptions, false information, and negative self-talk. This is your opportunity to write a new script. Both of you do this exercise separately and when things are in a good place, share it with your spouse.

1) Think about what, for you, would be a wonderful time together sexually. If you were the director and writer for a movie, what would be in the scene?

2) Write out your scene. Include details of where you would be, what it would smell like, what you would see and hear, what each of you would be doing and saying, and what you would be wearing and using. Give the details of the setting and atmosphere.

3) Include in your script how you would both be feeling and thinking, the meanings you would both be making of different parts of the script, and how you would be responding to each other. Remember, this is the script you would write when things are as you would hope them to be. You get to be the director and writer of your scene.

4) Make sure to be honest and specific about what you would like to be doing in the script. Include details of things you have perhaps thought about doing or having done to you that you have read about in these chapters.

5) Share your sexual scripts with each other.

19

The Practical and the Fantastical

You may wonder how you and your spouse can spice things up in your sex life. You may have come to this book wanting to explore some fun, creative ideas. Or perhaps there have been some things about sex that have been annoying, uncomfortable, or frustrating and you are wondering how to fix it. You might feel you are in a rut and want to make things more exciting so you have searched on Google for some answers. This chapter is devoted to some of the practical aspects of your sexual time together that can make things much more enjoyable. We have also included exploring sexual fantasy (the fantastical) and sexual positions in order to enhance the fun and romance of the previous chapter. Reminder: if you have jumped ahead to this chapter, we highly recommend that you read the rest of the book before exploring things found here. One of the best ways to make things great in your sexual relationship is to first make sure all the other areas of your marriage are bringing both of you joy and bringing God glory.

The Practical

Watch Your Expectations. Media, including movies, books, magazines, and TV, portrays sex in certain ways that gives the impression that what they do in the movie is always how it works. Both the man and woman always have an orgasm, and they always have it at the same time. It is always exciting and accompanied by a lot of heavy panting and clothes being thrown everywhere. Sex is always steak and lobster but never macaroni and cheese. It is always spontaneous and thrilling. Women always orgasm during intercourse and never experience sexual pain. Men never have erectile problems and always last long enough for both of them

223

to orgasm together. So watch your expectations and make sure they are based on reality rather than Hollywood.

Go to bed together. Whenever this is practically possible (if you don't work opposite shifts, etc.), we recommend for couples to go to bed together. There is a tremendous amount of intimacy that is missed when couples get into the routine of having separate sleeping schedules. Getting ready for bed together allows for intimate conversations, intimate, affectionate touches, and praying together. Pray together every day. For many couples, that means at night as they are going to bed. When you pray, always include in your prayers what you are thankful for about your spouse that happened *that day*. Think about what you saw that day in your spouse that you are grateful for. As you lay in your bed cuddling or holding hands, tell God about that in your prayer. Bedtime together can be such an intimate time. Prioritize it. Change your schedule around. If one of you is a night owl, or you have more work or studying to do after your spouse goes to sleep, either change your schedule (this is our first recommendation) or—on the nights you absolutely have to stay up later—learn to get ready for bed together, cuddle, talk, pray, and maybe have sex. Then, as your spouse drifts off to sleep, go down and continue your night.

Deal with fatigue. Take naps. If you prefer to have sex at night, naps can make a big difference. Mothers with small children, nap when they nap. Husbands and wives, when you get home from work, take a quick power nap so that you can have some energy not only for your evening, but for each other when you have sex. If you don't take a nap, plan on having sex earlier in the evening when you still have some energy left. This may take some creative thinking if you have children, but talk about it and determine your possibilities.

Explore. If your spouse agrees, explore available products: lubricants (Astroglide, Wet, Liquid Silk, Utopia, Uberlube, etc.), toys (vibrators, etc.), outfits, games, and other products (glow-in-the-dark body paint, edible lubricants and oils, edible underwear). There are websites that do not include any sexual pictures of people in their advertisements (covenantspice.com, bedroomblessings.com, thepurebed.com). Explore positions and playful scenarios (see *sexual positions* below for website information). Explore different places to make out and have sex. As men and women devoted to Jesus, it may be difficult to feel that focusing on being creative and spicing up your sex life fits with a focus on getting to heaven and helping others come with you. The reality is this: If anyone should be thoroughly enjoying the pleasures of the sexual relationship that God created, it should be those that follow the Creator.

Sex and aging bodies. There are a number of issues to pay attention to when your body is getting older and you still desire a fulfilling sex life. Have sex when you aren't exhausted. Consider other positions. Buy products that help as you age: vibrators, wedge pillows to help with back and knee problems, sex swings to help with thrusting difficulties associated with various disabilities, penile rings, Viagra/Cialis/Levitra, vibrating male sleeves, waterproof mattress pads, and vaginal moisturizers. Read the chapters on how to address the health challenges, medical issues, and sexual dysfunctions that occur when men and women age.

Sex is Messy and Awkward. Something that can really derail the enjoyment of sex is the messiness and awkwardness of sex. And sex is messy!

His sperm drips down my legs.
Sometimes there's a lot of fluid.
We used way too much lubricant and things got so sticky.
She farts in the middle of things.
His hands are so rough.
The sheets get all kinds of stuff on them.
Her fingernails and teeth scrape.
Sometimes there's blood.
It smells like urine.
He/she smells.
I hate that sound my vagina makes when he pulls out.
Her fluid is___.
His semen is____.

Sometimes the messiness of sex can actually stop people from having sex or cause them to avoid certain sexual practices that might otherwise be pleasurable. The first thing to do to help with how to respond to the mess and awkwardness is to *talk about it*. Start with asking each other, "Does anything about having sex and the messiness of sex make you feel uncomfortable?" Below are some practical things that can make the mess and awkwardness of sex more manageable. Read the section below and then find some time to talk together about how you feel regarding this topic.

Set things up ahead of time. Pull the lubricant out. Set the towels under the bed. Plug in the vibrator. Take a shower and brush your teeth. Shave. Use lotion or oil on rough hands and fingers. Try different ways and times to use your contraception to minimize the hassle, but talk about and learn to live with the hassle so that it doesn't steal the fun. Have the hand towels or wipes next to or under your bed and use them to wipe up the semen, the lubricant, the urine, the blood, or the outflowing contraceptive gel, foam, or suppository. Have a waterproof pad or towels under you during sex. Use flavored lubricants, scented oils, or whip cream during sex play to work your way around any of the scents and smells of sex that feel unpleasant to either of you. Be kind and laugh. During sex, if an elbow jabs you or a toenail gouges your thigh, groan and squeal, and go back to having fun. The typical adult passes gas multiple times during the day, and the friction and stimulation of sex can cause the body to do its work at awkward times. If someone farts during sex play, or if the vagina lets out its "queef" sound from trapped air, or if you hear the sloshing sound of various fluids during the thrusting and penetration of intercourse, learn to laugh about it, ignore it (you have more enjoyable things to focus on), and just go on.

For those who like to cuddle after sex, use the towels to clean up while in bed so that you can cuddle in comfort. For women, after sex, rather than doing a walking handstand to avoid the dripping of various liquids down your thighs, place a towel between your legs on the way to the bathroom. Use a panty liner after sex. For men, use the towel you've put under the bed or use the sink and some soap to clean up. Or take a shower together and soap each other up for post-play. Sex is messy and awkward, and you can make those aspects just another part of the overall wonderful experience of sexual intimacy.

The Fantastical: Sexual Fantasy

Purposefully fantasizing about your spouse and exploring sexual fantasies you could engage in can be a wonderful way to enrich your sex life. The Lover and the Beloved, in Song of Songs, fantasized about each other, expressing their longing for one another. Listen to the words of the Beloved and how she pictures and imagines things she would like to do and what she would like him to do to her:

"Let him kiss me with the kisses of his mouth" (1:2). "Take me away with you... Let the king bring me into his chambers" (1:4). "All night long on my bed I looked for the one my heart loves" (3:1). "Let my lover come into his garden and taste its choice fruits" (4:16). "Tell him I am faint with love" (5:8). "May the wine go straight to my lover, flowing gently over lips and teeth" (7:9). "Let us spend the night in the villages ... there I will give you my love" (7:11-12).

The Beloved even describes her erotic dream. "I slept but my heart was awake. Listen! My lover is knocking: 'Open to me, my sister, my darling.'"

Listen to the words of the Lover as he imagines what he would like to see, hear, and do:

"Show me your face, let me hear your voice" (2:14). "I will go to the mountain of myrrh and to the hill of incense" (4:6). "Come with me... my bride" (4:8). "I will climb the palm tree; I will take hold of its fruit" (7:8). "Let me hear your voice" (8:13).

We often equate fantasy with lust. And yes, when that fantasy is about anyone other than your spouse, that is what it is. When fantasizing is about your spouse, however, you are indulging in the longing and desire to be with your spouse sexually. Or you are reliving the special, erotic, or tingly moments that you experienced with your spouse in the past. As mentioned in chapter seventeen, *Low Desire and Arousal*, allowing yourself to fantasize about your spouse, to feel the blowing on your garden by letting your mind go there, to imagine your hands as they climb the palm tree of your spouse's body, is both biblical and helpful. Below, we include an exercise for purposefully fantasizing about your spouse.

The Fantastical: Sexual Positions

It is not uncommon that couples ask us how to spice up their sex life by adding more sexual positions. It is also not uncommon for these things to bring up conflict for a couple. "He wants to try positions that I am uncomfortable with." "She refuses to try any other positions." "I want to try some fun things, but he/she gets uncomfortable when I suggest it." Finding ways to work through feelings about using different sexual positions and opening yourself to being willing to explore can go a long way toward enhancing your time together sexually. It is also important, however, to make sure that you do not become overly focused on seeking novelty. Sometimes the hunger for constant variety and ever-changing levels of risk can be a worldly thing, rather than a godly desire for greater unity and fun. Pursue the novelty to enhance your relationship rather than to begin making demands or giving in just to make peace. Finding the balance is crucial, and it is vital that it is mutual.

If you have not yet done the *What's Allowed* exercise in chapter two, *So What Does the Bible Say About Marital Sex*, use that exercise to talk about the different positions you would like to try. Have an open, real conversation about how you feel. We also recommend that you spend some time on websites such as hotholyhumorous.com, christianfriendlysexpositions.com, and christiannymphos.org, which describe certain positions without using pornography or inappropriate nudity. As you decide to explore different positions, remember that you can change positions throughout your time together sexually to spice things up and make things fun. You can switch from missionary, to rear entry, to spooning, to 69 all in one evening (69 is a sexual position where partners simultaneously perform oral sex). Remember that many of these positions may be great for the husband but may not do anything for the wife's sexual stimulation. Always make sure you take care of your wife's pleasure and orgasm.

We have explored a lot and quickly in this chapter. Take some time to do the exercise on the following pages.

EXERCISES

The Practical and the Fantastical Exercise 1: Sexual Fantasy

Do this exercise sometime during your day, or as you are thinking about the sexual time you are planning to have with your spouse later in the day.

1) Sitting somewhere private, close your eyes.
2) Think about a particularly enjoyable time you had with your spouse when you experienced some enjoyable sexual feelings and sensations.
3) Purposefully picture what your spouse did to you that you enjoyed. Remember and picture what you did to your spouse that was arousing to you. Dwell on the specifics. What did their lips do, what did their hands do, what did their tongue do? What did you see? If you feel your body responding, let it.
4) Share with your spouse what you remembered and pictured.

The Practical and the Fantastical Exercise 2: Fantasy List - A Couples Exercise

*This is a couple's exercise. Make sure your spouse is open to doing it. If your relationship is not yet at the point where you feel comfortable doing this, then doing it can cause more harm than good. This is not an exercise that should ever be used to manipulate, coerce, demean, or humiliate. Be thoughtful, be kind, be loving. Doing this should be fun and lighthearted. Dream. Share your dream. Ask God to bless this exercise so that it can create the beautiful, lush garden He talks about in Isaiah 58:11 and the whole book of Song of Songs.

**When you respond to your spouse's list, be curious and avoid any kind of mockery or sarcasm. Your spouse is making him or herself vulnerable. Honor your spouse's dreams and imaginings.

1) Consider all of the possible toys, scenarios, beautiful places, and fun ideas this chapter and chapter eighteen, *The Fun and the Romance*, could have brought to mind for you. Now, each of you make a fantasy list. List the types of things you would enjoy doing with your spouse. Only include things on your list that you both agree on and feel comfortable with.
2) Think about the following: where, when, how, what. Where would

you be, when would you do this, how would you do it, what would you be doing?

3) As you make your list, make sure that you use what you learned from the *What's Allowed* exercise in the chapter on *So What Does the Bible Say About Marital Sex*. Include the things that would turn your spouse on and turn you on. Don't include anything that would violate either of your consciences, break a purity boundary, or is not mutually agreed on. Make the list fun and creative, thoughtful, and maybe a little crazy.

4) Share your list with your spouse. You can do this sitting at a table with something nice to drink, cuddling on a couch, or laying naked in bed. As you share, remember, this is a fantasy list, not a list of demands. As you listen to your spouse's list, remember that you have the right to decline to do anything on this list. Your spouse is sharing their dreams and fantasies. Enjoy sharing and listening.

20

Conclusion

"Let Me Hear Your Voice"
(Song of Songs 2:14)

We joke that talking about sex is often harder than having sex. If you have taken the time to utilize the exercises contained here, you have probably been talking about sex more than you have in your entire life. You may also have learned how to be intentional about your sexual relationship. The myth most of us hear and believe is that in order for sex to be great, it has to be spontaneous. Though there may have been more spontaneity early in your sexual relationship, the reality can be quite different in most mature, lasting relationships. For sex to be great, we need to intentionally plan, think, and pray how to be giving to our spouse. We also need to purposefully talk openly and honestly about what we love about our sex lives, what we genuinely need, and what we do not like.

God has great plans for us. He wants to prosper us and not to harm use (Jeremiah 29:11). He wants us to have a hope and a future. He created us, knows us, and cherishes us (Psalm 139; Isaiah 40:11). He wants us to know Him and He wants us to know the depth and width of His love for us (Ephesians 3:18). He is kind (Luke 6:35). He is generous (Ephesians 1:7-8). He longs to show His graciousness to us (Isaiah 30:18) and He wants us to enjoy a full and rich life (Ephesians 6:3; John 10:10). We have to remember that it was Jesus' goal that we enjoy life to the full. The way we show others that we are His disciples is by our love for one another (John 13:5). One way we can show the world that we are His disciples is by the depth of genuine, God-given intimacy we have in our marriage. Your marriage can be a light on the hill.

We all have challenges in our marriages. Let your light shine. Show the world how a disciple of Jesus repairs the injuries in their marriage. Show the world how the knowledge you have of your heavenly Father and His Son is reflected in your sexual love for each other. "[They] were naked... and not ashamed" (Genesis 2:25). This is the state that God created us in. This is what we can live out in our married life. Naked. Unashamed. Confident in our ability to share our body, committed to giving pleasure, reveling in the sensual enjoyment of our spouse's touch, and not embarrassed or reticent about erotic, sexual release. Not only can you overcome embarrassment, but now you can joyfully pursue sexuality as only God's people can. You can ask for what you need and like without being demanding and you can become the vessel that brings your spouse pleasure like no one else on this earth can.

Be intentional. Be purposeful. Watch your expectations. Remember that sometimes your sexual time together will be steak and lobster. Other times it will be macaroni and cheese. Being O.K. with macaroni and cheese can make the steak and lobster taste especially good.

You may have had some amazing victories as you traversed these passages. Please take some time to rejoice in those victories. Each little step you have taken and each little moment of joy you have had is a victory, so celebrate it. Do the victory dance! So how do you keep it up? How do you make sure that things continue to be like that flowing stream, always being refreshed? Here are some ideas. Keep reading. Read one of the many books on sex referenced here. Talk about it. Use your calendar. Keep your sexual times intentional. Put them on your calendar. There have been couples that Jennifer has worked with professionally who have shared about how their kids began to say "Oh my goodness, are you guys going to do more homework?" These kids had seen the "homework" notations on the family calendar and figured out what they meant. What a surprising testimony. Older, grown children of some of these couples began asking their parents to explain Validation to them and to share about what they had done to change their marriage and their sex lives. Couples have shared how they have told their grown, married children, "We have been renewed." What a way to show God to your children, to your friends, to other disciples of Jesus, to those you are reaching out to. So continue to work hard at honoring God with your sex life. You may be surprised at some of the unusual ways you will get to share your faith when you do.

"Keep the marriage bed pure" (Hebrews 13:4). The word *pure* here is *amiantos*, meaning undefiled, unstained. Work hard at keeping the world out and not allowing Satan to pollute the beauty that God has been creating in your sexual relationship. Don't let Satan win. Satan's greatest weapon is to divide. The unity and deep connection you have been forging in your marriage keeps him from getting a foothold. Purity does not mean boring and routine. Instead, it means keeping those waters refreshed. Fight for your intimacy. When it wanes, and it will, come back and reread what you have found here. Make sure you continue to go on dates and spend regular time in sensual touch that does not continue to sex. Come back and do again some of the exercises you found helpful and do others you may have skipped. If things begin to slip, or if the improvement you have made begins to fade, have an honest conversation about it and then put your eyes back on Jesus and once again renew your pursuit of closeness and connection with one another.

Your intimacy can mature and deepen with each passing year. Make that your goal. Great masterpieces take time, dedication, and heart. Go, create your masterpiece and ...

Let your song be sung!!

APPENDIX A: REFERENCES

Introduction

1   McCarthy, B. (1997). Strategies and techniques for revitalizing a non-sexual marriage. *Journal of Sex and Marital Therapy, 23*, 231–240.

2   L'Abate, L. (1999). Increasing intimacy in couples through distance writing and face-to-face approaches. In J. Carlson & L. Sperry (Eds.), *The intimate couple* (pp. 324-340). Philadelphia: Brunner/Mazel.

3   Konzen, J. (2013, November). *A phenomenological study of experiences of shame about sexuality for married, evangelical Christian women.* Poster session presented at the NCFR Annual Conference, San Antonio, TX.

4   Konzen, J. (2014). *The EIS model: A mixed methods research study of a multidisciplinary sex therapy treatment.* (Doctoral Dissertation). Available from ProQuest Dissertations and Theses database. (UMI No. 11722)

Chapter 1

1   Konzen, J. (2013, November). *A phenomenological study of experiences of shame about sexuality for married, evangelical Christian women.* Poster session presented at the NCFR Annual Conference, San Antonio, TX.
Konzen, J. (2014). *The EIS model: A mixed methods research study of a multidisciplinary sex therapy treatment.* (Doctoral Dissertation). Available from ProQuest Dissertations and Theses database. (UMI No. 11722)

2   Balswick, J., & Balswick, J. (2008). *Authentic human sexuality.* Downers Grove, IL: InterVarsity Press.
Konzen, J. (2014). *The EIS model: A mixed methods research study of a multidisciplinary sex therapy treatment.* (Doctoral Dissertation). Available from ProQuest Dissertations and Theses database. (UMI No. 11722)
Prager, K. (1995). *The psychology of intimacy.* New York, NY: Guilford Press.

3   Andersen, B., & Cyranowski, J. (1994). Women's sexual self-schema. *Journal of Personality and Social Psychology, 67,* 1079-1100. doi:10.1037/0022-3514.67.6.1079
Satir, V. (1983). *Conjoint family therapy* (3rd ed.). Palo Alto, CA: Science and Behavior Books.

4   Balswick, J., & Balswick, J. (2008). Authentic human sexuality. Downers Grove, IL: InterVarsity Press.

5   Prager, K. (1995). *The psychology of intimacy.* New York, NY: Guilford Press.

6   Konzen, J. (2014). *The EIS model: A mixed methods research study of a multidisciplinary sex therapy treatment.* (Doctoral Dissertation). Available from ProQuest Dissertations and Theses database. (UMI No. 11722)

7   Piper, J., & Taylor, J. (2005). *Sex and the supremacy of Christ.* Wheaton, IL: Crossway.

Chapter 2

1 Piper, J., & Taylor, J. (2005). *Sex and the supremacy of Christ*. Wheaton, IL: Crossway.
2 Laing, S. (2007). *The Five Senses of Romantic Love*. Springhill, TN: Discipleship Publications International: 60-61.

*Content paraphrased from Sex and the Supremacy of Christ, edited by John Piper and Justin Taylor, © 2005. Used by permission of Crossway, a publishing ministry of Good News Publishers, Wheaton, IL 60187. www. crossway.org.

Chapter 3

1 Batool, S., & Khalid, R. (2009). Role of emotional intelligence in marital relationship. *Pakistan Journal of Psychological Research, 24*(1-2), 43-62.
Leonard, L., Iverson, K., & Follette, V. (2008). Sexual functioning and sexual satisfaction among women who report a history of childhood and/or adolescent sexual abuse. *Journal of Sex & Marital Therapy, 34*, 375-384. doi:10.1080/00926230802156202
Metz, J., & Epstein, N. (2002). Assessing the role of relationship conflict in sexual dysfunction. *Journal of Sex & Marital Therapy, 28*, 139-164. doi:10.1080/00926230252851889
2 Roughan, P., & Jenkins, A. (1990). A systems-developmental approach to counseling couples with sexual problems. *Australia and New Zealand Journal of Family Therapy, 11*(3), 129-139.
3 Long, E. (1990). Measuring dyadic perspective-taking: Two scales for assessing perspective-taking in marriage and similar dyads. *Educational and Psychological Measurement, 50*, 91-103. doi:10.1177/0013164490501008
4 Metz, J., & Epstein, N. (2002). Assessing the role of relationship conflict in sexual dysfunction. *Journal of Sex & Marital Therapy, 28*, 139-164. doi:10.1080/00926230252851889
5 Webster, S., Bowers, L., Mann, R., & Marshall, W. (2005). Developing empathy in sexual offenders: The value of offense re-enactments. *Sexual abuse: A journal of research and treatment, 71*(1), 63-77. doi:10.1007/s11194-005-1211-y
Welton, G., Hill, P., & Seybold, K. (2008). Forgiveness in the trenches: Empathy, perspective taking, and anger. *Journal of Psychology and Christianity, 27*(2), 168-177.
6 Abernethy, A., Tadie, J., & Tilahun, B. (2014). Empathy in group therapy: Facilitating resonant chords. *International Journal of Group Psychotherapy, 64*(4), 517-535. doi:10.1521/ijgp.2014.64.4.516
Dimaggio, G., Lysaker, P. H., Carcione, A., Nicolò, G., & Semerari, A. (2008). Know yourself and you shall know the other...to a certain extent: Multiple paths of influence of self-reflection on mindreading. *Consciousness And Cognition: An International Journal, 17*(3), 778-789. doi:10.1016/j.concog.2008.02.005

Chapter 4

1   Tripp, D. (2001). *Age of opportunity.* Phillipsburg, NJ: Presbyterian and Reformed Publishing Company.

Chapter 6

1   MacNeil, S., & Byers, E. (2005). Dyadic assessment of sexual self-disclosure and sexual satisfaction in heterosexual dating couples. *Journal of Social and Personal Relationships, 22,* 169-181. doi:10.1177/0265407505050942

Chapter 7

1   Roughan, P., & Jenkins, A. (1990). A systems-developmental approach to counseling couples with sexual problems. *Australia and New Zealand Journal of Family Therapy, 11*(3), 129-139.
     Schaefer, M., & Olson, D. (1981). Assessing intimacy: The PAIR inventory. *Journal of Marital and Family Therapy, 7*(1), 47-60. doi:10.1111/j.1752-0606.1981.tb01351.x
     Verhulst, J., & Heiman, J. (1979). An interactional approach to sexual dysfunctions. *American Journal of Family Therapy, 7*(4), 19-36. doi:10.1080/01926187908250334
2   Konzen, J. (2014). *The EIS model: A mixed methods research study of a multidisciplinary sex therapy treatment.* (Doctoral Dissertation). Available from ProQuest Dissertations and Theses database. (UMI No. 11722)
3   Gottman, J. (2000). The seven principles for making marriage work.
4   Meneses, C., & Greenberg, L. (2011). The construction of a model of the process of couple's forgiveness in emotion focused therapy for couples. *Journal of Marital and Family Therapy, (37)*4, 491-502. doi: 10.1111/j.1752-0606.2011.00234.x
5   Greenberg, L. (2011). The construction of a model of the process of couple's forgiveness in emotion focused therapy for couples. *Journal of Marital and Family Therapy, (37)*4, 491-502. doi: 10.1111/j.1752-0606.2011.00234.x
6   Gottman, J. (2000). The seven principles for making marriage work.

Chapter 8

1   1 Holt-Lunstad, J., Birmingham, W., & Light, K. (2008). Influence of "warm touch" support enhancement intervention among married couples on ambulatory blood pressure, oxytocin, alpha amylase, and cortisol. *Psychosomatic Medicine, 70,* 976-985. doi:10.1097/PSY.0b013e318187aef7
2   Field, T. (2003). *Touch.* Cambridge, MA: MIT Press.
3   Crusco, A., & Wetzel, C. (1984) The Midas touch: The effects of interpersonal touch on restaurant tipping. *Personal Social Psychology Bulletin, 4*(10), 512-51.
4   Fletcher, G. & Overall, N. (2010). Intimate Relationships. In Baumeister, R. & Finkel E. (Eds.), *Advanced Social Psychology.* New York: Oxford University

Press.

5 Johnson, S., & Zuccarini, D. (2009). Integrating sex and attachment in emotionally focused couple therapy. *Journal of Marital and Family Therapy, 36*(4), 431-445. doi:10.1111/j.1752-0606.2009.00155.x

6 Smith, J., Vogel, D., Madon, S., & Edwards, S. (2011). The power of touch: Nonverbal communication within married dyads. *The Counseling Psychologist, 39*(5), 764-787. doi:10.1177/0011000010385849

7 Mosier, W. (2006). Intimacy: The key to a healthy relationship. *Annals of The American Psychotherapy Association, 9*(1), 34-35.

8 Fletcher, G. & Overall, N. (2010). Intimate Relationships. In Baumeister, R. & Finkel E. (Eds.), *Advanced Social Psychology*. New York: Oxford University Press.

9 Heiman, J., Long, J., Smith, S., Fisher, W., Sand, M., & Rosen R. (2011). Sexual satisfaction and relationships happiness in midlife and older couples in five countries. *Archives of Sexual Behavior, 40,* 741-753.

10 Heiman, J., Long, J., Smith, S., Fisher, W., Sand, M., & Rosen R. (2011). Sexual satisfaction and relationships happiness in midlife and older couples in five countries. *Archives of Sexual Behavior, 40,* 741-753.
Punyanunt-Carter, N. (2004). Reported affectionate communication and satisfaction in marital and dating relationship. *Psychological Reports, 95,* 1154-1160. doi:10.2466/PR0.95.7.1154-1160
Schwartz, P., & Young, L. (2009). Sexual satisfaction in committed relationships. *Sexuality Research & Social Policy: A Journal of The NSRC, 6*(1), 1-17. doi:10.1525/srsp.2009.6.1.1

11 Holt-Lunstad, J., Birmingham, W., & Light, K. (2008). Influence of "warm touch" support enhancement intervention among married couples on ambulatory blood pressure, oxytocin, alpha amylase, and cortisol. *Psychosomatic Medicine, 70,* 976-985. doi:10.1097/PSY.0b013e318187aef7

12 McCabe, M., & Cobain, M. (1998). The impact of individual and relationship factors on sexual dysfunction among males and females. *Sexual and Marital Therapy, 13*(2), 131-143. doi:10.1080/026746598084065541

13 Renaud, C., Byers, E., & Pan, S. (1997). Sexual and relationship satisfaction in mainland China. *The Journal of Sex Research, 34*(4), 399-410. doi:10.1080/00224499709551907

14 Hanzal, A., Segrin, C., & Dorros, S. (2008). The role of marital status and age on men's and women's reactions to touch from a relational partner. *Journal of Nonverbal Behavior, 32,* 21-35. doi:10.1007/s10919-007-0039-1

Chapter 9

1 Basson, R., Rees, P., Wang, R., Montejo, A., & Incrocci, L. (2009). Sexual function in chronic illness. *Journal of Sexual Medicine, 7,* 374-388. doi:10.1111/j.1743-6109.2009.01621.x
Clayton, A., & Balon, R. (2009). The impact of mental illness and psychotropic medications on sexual functioning: The evidence and

management. *Journal of Sexual Medicine, 6*(5), 1200-1211. doi:10.1111/j.1743-6109.2009.01255.x

Goldstein, A., Pukall, C., & Goldstein, I. (2011). *When sex hurts: A woman's guide to banishing sexual pain.* Philadelphia, PA: Da Capo Press.

2   Basson, R., Rees, P., Wang, R., Montejo, A., & Incrocci, L. (2009). Sexual function in chronic illness. *Journal of Sexual Medicine, 7,* 374-388. doi:10.1111/j.1743-6109.2009.01621.x

Clayton, A., & Balon, R. (2009). The impact of mental illness and psychotropic medications on sexual functioning: The evidence and management. *Journal of Sexual Medicine, 6*(5), 1200-1211. doi:10.1111/j.1743-6109.2009.01255.x

Goldstein, A., Pukall, C., & Goldstein, I. (2011). *When sex hurts: A woman's guide to banishing sexual pain.* Philadelphia, PA: Da Capo Press.

3   Cobia, D., Sobansky, R., & Ingram, M. (2004). Female survivors of childhood sexual abuse: Implications for couples' therapists. *The Family Journal: Counseling and Therapy for Couples and Families, 12*(3), 312-318. doi:10.1177/1066480704264351

Leclerc, B., Bergeron, S., Binik, Y., & Khalife, S. (2009). History of sexual and physical abuse in women with dyspareunia: Association with pain, psychosocial adjustment, and sexual functioning. *Journal of Sexual Medicine, 7,* 971-980.

4   Cobia, D., Sobansky, R., & Ingram, M. (2004). Female survivors of childhood sexual abuse: Implications for couples' therapists. *The Family Journal: Counseling and Therapy for Couples and Families, 12*(3), 312-318. doi:10.1177/1066480704264351

Maltz, W. 2012. The sexual healing journey (3rd ed). New York: HarperCollins.

5   Maltz, W. 2012. The sexual healing journey (3rd ed): p.7. New York: HarperCollins.

6   McCarthy, B., & McCarthy, E. (2003). *Rekindling desire.* New York, NY: Brunner Routledge.

Chapter 10

1   Konzen, J. (2014). *The EIS model: A mixed methods research study of a multidisciplinary sex therapy treatment.* (Doctoral Dissertation). Available from ProQuest Dissertations and Theses database. (UMI No. 11722)

2   Koch, P., Mansfield, P., Thurau, D., & Carey, M. (2005). "Feeling Frumpy": The relationship between body image and sexual response changes in midlife women. *The Journal of Sex Research, 42*(3), 215-223. doi:10.1080/00224490509552276

Montemurro, B., & Gillen, M. (2013). Wrinkles and sagging flesh: Exploring transformations in women's sexual body image. *Journal of Women & Aging, 25,* 3-28. doi:10.1080/08952841.2012.702179

Reissing, R., Laliberte, G., & Davis, H. (2005). Young women's sexual adjustment: The role of sexual self-schema, sexual self-efficacy, sexual aversion and body attitudes. *The Canadian Journal of Human Sexuality, 14,* 3. Retrieved from http://www.sieccan.org/index.html

Sanchez, D., & Kiefer, A. (2007). Body concerns in and out of the bedroom: Implications for sexual pleasure and problems. *Archives of Sexual Behavior, 3,* 808–820.

3   Calvert, E. (2008). *Women's sexual satisfaction: The impact of religious affiliation, religious influence, and the nature of religious messages about sexuality* (Doctoral dissertation). Available from ProQuest Dissertations and Theses database. (UMI No. 3328184)

Reissing, R., Laliberte, G., & Davis, H. (2005). Young women's sexual adjustment: The role of sexual self-schema, sexual self-efficacy, sexual aversion and body attitudes. *The Canadian Journal of Human Sexuality, 14,* 3. Retrieved from http://www.sieccan.org/index.html

Wagner, J., & Rehfuss, M. (2008). Self-injury, sexual self-concept, and a conservative Christian upbringing: An exploratory study of three young women's perspectives. *Journal of Mental Health Counseling, 30*(2), 173-188. Retrieved from http://www.amhca.org/news/journal.aspx

4   Koch, P., Mansfield, P., Thurau, D., & Carey, M. (2005). "Feeling Frumpy": The relationship between body image and sexual response changes in midlife women. *The Journal of Sex Research, 42*(3), 215-223. doi:10.1080/00224490509552276

5   Koch, P., Mansfield, P., Thurau, D., & Carey, M. (2005). "Feeling Frumpy": The relationship between body image and sexual response changes in midlife women. *The Journal of Sex Research, 42*(3), 215-223. doi:10.1080/00224490509552276

6   Sanchez, D., & Kiefer, A. (2007). Body concerns in and out of the bedroom: Implications for sexual pleasure and problems. *Archives of Sexual Behavior, 3,* 808–820.

7   Basson, R. (2007). Sexual desire/arousal disorders in women. In S. Leiblum (Ed.), *Principles and practice of sex therapy* (4th ed., pp. 25-53). New York, NY: Guilford Press.

8   Stadter, M. (2011). The inner world of shaming and ashamed: An object relations perspective and therapeutic approach. In R. Dearing & J. Tangney (Eds.), *Shame in the Therapy Hour.* Washington, DC: American Psychological Association.

Tangney, J., & Dearing, R. (2011). Working with shame in the therapy hour: Summary and integration. In R. Dearing & J. Tangney (Eds.), *Shame in the therapy hour.* Washington, DC: American Psychological Association.

9   www.plasticsurgery.org

10 Bacon, L. (2010). *Health at every size: The surprising truth about your weight.* Dallas, TX: BenBella Books.

Chapter 11

1   1 Johnson, S., & Zuccarini, D. (2009). Integrating sex and attachment in emotionally focused couple therapy. *Journal of Marital and Family Therapy, 36*(4), 431-445. doi:10.1111/j.1752-0606.2009.00155.x

Makinen, J., & Johnson, S. (2006). Resolving attachment injuries in couples using emotionally focused therapy: Steps toward forgiveness and reconciliation. *Journal of Consulting and Clinical Psychology, 74*(6), 1055-1064. doi:10.1037/0022-006X.74.6.1055

2   O'Farrell, T. & Fals-Stewart W. (2006). Behavioral Couples Therapy for Alcoholism and Drug Abuse. New York: Guildford Press.

Chapter 12

1   Kaplan, H. (1974). *The new sex therapy: Active treatment of sexual dysfunctions.* New York, NY: Random House.

2   Masters, W., & Johnson, V. (1966). *Human sexual response.* Philadelphia: Lippincott Williams & Wilkins.

3   Basson, R. (2000). The female sexual response: A different model. *Journal of Sex & Marital Therapy, 26*, 51-65.
Heiman, J. (2007). Orgasmic disorders in women. In S. Leiblum (Ed.), *Principles and practice of sex therapy* (pp. 84-123). New York, NY: Guilford Press.
Hyde, J., & DeLamater, J. (2008). *Understanding human sexuality.* New York, NY: McGraw-Hill.

4   Hyde, J., & DeLamater, J. (2008). *Understanding human sexuality.* New York, NY: McGraw-Hill.
Moreland, R. B. (2004). Molecular basis of veno-occlusion and the molecular pathology of vasculogenic erectile dysfunction. *Sexuality And Disability, 22*(2), 143-149. doi:10.1023/B:SEDI.0000026754.61650.3a
Tajkarimi, K., & Burnett, A. (2011). The role of genital nerve afferents in the physiology of the sexual response and pelvic floor function. *Journal of Sexual Medicine, 8*, 1299-1312. doi:10.1111/j.1743-6109.2011.02211.x

5   Calabrò, R., Gervasi, G., & Bramanti, P. (2011). Male sexual disorders following stroke: An overview. *International Journal Of Neuroscience, 121*(11), 598-604. doi:10.3109/00207454.2011.600647

6   Basson, R., Leiblum, S., Brotto, L., Derogatis, L., Fourcroy, J., Fugl-Meyer, K., & ... Schultz, W. (2003). Definitions of women's sexual dysfunction reconsidered: Advocating expansion and revision. *Journal Of Psychosomatic Obstetrics & Gynecology, 24*(4), 221-229. doi:10.3109/01674820309074686
Hyde, J., & DeLamater, J. (2008). *Understanding human sexuality.* New York, NY: McGraw-Hill.
Pastor, Z. (2013). Female ejaculation orgasm vs. coital incontinence: A systematic review. *Journal of Sexual Medicine, 10*(7), 1682-1691. doi:10.1111/jsm.12166

7   Heiman, J. (2007). Orgasmic disorders in women. In S. Leiblum (Ed.), *Principles and practice of sex therapy* (pp. 84-123). New York, NY: Guilford Press.
Hyde, J., & DeLamater, J. (2008). *Understanding human sexuality.* New York, NY: McGraw-Hill.
Meston, C., Levin, R., Sipski, M., Hull, E., & Heiman, J. (2004). Women's orgasm. *Annual Review of Sex Research, 15*, 173-257.

8   Pastor, Z. (2013). Female ejaculation orgasm vs. coital incontinence: A systematic review. *Journal of Sexual Medicine, 10*(7), 1682-1691. doi:10.1111/jsm.12166
Wimpissinger, F., Tscherney, R., & Stackl, W. (2009). Magnetic resonance imaging of female prostate pathology. *Journal of Sexual Medicine, 6,* 1704–1711.

9   Giuliano, F. (2011). Neurophysiology of erection and ejaculation. *Journal of Sexual Medicine, 8*(4), 310-315. doi:10.1111/j.1743-6109.2011.02450.x

10 Banner, L., & Anderson, R. (2007). Integrated sildenafil and cognitive-behavior sex therapy for psychogenic erectile dysfunction: A pilot study. *Journal of Sexual Medicine, 4,* 1117-1125. doi:10.1111/j.1743-6109.2007.00535.x
Basson, R., Rees, P., Wang, R., Montejo, A., & Incrocci, L. (2009). Sexual function in chronic illness. *Journal of Sexual Medicine, 7,* 374-388. doi:10.1111/j.1743-6109.2009.01621.x
Binik, Y., Bergeron, S., & Khalifé, S. (2007). Dyspareunia and vaginismus: So-called sexual pain. In S. Leiblum (Ed.), *Principles and practice of sex therapy* (pp. 124-154). New York, NY: Guilford Press.
Stevenson, R., & Elliott, S. (2007). Sexuality and illness. In S. Leiblum (Ed.), *Principles and practice of sex therapy* (pp. 313-349). New York, NY: Guilford Press.

11 Binik, Y., & Meana, M. (2009). The future of sex therapy: Specialization or marginalization? *Archives of Sexual Behavior, 38,* 1016-1027. doi:10.1007/s10508-009-9475-9
Goldstein, A., Pukall, C., & Goldstein, I. (2011). *When sex hurts: A woman's guide to banishing sexual pain.* Philadelphia, PA: Da Capo Press.

12 Ponsford, J. (2003). Sexual changes associated with traumatic brain injury. *Neuropsychological Rehabilitation, 18,* 275-289

13 Sandel, M., Williams, K., Dellapietra, L., & Derogatis, L. (1996). Sexual functioning following traumatic brain injury. *Brain Injury, 10,* 719-728.

14 Hyde, J., & DeLamater, J. (2008). *Understanding human sexuality.* New York, NY: McGraw-Hill.

15 Heiman, J. (2007). Orgasmic disorders in women. In S. Leiblum (Ed.), *Principles and practice of sex therapy* (pp. 84-123). New York, NY: Guilford Press.
Komisaruk, B., & Whipple, B. (2005). Brain activity imaging during sexual response in women with spinal cord injury. In J. Hyde (Ed.), *Biological substrates of human sexuality* (pp. 109-145). Washington: American Psychological Association.

16 Kreuter, M., Dahllof, A., Gudjonsson, G., Sullivan, M., & Siosteen, A. (1998). Sexual adjustment and its predictors after traumatic brain injury. *Brain Injury, 12,* 349-368.
Kreutzer, J., & Zasler, N. (1989). Psychosexual consequences of traumatic brain injury: Methodology and preliminary findings. *Brain Injury, 3*(2), 177-186.

17 Sandel, M., Williams, K., Dellapietra, L., & Derogatis, L. (1996). Sexual functioning following traumatic brain injury. *Brain Injury, 10,* 719-728.

18 Ponsford, J. (2003). Sexual changes associated with traumatic brain injury.

Neuropsychological Rehabilitation, 18, 275-289.

19   Hibbard, M., Gordon, W., Flanagan, S., Haddad, L., & Labinsky, E. (2000). Sexual dysfunction after traumatic brain injury. *NeuroRehabilitation, 15,* 107-120.

20   McKenna, K. (2005). The central control and pharmacological modulation of sexual function. In J. Hyde (Ed.), *Biological substrates of human sexuality* (pp. 75-108). Washington: American Psychological Association.

21   Carlson, N. (2008). *Foundations of Physiological Psychology.* New York: Pearson.
McKenna, K. (2005). The central control and pharmacological modulation of sexual function. In J. Hyde (Ed.), *Biological substrates of human sexuality* (pp. 75-108). Washington: American Psychological Association.
Swaab, D. (2005). The role of the hypothalamus and endocrine system in sexuality. In J. Hyde (Ed.), *Biological substrates of human sexuality* (pp. 21-74). Washington: American Psychological Association.

22   Frohman, E., Frohman, T., & Moreault, A. (2002). Acquired sexual paraphilia in patients with multiple sclerosis. *Archives of Neurology, 50,* 1006-1010.

23   Simpson, G., Tate, R., Ferry, K., Hodkinson, A., & Blaszczynski, A. (2001). Social, neuroradiologic, medical and neuropsychologic correlates of sexually aberrant behavior after traumatic brain injury: A controlled study. *The Journal of Head Trauma Rehabilitation (16)*6, 556-572.

Chapter 13

1   Heiman, J., Long, J., Smith, S., Fisher, W., Sand, M., & Rosen R. (2011). Sexual satisfaction and relationships happiness in midlife and older couples in five countries. *Archives of Sexual Behavior, 40,* 741-753.
Punyanunt-Carter, N. (2004). Reported affectionate communication and satisfaction in marital and dating relationship. *Psychological Reports, 95,* 1154-1160. doi:10.2466/PR0.95.7.1154-1160
Schwartz, P., & Young, L. (2009). Sexual satisfaction in committed relationships. *Sexuality Research & Social Policy: A Journal of The NSRC, 6*(1), 1-17. doi:10.1525/srsp.2009.6.1.1

2   Konzen, J. (2014). *The EIS model: A mixed methods research study of a multidisciplinary sex therapy treatment.* (Doctoral Dissertation). Available from ProQuest Dissertations and Theses database. (UMI No. 11722)

3   Hanzal, A., Segrin, C., & Dorros, S. (2008). The role of marital status and age on men's and women's reactions to touch from a relational partner. *Journal of Nonverbal Behavior, 32,* 21-35. doi:10.1007/s10919-007-0039-1

4   Konzen, J. (2014). *The EIS model: A mixed methods research study of a multidisciplinary sex therapy treatment.* (Doctoral Dissertation). Available from ProQuest Dissertations and Theses database. (UMI No. 11722)

5   Konzen, J. (2014). *The EIS model: A mixed methods research study of a multidisciplinary sex therapy treatment.* (Doctoral Dissertation). Available from ProQuest Dissertations and Theses database. (UMI No. 11722)

Chapter 14

1   Smith, J., Vogel, D., Madon, S., & Edwards, S. (2011). The power of touch: Nonverbal communication within married dyads. *The Counseling Psychologist, 39*(5), 764-787. doi:10.1177/0011000010385849
Stephenson, K., Rellini, A., & Meston, C. (2013). Relationship satisfaction as a predictor of treatment response during cognitive behavioral sex therapy. *Archives of Sexual Behavior, 42*, 143-152. doi:10.1007/s10501-102-9961-3

2   Bridges, S., Lease, S., & Ellison, C. (2004). Predicting sexual satisfaction in women: Implications for counselor education and training. *Journal of Counseling & Development, 82*, 158-166. doi:10.1002/j.1556-6678.2004.tb00297.x

3   Curtis, Y., Eddy, L., Ashdown, B., Feder, H., & Lower, T. (2012). Prelude to coitus: Sexual initiation cues among heterosexual married couples. *Sexual and Relationship Therapy, 27*(4), 322-334. doi:10.1080/14681994.2012.734604
Schwartz, P., & Young, L. (2009). Sexual satisfaction in committed relationships. *Sexuality Research & Social Policy: A Journal of The NSRC, 6*(1), 1-17. doi:10.1525/srsp.2009.6.1.1

4   Miller, S., & Byers, E. (2004). Actual and desired duration of foreplay and intercourse: Discordance and misperceptions within heterosexual couples. *The Journal of Sex Research, 41*(3), 301-309. doi:10.1080/00224490409552237
Renaud, C., Byers, E., & Pan, S. (1997). Sexual and relationship satisfaction in mainland China. *The Journal of Sex Research, 34*(4), 399-410. doi:10.1080/00224499709551907

5   Heiman, J., Long, J., Smith, S., Fisher, W., Sand, M., & Rosen R. (2011). Sexual satisfaction and relationships happiness in midlife and older couples in five countries. *Archives of Sexual Behavior, 40*, 741-753.

6   Heiman, J., Long, J., Smith, S., Fisher, W., Sand, M., & Rosen R. (2011). Sexual satisfaction and relationships happiness in midlife and older couples in five countries. *Archives of Sexual Behavior, 40*, 741-753.
Konzen, J. (2014). *The EIS model: A mixed methods research study of a multidisciplinary sex therapy treatment.* (Doctoral Dissertation). Available from ProQuest Dissertations and Theses database. (UMI No. 11722)

Chapter 15

1   American Psychiatric Association. (2013). *Diagnostic and statistical manual of mental disorders* (5th ed.). Washington, DC: Author.

2   Kirby, R., Carson, C., & Goldstein, I. (1999). *Erectile dysfunction: A clinical guide.* Oxford, UK: Isis Medical Media Ltd.

3   American Psychiatric Association. (2013). *Diagnostic and statistical manual of mental disorders* (5th ed.). Washington, DC: Author.

4   Hartman, U., & Waldinger, M. (2007). Treatment of delayed ejaculation. In. S. Leiblum (Ed.), *Principles and practice of sex therapy* (pp. 241-276). New York, NY: Guilford Press.

Chapter 16

1 Heiman, J. (2007). Orgasmic disorders in women. In S. Leiblum (Ed.), *Principles and practice of sex therapy* (pp. 84-123). New York, NY: Guilford Press.
2 American Psychiatric Association. (2013). *Diagnostic and statistical manual of mental disorders* (5th ed.). Washington, DC: Author.
3 Clayton, A., & Balon, R. (2009). The impact of mental illness and psychotropic medications on sexual functioning: The evidence and management. *Journal of Sexual Medicine, 6*(5), 1200-1211. doi:10.1111/j.1743-6109.2009.01255.x
Gossman, I., Julien, D., Mathieu, M., & Chartrand, E. (2003). Determinants of sex initiation frequencies and sexual satisfaction in long-term couples relationships. *The Canadian Journal of Human Sexuality, 12*(3-4), 169-181.
Laumann, E., Paik, A., Glasser, D., Kang, J. Wag, T., Levinison, B. . . . & Gingell, C. (2006). A cross-national study of subjective sexual well-being among older women and men: Findings from the global study of sexual attitudes and behaviors. *Archives of Sexual Behavior, 35*(2), 145-161. doi:10.1007/s10508-005-9005-3
Matevosyan, N. (2010). Evaluation of perceived sexual functioning in women with serious mental illness. *Sexual Disability, 28,* 233-243. doi:10.1007/s11195-010-9166-4
Ostman, M. (2008). Severe depression and relationships: The effect of mental illness on sexuality. *Sexual and Relationship Therapy, 23*(4), 355-363. doi:10.1080/14681990802419266
4 Hinchliff, S., & Gott, M. (2010). Seeking medical help for sexual concerns in mid-and later life: A review of the literature. *Journal of Sex Research, 48,* 106-117. doi:10.1080/00224499.2010.548610
Lindau, S., Schumm, L., Laumann, E., Levinson, W., O'Muircheartaigh, C., & Waite, L. (2007). A study of sexuality and health among older adults in the United States. *The New England Journal of Medicine, 357*(8), 762-775.
5 Haning, R., O'Keefe, S., Randall, E., Kommor, M., Baker, E., & Wilson, R. (2007). Intimacy, orgasm likelihood, and conflict predict sexual satisfaction in heterosexual male and female respondents. *Journal of Sex & Marital Therapy, 33,* 93-113. doi:10.1080/00926230601098449
Kelly, M., Strassberg, D., & Turner, C. (2004). Communication and associated relationship issues in female anorgasmia. *Journal of Sex & Marital Therapy, 30*(4), 263-276. doi:10.1080/00926230490422403
Schwartz, P., & Young, L. (2009). Sexual satisfaction in committed relationships. *Sexuality Research & Social Policy: A Journal of The NSRC, 6*(1), 1-17. doi:10.1525/srsp.2009.6.1.1
6 American Psychiatric Association. (2013). *Diagnostic and statistical manual of mental disorders* (5th ed.). Washington, DC: Author.

Chapter 17

1 American Psychiatric Association. (2013). *Diagnostic and statistical manual of mental disorders* (5th ed.). Washington, DC: Author.

2   Byers, S. (2005). Relationship satisfaction and sexual satisfaction: A
     longitudinal study of individuals in long-term relationships. *The Journal of
     Sex Research, 42*(2), 113-118. doi:10.1080/00224490509552264
     Leonard, L., Iverson, K., & Follette, V. (2008). Sexual functioning and sexual
     satisfaction among women who report a history of childhood and/or
     adolescent sexual abuse. *Journal of Sex & Marital Therapy, 34*, 375-384.
     doi:10.1080/00926230802156202
     Metz, J., & Epstein, N. (2002). Assessing the role of relationship conflict
     in sexual dysfunction. *Journal of Sex & Marital Therapy, 28*, 139-164.
     doi:10.1080/009262302252851889
3   Gossman, I., Julien, D., Mathieu, M., & Chartrand, E. (2003). Determinants
     of sex initiation frequencies and sexual satisfaction in long-term couples
     relationships. *The Canadian Journal of Human Sexuality, 12*(3-4), 169-181.
     Koch, P., Mansfield, P., Thurau, D., & Carey, M. (2005). "Feeling Frumpy":
     The relationship between body image and sexual response changes
     in midlife women. *The Journal of Sex Research, 42*(3), 215-223.
     doi:10.1080/00224490509552276
     Schwartz, P., & Young, L. (2009). Sexual satisfaction in committed
     relationships. *Sexuality Research & Social Policy: A Journal of The NSRC, 6*(1),
     1-17. doi:10.1525/srsp.2009.6.1.1
     Trudel, G., Marchand, A., Ravart, M., Aubin, S., Turgeon, L., & Fortier, P.
     (2001). The effect of a cognitive-behavioral group treatment program on
     hypoactive sexual desire in women. *Sexual and Relationship Therapy, 16*(2),
     145-164. doi:10.1080/14681990120040078
4   Atwood, J., & Weinstein, E. (1989). The couple relationship as the focus of
     sex therapy. *Australian and New Zealand Journal of Family Therapy, 10*(3),
     161-168.
     Haavio-Mannila, E., & Kontula, O. (1997). Correlates of increased
     sexual satisfaction. *Archives of Sexual Behavior, 26*, 399–419.
     doi:10.1023/A:1024591318836
     Heiman, J., Gladue, B., Roberts, C., & Lo Piccolo, J. (1986). Historical
     and current factors discriminating sexually functional from sexually
     dysfunctional married couples. *Journal of Marital and Family Therapy, 12*,
     163–174. doi:10.1111/j.1752-0606.1986.tb01633.x
5   Kaplan, H. (1979). *Disorders of sexual desires.* New York, NY: Simon &
     Schuster.
     Montesi, J., Conner, B., Gordon, E., Fauber, R., Kim, K., & Heimberg, R. (2013).
     On the relationship among social anxiety, intimacy, sexual communication,
     and sexual satisfaction in young couples. *Archives of Sexual Behavior, 42*, 81-
     91. doi:10.1007/s10508-012-9929-3
6   Leonard, L., Iverson, K., Follette, V. (2008). Sexual functioning and sexual
     satisfaction among women who report a history of childhood and/or
     adolescent sexual abuse. *Journal of Sex & Marital Therapy*, 34:375–384. DOI:
     10.1080/00926230802156202
7   Basson, R. (2000). The female sexual response: A different model. *Journal of
     Sex & Marital Therapy, 26*, 51-65.
8   Basson, R. (2000). The female sexual response: A different model. *Journal of*

Sex & Marital Therapy, 26, 51-65.

9   Basson, R., Rees, P., Wang, R., Montejo, A., & Incrocci, L. (2009). Sexual function in chronic illness. Journal of Sexual Medicine, 7, 374-388. doi:10.1111/j.1743-6109.2009.01621.x

10   Hayes, R., & Dennerstein, L. (2005). The impact of aging on sexual function and sexual dysfunction in older women: A review of population-based studies. *Journal of Sexual Medicine, 2,* 317-330.
      Lindau, S., Schumm, L., Laumann, E., Levinson, W., O'Muircheartaigh, C., & Waite, L. (2007). A study of sexuality and health among older adults in the United States. *The New England Journal of Medicine, 357*(8), 762-775.
      Trompeter, S., Bettencourt, R., & Barrett-Connor, E. (2012). Sexual activity and satisfaction in healthy community-dwelling older women. *American Journal of Medicine, 125*(1), 37-43. doi:10.1016/j.amjmed.2011.07.036

11   Hinchliff, S., & Gott, M. (2010). Seeking medical help for sexual concerns in mid-and later life: A review of the literature. *Journal of Sex Research, 48,* 106-117. doi:10.1080/00224499.2010.548610
      Kaplan, H. (1990). Sex, intimacy, and the aging process. *Journal of The American Academy Of Psychoanalysis, 18(*2), 185-205.
      Lindau, S., Schumm, L., Laumann, E., Levinson, W., O'Muircheartaigh, C., & Waite, L. (2007). A study of sexuality and health among older adults in the United States. *The New England Journal of Medicine, 357*(8), 762-775.
      Stone, J. (1987). Marital and sexual counseling of elderly couples. In G. Weeks & L. Hof (Eds.), *Integrating sex and marital therapy,* (pp.221-244). New York, NY: Brunner/Mazel.

12   Basson, R., Rees, P., Wang, R., Montejo, A., & Incrocci, L. (2009). Sexual function in chronic illness. Journal of Sexual Medicine, 7, 374-388. doi:10.1111/j.1743-6109.2009.01621.x
      Binik, Y., Bergeron, S., & Khalifé, S. (2007). Dyspareunia and vaginismus: So-called sexual pain. In S. Leiblum (Ed.), *Principles and practice of sex therapy* (pp. 124-154). New York, NY: Guilford Press.
      Stevenson, R., & Elliott, S. (2007). Sexuality and illness. In S. Leiblum (Ed.), *Principles and practice of sex therapy* (pp. 313-349). New York, NY: Guilford Press.

APPENDIX B:
IDENTIFYING HOW YOU FEEL

Something happened between you and your spouse. You want to talk about it, or use the Validation exercise, and so you are trying to figure out how you felt. Take some time to identify your emotions. Here is a list to get you started. You can even grab a pen and circle the things you are feeling and have them ready for when you are the Speaker. Emotions that tend to be the first ones we recognize and the ones we are most likely to identify and verbalize:

Mad
Furious
Angry
Frustrated

Disappointed
Impatient
Irritated
Annoyed

*Note: It is important that if you are feeling these emotions, say it, without attacking or blaming. However, make sure to share some of the more vulnerable words below as well.

Underlying emotions:

Hurt	Embarrassed	Misunderstood
Small	Guilty	Ashamed
Like a kid	Empty	Afraid
Disrespected	Not thought of	Defensive
Anxious	Ignored	Worried
Unheard	Rejected	Discouraged
Unloved	Insecure	Alone
Not cared for	Like a failure	Unsafe
Confused	In trouble	Panicked
Inadequate	Unappreciated	Not needed
Defective	Helpless	Left out
Useless	Powerless	Insignificant
Incompetent	Uncomfortable	Frightened
Judged	Inferior	Worthless
Unimportant	Less than	Pressured
Abandoned	Not valued	Accused
Unwanted	Overwhelmed	Disconnected
Sad	Undesired	Self-conscious
Devastated	Unattractive	Trapped
Distant	Invisible	Disregarded
Crushed	Stupid	Dismissed
Weary	Forgotten	
Lost	Belittled	
Lonely	Not good enough	

THE *Art* OF
INTIMATE
MARRIAGE

*The Intimate Marriage Cards referenced in this book
can be ordered online at the following sites:

www.theartofintimatemarriage.com
or through Amazon.com

Made in the USA
Middletown, DE
26 June 2016